The Hidden History of Capoeira

The
HIDDEN HISTORY
OF CAPOEIRA

A Collision of Cultures in the
Brazilian Battle Dance

Maya Talmon-Chvaicer

UNIVERSITY OF TEXAS PRESS   AUSTIN

The main ideas in the second part of Chapter 2
were first published in "The Criminalization of
Capoeira in Nineteenth-Century Brazil," in
Hispanic American Historical Review 82:3, 525–547.
The major theme of Chapter 5 was first published
in "Verbal and Non-verbal Memory in Capoeira,"
in *Sport and Society* 7 (2004): 49–68, www.tandf
.co.uk/journals.

Requests for permission to reproduce material
from this work should be sent to:
   Permissions
   University of Texas Press
   P.O. Box 7819
   Austin, TX 78713-7819
   www.utexas.edu/utpress/about/bpermission.html

⊗ The paper used in this book meets the minimum
requirements of ANSI/NISO Z39.48-1992 (R1997)
(Permanence of Paper).

Library of Congress Cataloging-in-Publication Data
Talmon-Chvaicer, Maya, 1968–
   The hidden history of capoeira : a collision
of cultures in the Brazilian battle dance / Maya
Talmon-Chvaicer. — 1st ed.
      p.   cm.
   Includes bibliographical references and index.
   ISBN 978-0-292-71724-4 (pbk. : alk. paper)
   1. Capoeira (Dance)—Social aspects—
Brazil—History.   2. Brazil—Social life and
customs.   I. Title.
GV1796.C145T35   2007
793.3′1981—dc22
2007008882

To my parents, Ruth and Dan, my husband, José (Yossi),

and my sons, Lavy and Naveh,

for their support, encouragement, and patience

CONTENTS

OVER THE PAST decade I have seen Maya Talmon-Chvaicer's interest in Capoeira and in the Portuguese enslavement of Africans come together in an extraordinary fashion as she came to realize that an analysis of the history and anthropology of Capoeira could provide a new entrée into Brazilian cultural development.

This book presents us with many voices, and combines them in an a capella performance of great artistry. We hear the voices of the white authorities, of the enslaved Africans, and of the black, mixed-race, and white Capoeiras, all changing over time, all interacting. In the authorities' view Capoeira changed from the play of the enslaved to the violent war games of "disruptive bandits," and then, remarkably, it was rehabilitated and eventually became the Brazilian national sport. In early participants' eyes it was preparation for a difficult life and a way to publicly express scorn and disrespect for authority. But for some it became a school for immersion in African values, for others a means of finding a shared "Brazilian" experience.

Maya Talmon-Chvaicer has brought together the changing attitudes of both those in power and participants, along with a deep analysis of the African religious beliefs and the Catholicism that are part and parcel of this ritualized "game of life." The result is a lucid analysis of the change over time in light of the political and social history of Brazil and the changes from within as Kongolese, Yoruban, and Portuguese values and beliefs affected the ritual dance and martial art. All of these are an integral part of contemporary Capoeira, both in Brazil and abroad, but in Brazil Capoeira still plays a significant role in symbolizing national identity and is the subject of a proprietary fight that has national significance. Talmon-Chvaicer analyzes all these complex issues, both over time and in relation to the many varied cultures and peoples. She retains from start to finish her respect and admiration for Capoeira, which she views as containing "all the necessary ingredients for living well, both physically and spiritually," but this does not constrain her from examining the disparate roots and meanings of the rituals, often very far from the cultures of contemporary participants. But this, too, is an important historical development in the modern world.

Mechal Sobel

ACKNOWLEDGMENTS

THIS BOOK, WRITTEN over the past five years, has succeeded because of the many people who have helped me along the long road and whom I wish to thank.

First, I would like to express my sincere appreciation and gratitude to Professor Mechal Sobel, who shared with me her remarkable expertise as my Ph.D. supervisor and afterward supported, advised, and encouraged me throughout the whole process until publication.

The initial impetus to modify my dissertation into a book in English was a special scholarship awarded by the Helena Lewin Cathedra for Latin American Studies at the University of Haifa. Thanks to the professional efforts and skills of Hanita Rosenbluth, who translated this work; Rena Minkoff, who edited it; and Yael Slomovic, who edited all the illustrations, so that capoeiras, scholars and people all over the world now have access to a better book.

I thank all the wonderful people who helped me in the research process: Jacob Chvaicer accompanied me during my research in Rio and collected material in the various archives and libraries; Dr. Angelo Decânio and his wife, Isabela, opened their home and hearts and introduced me to capoeira *rodas* and *terreiros de Candomblé* in Salvador; the capoeira *mestres* Cobra Mansa, Bogado, Camisa, Acordeon, Itapoan, Angolinha, João Grande, Curió, and Mestre Valmir agreed to be interviewed and to engage me in their world. I am also indebted to some very special scholars who shared their knowledge and research with me, and eagerly engaged in discussions that opened my eyes to new visions and ways of thinking. I offer special thanks to Kia Bunseki Fu-Kiau, Carlos Eugênio Líbano Soares, Antônio Liberac Pires, Jair Moura, Mary Karasch, João José Reis, Doron Lux (Calunga), and others.

Finally, I am grateful to my family, who have supported me in every possible way. My parents, Ruth and Dan Talmon, in addition to their endless love, support, and encouragement, have assisted wherever and whenever necessary—even when I was thousands of miles away. Tuba, Jacob, and Paulo Chvaicer, my "in-laws," helped me during long research periods in Rio. I especially want to thank my husband, José (Yossi), for his uncompromising support and for translations, letters, designs, and so much more. And last but not least, I thank my dear sons, Lavy and Naveh, for their unconditional love, patience, and understanding.

Together we can "take a turn around the world, comrade."

The Hidden History of Capoeira

CAPOEIRA IS A Brazilian battle dance, a national sport that is part of Brazilian folklore, and, in recent decades, has been taught in schools, universities, and private health clubs. Today it is popular all over the world, and increasing interest has given rise to a large number of historical, anthropological, and sociological studies examining its various aspects and manifestations. In the nineteenth century players, or participants, in capoeira were known as Capoeiras. To avoid confusion I use the same terms: those who play capoeira are Capoeiras (plural) or Capoeirista (singular).

The new historiography looks for and studies the Other, marginal groups ignored and unheard by historians for hundreds of years. Though they sometimes constitute a numerical majority, these groups have been virtually disregarded by scientific research because of their inferior social status, and their story, if told at all, was told by external observers. Since the last part of the twentieth century, however, efforts have been made to listen to the voices of these minorities. Using new and innovative approaches, scientists have begun to investigate the effect of the Other on dominant cultures. In Brazil it has been found that despite the differences between masters and slaves, rulers and subjects, the intercultural encounter has engendered mutual influences, integration, and radical changes in all facets of the cultural and social fabric. In other words, a belief in the superiority of European culture and a homogeneous Brazilian culture no longer exists. This study supports the view that Brazil's social and cultural reality, molded in the dynamic processes of multiculturalism, is influenced by diverse philosophies of life that are still changing.

During the nineteenth century, consistent efforts were made to obliterate capoeira by a variety of methods. White people's sense of superiority induced them to segregate themselves from those they had subjugated, slaves who had brought with them the ancient traditions and cultures of their homeland. Consequently, official descriptions, as well as reports by tourists and the press, of blacks' performances and of capoeira were merely synoptic, superficial, and incomplete. Capoeiras were stigmatized as dangerous drifters who committed criminal acts and threatened public order, as can be seen in the writings of Barreto Mello Filho e Lima, Plácido de Abreu, Allain Emile, Azevedo Aluizo, and others.[1] However, in the early twentieth century, a few army and police officers demonstrated the advantages of capoeira as a martial art and published the first capoeira instruction booklets.[2]

In the 1930s and 1940s Gilberto Freyre, Artur Ramos, Viriato Correia, Edison Carneiro, and other scholars began emphasizing the beneficial influence of African and Indian cultures on Brazilian society.[3] There began an intensive preoccupation with creating a Brazilian national identity, with emphasis on homogeneity as embodied in the new mixed type, or Mestiço. Capoeira, like other popular manifestations such as samba, carnival, and the African-Brazilian religions, gained legitimacy as part of Brazil's national identity and was practiced extensively. Capoeira was recognized as the Brazilian martial art, as the national sport, and as a Brazilian product worthy of the public's attention and involvement. As an extension of this approach and because of the significant social changes that have occurred over the past seventy years, capoeira has become very popular among the middle and upper classes. In the 1980s and especially in the 1990s many studies of capoeira were undertaken. The anthropologists Iria D'aquino, Lewis Lowell, Leticia Reis, and Gregory John Downey focused on social relationships among Brazilian Capoeiras, discussing the role of the capoeira schools in achieving status, power, and identity; capoeira as a tool in the struggle for equality; racial relationships between whites and blacks in capoeira; and the differences in capoeira movements as a result of social and political diversity.[4] The historians Thomas Holloway, Marcos Luíz Bretas, Luis Sergio Dias, Antonio Liberac Pires, Carlos Eugênio Líbano Soares, Maria Burges Salvadori, Luís Renato Vieira, and Mathias Röhring Assunção wrote histories of nineteenth- and twentieth-century capoeira, focusing on the authorities' policies against capoeira during colonial and imperial times and the first republic and the development of capoeira from an outlawed activity to an integral part of twentieth-century Brazilian popular culture.[5] Likewise, Brazilian Capoeiras such as Almeida Bira, Nestor Capoeira, Angelo Augusto Decanio, Oliveira José Luis have written about capoeira from their own experiences.[6]

The authorities and the Regionais (those who practice Capoeira Regional) have tried to characterize capoeira as a national activity originating in Brazil, the country's national sport, and part of Brazilian folklore. Slogans such as "Capoeira é uma só" (There is only one capoeira) and claims that in schools of Capoeira Regional both styles (Angola and Regional) are being taught suggest that the prevailing view among the ruling circles has been accepted. They have tried to force their convictions on the rest of the population and have thus redefined capoeira according to their needs and interests. Today this is not enforced through legislation and oppression as had occurred during the nineteenth and early twentieth century but through the inculcation of values and the emphasis on aspects of capoeira that coincide with the prevailing views. In other words, most of the available written sources reflect the convictions of the elite and the ruling circles. Consequently, due to the marginal social status of slaves and former slaves in Brazil, the importance and influence of the Kongolese[7] and Yoruban cultures have not found expression in these sources. Few authors have attempted to demonstrate the connection between Brazilian capoeira and African cultures. Júlio Cesar de Souza Tavarez, in "Dança de guerra" (War Dance) claimed that slaves preserved their African traditions through body movements.[8] Kenneth Dossar analyzed African aesthetics and dance elements in Capoeira Angola, and in a recent work T. J. Desch-Obi developed a connection between capoeira and twentieth-century southwestern Angolan martial arts (*kandeka* and *engolo*) and the seventeenth-century military culture of the Imbangala groups.[9]

The object of this book is to reveal narratives that have been repressed and excluded from the history books and thus to present a far more intricate and detailed study of the development and meaning of capoeira than has been available previously.

This is a historical-cultural-social study combined with anthropological research. It is an intricate and detailed examination of primary written sources, analyzing the outlooks, symbols, and rituals of the three major cultures that inspired capoeira—Kongolese, Yoruban, and Catholic Portuguese. It also discusses the depth, wealth, and differences of the various capoeira languages, which arise from their different social and cultural heritages and from encounters, collisions, and fusion. Capoeira has become diversified; the variations on the theme incorporate numerous traditions that are influenced by many aesthetic, spatial, and time perceptions and teaching methods, as well as by African, African-Brazilian and Catholic-Christian convictions, rituals, symbols, and religious beliefs.

Kongolese culture formed the background for most of the capoeiras from the early nineteenth century and is probably where they originated.[10] Many of the rich elements of that culture were hidden, repressed, misunderstood, or underestimated by Europeans and their descendants.

Yoruban culture has had a great influence on slave life and culture in Rio de Janeiro and Bahia, mainly since the second half of the nineteenth century, after the massive forced immigration of slaves from western Africa who, due to their sheer number and subsequently elevated social status, have left their mark on capoeira to this day.

Portuguese Catholics, among whom were the elite and ruling classes and therefore determined policies regarding capoeiras, also exerted great influence on the form. The increasing number of Brazilian Catholics active in capoeira groups has brought about meaningful changes in its cultural manifestations.

By studying the changes that have taken place in the goals of capoeira, as well as its symbols and characteristics since the beginning of the nineteenth century, we can perhaps detect the influences of these cultures on each of these aspects.

The five chapters that constitute this study examine the various processes that capoeira has undergone, from different points of view in different eras. The first part of each chapter depicts capoeira as it was experienced, observed, and understood by Europeans and their descendants who considered this activity in relation to their own interests. The second part of each chapter discusses the covert aspects and the further numerous meanings of capoeira.

Chapter 1 discusses capoeira in Rio de Janeiro in the early nineteenth century, up to the 1840s. It deals with the nature of capoeira—which was initially perceived as a slave pastime but soon became a means of disturbing the peace—and the way in which authorities tried to tackle this development. At the time capoeira was regarded as an insignificant slave activity, one among many, and contemporary myths linking capoeira with rebellion are inaccurate, to say the least. The second part of the chapter introduces the concept of capoeira as reflecting the outlook of its practitioners, who were, by and large, slaves originating from West Central Africa. The significance of play in these cultures, particularly as connected with the spiritual and symbolic features of capoeira, is also discussed.

The second chapter, covering the period 1840–1880, examines differences in the Capoeiras' countries of origin, skin color, and social status and how the authorities perceived them as bloodthirsty murderers who used capoeira to kill and maim innocent citizens just for fun. Another interpretation of their behavior suggests that capoeira was used in some instances to protect the regional and social interests of gangs struggling for control of urban space. The second part deals with the hidden aspects of capoeira. Despite the authorities' attempts to present the Capoeiras as a threat to public order and as enemies of society, the masses admired their skillful mastery of the game, played in the squares on festival days and in religious processions, which made fun of the authorities, turning them into objects of scorn and derision.

Chapter 3, covering the period from the 1870s to the 1930s, examines the characteristics of Capoeiras, who split into two major subgroups based on ethnic and socioeconomic rivalries. The circumstances that made Capoeiras an influential factor in local politics and their suppression after the fall of the monarchy are discussed. The second part discloses some secrets of capoeira, the use of the occult, and the growing influence of Yoruban culture and the Catholic Church on beliefs, customs, amulets, and rituals.

Chapter 4 discusses the shift in the focus of capoeira from Rio de Janeiro to Bahia in the 1930s and the change in the authorities' attitude toward it—from treating it as a crime punishable by law to declaring it the national sport of Brazil. Two quite different capoeira styles developed: Capoeira Regional in the 1930s and Capoeira Angola in the 1940s. The second part of the chapter presents the spiritual aspect of capoeira, including rituals, music, and musical instruments and shows how new traditions evolved as a result of the encounter, clash, and integration of the diverse cultures, mainly Catholic Christianity and Yoruban. It is evident that various spiritual aspects are still preserved in local memory, although explanations of and insights into their meanings have faded with time.

Chapter 5 deals with the increasing tensions arising from the different philosophies of life, values, traditions, and customs that led to the changing expressions, goals, and characteristics of capoeira in the 1940s and 1980s.

An examination of the original myth, the essence, goals, and teaching methods, as well as the kinesthetic aspects of capoeira and the major changes in perception of aesthetics, time, and space sheds light on the historical and social processes that capoeira and the Capoeiras have undergone. Despite all attempts to effect uniformity and impose the image of capoeira as a national sport endemic to Brazil, the conflicting outlooks of rulers and subjects, of Brazilians and African-Brazilians have not disappeared.

ONE

A Rio de Janeiro Slave Game

PART 1. CAPOEIRA AS VIEWED BY STRANGERS

The Game of Capoeira and Disturbances of the Peace

IN THE EARLY nineteenth century, travelers and foreign diplomats noted in their memoirs that on arriving in Rio de Janeiro for the first time, people might think they had landed by mistake in an African town as there were more blacks than whites in the streets at all hours, day and night. This became evident in 1808, when the Portuguese court, fleeing from Napoleon's troops, arrived in Rio. The enslaved population, numbering 12,000 at that time—about 20 percent of the urban population—grew rapidly, and by 1821 it was estimated at over 36,000, about 45 percent of the city's inhabitants.[1] The Africans living in the city were mostly slaves engaged in heavy manual labor as servants, porters, sailors, peddlers, and so on. In their free time, mainly on Sundays and holidays, they would gather in public squares to participate in their traditional dances. John Robertson, who traveled in Brazil in 1808, gives a detailed description of groups of slaves congregating in the squares, each according to their nation, and dancing in separate circles of 300 to 400 people each: "There were natives of Mozam-

bique and Quilumana, Cabinda and Luanda, Benguela and Angola."[2] At least
six nations took part in these events; with each of the six circles comprising
300 dancers, there were 1,800 dancers altogether. The German painter Johann
Moritz Rugendas (João Maurício Rugendas), who traveled in Brazil between
1822 and 1824, described the blacks' celebrations, which began as soon as the
working day was done, as well as on holidays and feast days.[3] He described the
tradition of electing a "King of Kongo" during the festival of Nossa Senhora
do Rosário and the dances: the batuque, which was the most popular, and the
lundu, fandango, and capoeira. He described the capoeira as a "warlike, much
more aggressive dance":

> Two contestants face each other, each trying to butt his adversary in the
> chest with his head and knock the opponent down. They turn cartwheels
> and pause as they launch into an attack. Sometimes they stand like he-goats,
> butting at each other. The game often turns into a wild brawl when knives
> are drawn and blood is shed.[4]

This violent game annoyed the authorities so much that they were determined to root it out with all the means at their disposal. Writs were signed stat-
ing that Capoeiras must be arrested and severely punished.[5] Urgent letters were
addressed to police inspectors and army officers, demanding that they tighten
up patrols and vigilance in trouble spots. Anybody suspected of violating these
orders was arrested.[6] On September 30, 1812, Pedro Benguela, slave of José Joaquim, was arrested "for being in Carioca Square and playing capoeira with a
sharp razor."[7] He was sentenced to 100 lashes. On January 2, 1813, three consecu-
tive charges were brought against detainees "caught playing capoeira." The first
was a slave captured in the Botafogo neighborhood who was sentenced to 200
lashes; the second, a slave named Tomas, received 50 lashes; and the sentence of
the third, João, was 200 lashes.[8] On January 15, 1819, a slave named Alexander
Mozambique was arrested and accused of practicing capoeira. He was sentenced
to three months in jail and 300 lashes.[9] In January 1821, Ignácio Mossange, Antônio da Cunha's slave, was arrested and punished for "playing capoeira with a
razor—300 lashes and three months in the penitentiary."[10] Leila Mezan Algranti's study established that between 1810 and 1821, of a total of 4,853 arrests 438
were Capoeiras. Participating in capoeira was the second most common cause
for arrest after attempted escape, which accounted for 751 entries in the records.[11]
Numerous sources indicate that as early as 1815 delinquent slaves were exploited
as laborers in public works projects. Many were sent to work on the Estrada da
Tijuca—a large-scale road construction project that started during the reign of
King João VI. It was designed to connect Rio de Janeiro to the immense arid re-

FIGURE 1.1. *Capoeira Game.* From João Maurício Rugendas, *Viagem pitoresca através do Brasil* (São Paulo: Livraria Martins Editôra, 1954), FIGURE 4/18. Reproduced by kind permission of the British Library.

gions to the east (Sertão Carioca) and the new road to Minas Gerais. The historian Carlos Eugênio Líbano Soares thinks that these punishments were meant to remove from the city the criminals considered most dangerous, and Capoeiras constituted a large percentage of them.[12] Another public works project in which Capoeiras were employed as forced labor was the construction of a dam. This huge project took thirty-seven years (1824–1861) to complete and was executed by the navy. Because of the importance of the dam and the difficulties involved in its construction, the authorities tended to exchange the regularly imposed floggings for hard labor on the dam. Resolution 182, dated August 30, 1824, stated, "Send the black Capoeiras arrested for disturbing the peace to work on the dam instead of flogging them."[13] The simple option of exploiting the prisoners' extremely cheap labor to carry out difficult, strenuous, and dangerous work was the main motive behind these rulings. The authorities obviously preferred to employ healthy prisoners rather than those who had been whipped 100, 200, or even 300 times, which might even have killed them.

In the 1820s and 1830s, the slave game and pastime capoeira, according to whites, became a means of disturbing the peace. A letter addressed to the police commissioner in 1816 indicates the change in the government's policies:

FIGURE 1.2. *São Salvador.* From João Maurício Rugendas, *Viagem pitoresca através do Brasil* (São Paulo: Livraria Martins Editôra, 1954), FIGURE 1/27. Reproduced by kind permission of the British Library.

> The office of this inspectorate has been apprised that the black Capoeiras in this city, especially in Direita Street, commit disturbances of the peace and throw rocks during their games that are held in various places. Your Highness is required to arrange for security escorts, especially on festive days, so that they can arrest all those who participate in the games as well as those who cause disturbances of the peace.[14]

This letter suggests a clear distinction between the Capoeiras' games and the disturbances arising from them. But as regards the authorities, arrest was mandatory in any case of disturbance caused by or connected to the games. The terms used by the authorities were modified accordingly. The term "capoeira game," widely used in police records in the first two decades of the century, was almost entirely absent in the 1830s, replaced by "Capoeiras" or "black Capoeiras."

Early in December 1821, six people were murdered, and Capoeiras were accused of the crime. A military committee investigating the "capoeira phenomenon" recommended that the minister of war "publicly and relentlessly punish the black Capoeiras arrested by military escorts for disturbing the peace. We absolutely denounce the Police General Inspector's practice of releasing Capoeiras if no specific paragraph in the penal code is found."[15] This recommendation clearly reflects the committee's disapproval of the prevailing policy toward Capoeiras and the ambiguity regarding their punishments. Black Capoeiras were arrested, then, for disturbing the peace. This policy apparently gave license to release those who had not been charged with crimes such as robbery, larceny, and murder. This was due to pressure exerted by the slave owners, who had to pay prison expenses and needed to get their slaves back as soon as possible. Further complaints about the slaves' crimes were routine matters. Resolution 122, dated May 28, 1824, states, "We have been apprised that black slaves called Capoeiras continue their insolent deeds and disturb the peace in the streets of this city."[16] In December of the same year, Police Inspector Estevão Ribeiro de Resende wrote a letter to Superintendent Miguel Nunes Vidigal:

> Last Sunday large gangs of black Capoeiras disturbed the peace in scandalous collaboration. . . . I have noticed that on Sundays and feast days these despicable persons congregate and that more knifings, casualties, and robberies are registered. It is not enough for the police patrols to disperse the crowds. The culprits must be punished instantly and publicly, which is why I recommend that the mounted patrols be doubled on such days.[17]

The clashes among Capoeiras themselves or with peaceful citizens sometimes had deplorable results. In June 1833 the Rio de Janeiro police chief, Eusébio de Queiróz Coutinho Matoso Câmara (1833–1844), complained that "the Capoeiras' gall has reached such a point that incidents of stone throwing in Campo de Santana certainly endanger peaceful passersby."[18] He requested that the minister of justice grant permission to extend police authority regarding the incarceration and flogging of slaves arrested for capoeira. Sometimes there were fatalities. For example, on November 18, 1833, "two black men were found stabbed to death on São Lourenço Street, and in Principe . . . two wounded men said that Capoeiras had stabbed them."[19] On July 27, 1831, because of the inability of the police to deal with these crimes, Justice of the Peace Diego Antônio Feijó, assistant to the general inspector of police, recommended that citizens should assist the police in outlying areas of the city and in the suburbs. Citizens who met the requirements (tavern owners, cashiers, tenured employees who proved themselves responsible and reliable) were given special training, and they were granted permission to use firearms and arrest Capoeiras and others who had committed or plotted to commit crimes. It is noteworthy that the judge demanded that they "arrest active black Capoeiras as well as those who train for it (capoeira) even for purposes of entertainment."[20] Although the authorities distinguished between forbidden activities such as disturbing the peace and innocuous activities such as training for fun and recreation, all such activities were prohibited.

In the first decade of the nineteenth century, slave owners allowed their slaves to celebrate and while away their time, especially on Sundays and feast days, in the city squares and to dance their traditional dances. For a long time whites' attitude to the slaves' social and cultural activities was quite dismissive. Travelers shared this view, as can be seen in the account of Charles Ribeyrolls, a Frenchman who visited Brazil in the mid-nineteenth century and described the dances he saw:

> Here capoeira is a kind of war dance, with the Congo drum beating out a powerful, militant rhythm. Then there is the batuque with its sensual movements (*laçiva*), with the *urucungo* (the berimbau) intensifying or slowing down the rhythm. Farther on I see another wild dance, with taunting eyes, waists, and thighs. This kind of intoxicating undulation is called lundu. Primitive joy, disgusting lasciviousness, lustful heat. All this is debased and pitiful. But the blacks love to dance and others benefit from it.[21]

Some slave owners were reassured by this, claiming that the dances embodied the blacks' happiness and satisfaction despite their enslavement—the best proof that slavery should not be abolished.[22] But with time and increasing numbers of slaves, their masters became convinced that such gatherings were fertile ground for subversive activities, and outbursts of rioting sometimes caused disturbances, injuries, and casualties. This reversal of attitude soon led to banning the dances. Records of prohibitions imposed on various dances and games in Rio de Janeiro as of the 1810s are quite frequent. For example, after the death of Queen Maria I in 1816, Police Commissioner Paulo Fernando Viana prohibited blacks from holding the customary celebrations after the death of a dignitary. He banned "fights and games that blacks customarily perform at such events."[23] A year later, in 1817, the dances of the Nossa Senhora do Rosário Brotherhood in Campo de Santana were prohibited because of drunkenness and disturbing the peace. Dancing the batuque was also forbidden.[24] In 1821 Police Commissioner Viana again banned "once and for all the blacks' dances . . . and anything else performed on feast days in certain homes, which encourages drunkenness, insults, and disturbances of the peace."[25] The newspaper *O Universo* reported on August 15, 1825, "A slave found playing, either by day or by night, will be arrested and punished with 25 lashes."[26]

What the authorities feared most were not the dances and games themselves but the gathering of slaves in large numbers.

Capoeira was not unique, as can be deduced from another letter dated October 9, 1816:

> Disturbances of the peace caused by blacks have increased. They follow the peels game (*casquinha*) publicly played in squares and on street corners, especially in the vicinity of taverns. The neighbors are furious and scandalized by the noise and screams heard in the place following the excessive drinking. His Highness should dispatch patrol units to various places in the city to restore order. Those found participating in these games must be arrested and immediately punished by flogging and then sentenced to do public works. The prisons are filled with blacks found at tavern doors, sitting at the bar where water is transported, and it is in such gatherings that numerous disturbances of the peace are recorded. Why do they congregate around taverns? It is known that tavern owners approve of such gatherings because of the profits they make from serving drinks and providing other services connected to taverns. . . . These gatherings in the city squares and around tavern doors are the cause of daily disturbances of the peace and of the neighbors' complaints.[27]

This letter not only expresses objection to the peels game but also to slaves or blacks gathering around the taverns to drink. Despite writs and numerous arrests, the authorities felt that the situation was getting out of hand. They therefore prohibited all games, including the pancada (palm games), dice, and gambling games. In addition to orders banning gatherings of blacks at celebrations, funerals, games, and other occasions, slaves were forbidden to carry arms. Blacks, both slaves and free men, were not allowed to be out at night after curfew, and slaves were denied the right to wear shoes so that they could be distinguished from the rest of the population. The reason for these orders was control over the slaves and prevention of illicit activities that might be dangerous to their masters and the government.[28] The list of edicts issued in 1830 to control undesired activities reflects the internal hierarchy set up by the police regarding degrees of disturbances of the peace:

> The commander of the Imperial Police Force has issued strict orders to the units under his command to enforce the laws and edicts, . . . especially those forbidding slave gatherings or participation in funerals with superstitious rites that involve crowding, depraved actions, and lewd verbal expressions; those that forbid crowding and games in taverns, streets, and public squares; those relating to slave nudity or littering in the squares and streets; those relating to Capoeiras and to searching slaves in order to prevent the

use of weapons and sticks; and finally to all those edicts designed to assure public safety and security.[29]

It should be noted that capoeira and possession of arms are almost last on this detailed list, after littering and nudity.

Regarded in the early nineteenth century as a game that could erupt into violence, as early as the 1820s capoeira was considered a real threat to public peace—as were many other slave activities. Capoeiras were perceived as dangerous and violent offenders when they trained for purposes of recreation, and even more so when their gatherings ended in rioting. Who were these people who upset the authorities so much?

Origins of the Capoeiras

The Capoeiras of the early nineteenth century were black slaves, mainly from West Central Africa. The number of slaves brought from Africa to the New World has not yet been established, but many studies have attempted to determine the extent of the slave trade. The question is still unresolved, but some data may give a general picture of the numbers involved. Herbert Klein conjectures that the number of slaves transported from Africa between 1451 and 1870 was more than 10 million. In his opinion, more than 4 million, that is, 40 percent, were brought to the shores of Brazil. Rio de Janeiro was the prime "consumer" of this "commodity" between 1795 and 1811. More than 96 percent of all slaves landing here were brought from ports in West Central Africa (see Table 1.1).

Philip D. Curtin found in his study that between 1817 and 1843, 70 percent of all the slaves brought to Rio de Janeiro were transported from the shores of West Central Africa (Table 1.2 and Map 1.1).

In the nineteenth century West Central Africa was divided into three main regions: northern Congo (Cabinda), Angola, and Benguela. The northern Congo stretched from Cape Lopes to the estuary of the Zaire River. These definitions are not entirely accurate. The slave traders collected slaves of diverse origins at various ports in the same area, categorizing all of them as a single "cargo" of common origin. This means that slaves with diverse cultures, languages, and customs may have been taken from areas in the northern Congo and transported on foot or by boat to Cabinda, where they were transferred to larger vessels. On arrival in Rio de Janeiro they were lumped together and known as Cabinda. Until 1830 more than 28 percent of all slave ships dropping anchor at Rio sailed from this port. A decade later, when slave trading from the port of Luanda declined owing to pressure exerted by the English beginning in the 1840s,

Table 1.1. Slaves Brought to Rio de Janeiro, 1795–1811

Port of Departure	Number Brought to Brazil	Percentage	Number of Ships Arriving in Brazil
West Africa	**1,797**	**1.2**	**8**
Mina Coast	583		2
Calabar	639		2
São Tomé	575		4
West Central Africa	**148,576**	**96.2**	**329**
Cabinda	898		2
Angola	73,175		162
Benguela	74,503		165
East Africa	**3,577**	**2.3**	**13**
Unknown	**549**	**0.3**	**1**
Total	**154,489**	**100**	**351**

Source: Klein, "The Trade in African Slaves to Rio de Janeiro, 1795–1811," p. 540.

Table 1.2. Origin of Slaves Brought to Rio de Janeiro, 1817–1843

Port of Departure	Number of Slaves	Percentage
West Africa	**2,700**	**0.7**
Benin Bay	600	
Biafra Bay	1,000	
São Tome & Principe	900	
Senegambia & Sierra Leone	200	
West Central Africa	**268,500**	**71.1**
Angola	172,600	
Northern Congo	95,900	
East Africa	**92,400**	**24.5**
Unknown	**14,000**	**3.7**
Total	**377,600**	**100**

Source: Curtin, *The Atlantic Slave Trade*, p. 240.

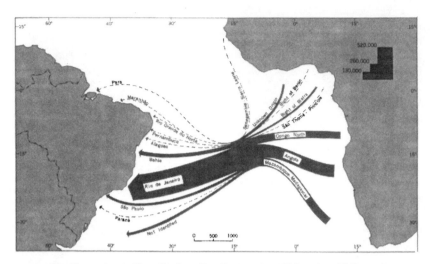

MAP 1.1. The Transatlantic Slave Trade to Brazil, 1817–1843. University of Wisconsin Cartography Lab.

Cabinda played a central role in the slave trade. Besides Cabinda, several other ports in the same region supplied slaves to meet the increasing demand: Loango, Mayumba, and Malemba (Map 1.2).[30] Slaves from Gabon (called Gabão) and from Boma, Tio Kingdom, the Zaire River, and Ubangi were all categorized as northern Kongolese. The name "Congo" was commonly given to slaves from the northern Congo, although the network of slave trading collected them from hundreds of diverse nations along the Zaire River. Slaves from Bakongo, northern Angola, and southern Zaire were also called "Congo." Another group, constituting about a third of all the slaves brought to Rio, were known as "Angola." In the nineteenth century the Angola slaves came mainly from Luanda, which was at the time a major Portuguese port, and from Cassange. Although this area was quite small, it comprised several ethnic groups. After the British put a stop to shipping slaves from there, the volume of the slave trade in the neighboring port of Ambriz increased. Slaves known as Cassange were transported from the markets of Cassange in eastern Angola. The names Ambaca, Rebolo, Quissama, and Luanda were also well known and widespread. The Benguela, in modern-day Angola, constituted a separate group, the largest, brought to Rio de Janeiro. They were named for their port of departure, Benguela, in southern Angola, and this port also became an important slave trading center after the English closed the port of Luanda to slave ships. Included in this category were the Ovimbundu and the Ganguela.

West Central Africa is divided into four main linguistic groups: the BaKongo of northern Angola, who were transported on the Zaire River; the Mbundu of central Angola, who were shipped from the ports of Luanda and Ambriz; the Lunda-Tchokwe of eastern Angola, who were traded through the markets of Cassange and Luanda; and the Ovimbundu and the Ngangela of southern Angola, who were sold at Benguela (Map 1.2). As shown in Tables 1.1 and 1.2, until 1811 most of the slaves from West Central Africa were Angolans. The number diminished later to about 45 percent.[31]

In the early nineteenth century it was customary to call slaves by first name and port of departure or nation, so that, for example, Manuel Cabinda was a slave who was transported from Cabinda and Antônio Mozambique was probably shipped from Mozambique.

Soares suggests that most of the slaves arrested on account of capoeira were

Africa: The Origins of the African Nations
of Rio de Janeiro.

MAP 1.2. The Origin of the African Nations of Rio de Janeiro. From Mary C. Karasch, *Slave Life in Rio de Janeiro, 1808–1850*, p. 16. © 1987 Princeton University Press. Reprinted by permission of Princeton University Press.

Table 1.3. Origin of Arrested Capoeiras, 1810–1821

West Central Africa	*West Africa*
Congo: 62	Mina: 16
Benguela: 59	Calabar: 7
Cabinda: 45	
Angola: 34	
Cassange: 16	
Cabonda: 8	
Rebolo: 21	
Monjulo: 10v	
Songo: 5	
Mofumba: 3	
Ganguela: 3	
Kisama: 3	
Total: 269	**Total: 23**

Source: Soares, *A capoeira escrava*, p. 599.

named "Congo." Then came those labeled "Benguela," and slightly fewer were those transported from Cabinda (Table 1.3).[32]

More than one-third of the slaves brought to Rio de Janeiro were shipped from Benguela. Many slaves nicknamed Congo were abducted and transported via the Zaire River, and Cabinda was also a major slave trading port on the estuary of the Zaire River. Although the area itself was quite small, its population maintained mutual economic connections, and each tribe was acquainted with the traditions and customs of its neighbors, thus exerting mutual cultural influence.

Although it is generally agreed that the first Capoeiras in Brazil were of West Central African origin, there is no consensus as to the origin of capoeira itself. There are those who see it as an expression of the slaves' reaction to oppression and slavery (the "Brazilianists") and those who regard it as emphasizing African roots, traditions, and heritage (the "Africanists").[33] Many Brazilianists maintain that it began in the *quilombos* (settlements of runaway slaves), though no documents have been found to substantiate this premise.[34] Some see the plantations as its birthplace, while others base their argument on written sources and believe that it began in the marketplaces of the city.[35]

Some Africanists believe capoeira is rooted in West Central African warfare traditions. Written sources from the sixteenth century, when Portuguese involvement commenced in Congo-Angola, describe war dances and martial training that present some similarities to capoeira. A Jesuit priest described the Ndongo soldiers' abilities as follows: "Their defense consists of 'sanguar'—leaping from side to side with a thousand twists and such agility that they can dodge arrows and spears."[36] Another theory suggests that it was based on a contemporary war dance, the *n'golo* (the zebra dance), performed during the Efundula, a puberty rite for girls of the Mucope, Muxilenge, and Muhumbè tribes of southern Angola. The Angolan artist Albano Neves e Souza, who visited Brazil in the 1960s, pointed out some resemblances between capoeira and the *n'golo*.[37] Recently, T. J. Desch-Obi developed a connection between martial techniques and combat games by suggesting a correlation between the southwestern Angolan twentieth-century striking arts (*kandeka* and *engolo*) and the seventeenth-century military culture of the Imbangala groups.[38] This theory has many weaknesses, including lack of evidence, other games that resemble capoeira that could indicate different roots, and the broad changes in West Central African cultures, especially that of the Imbangala, that have occurred over time.[39] It does indeed seem simplistic to specify a single performance, place, date, and people as the source of capoeira. Since the Congo-Angola population maintained relationships of exchange, I believe that, through the Atlantic slave trade, the West Central African fighting techniques, war dances, and combat games reached Brazil and combined to form the basis of capoeira.

Characteristics of Capoeiras

In addition to sharing African origin, Capoeiras shared certain group activities, social loyalty, and the use of light arms. They also used unique symbols and methods of communication.

As a game, capoeira was a social activity involving a number of participants. On May 31, 1815, for example, the Guarda Real captured a group of ten enslaved Capoeiras. Five of them were from the Congo, one from Mina, one from Mozambique, one from Angola, one mulatto from Brazil, and one from Ganguela.[40] On February 4, 1818, five slaves—Bento Congo, Manuel Congo, Francisco Congo, Jorge Cabinda, and Francisco Mozambique—were arrested for playing capoeira.[41] Apart from whiling away their time together, they considered themselves comrades in misfortune. They were loyal to their fellow sufferers and tried to help each other in times of trouble. A case in point is the occurrence on March 20, 1820, when Bernardo Mina was arrested, and his friend, Brazilian-born Estanislao, tried to resist arrest and called out to his capoeira comrades, who hurled stones at the patrol and surrounded it. Sadly, these attempts to free Bernardo and Estanislao failed.[42]

Resistance was not directed solely against the authorities but also against other rival groups. Around seven o'clock on the evening of July 26, 1831, two capoeira groups consisting of two hundred men came to blows in the São José neighborhood by the beach. When the civil guard intervened and before the group dispersed, a Capoeirista threw a stone at the patrol captain's head and wounded him. Two blacks and one mulatto were arrested and brought to trial. Later that evening the parties regrouped and continued to fight in another area of the city.[43] The reasons for the fighting are not specified in the report, but on the arrival of a third party, representing the authorities, they joined forces in resistance. Once the patrol had gone, they began fighting each other again.

The hierarchy within these groups was clearly defined, accepted by the group members, and known to the authorities. For example, José Angola, slave of João Alves, was arrested on November 25, 1819, for playing capoeira: "Along with others who escaped, he is a recognized capoeira leader."[44] In most cases of arrest, the authorities cited use of cold arms, for example, stones, knives, razors, clubs, and sticks. Such was the case in the arrest of a slave on April 14, 1812, for playing capoeira and hurling stones.[45] On July 25, 1817, José Benguela was arrested for playing capoeira and having in his possession a *faca de ponta* (a large, very sharp knife).[46] On the same day, Joaquim Augusto was arrested for playing capoeira and carrying an *estoque* (saber).[47] On February 4, 1818, five slaves playing capoeira were captured with a *navalha de ponta* (a kind of razor).[48] On January 3, 1820, the slave Joaquim Angola was arrested for possessing "a razor and a capoeira club."[49]

On November 16, 1832, the police inspector warned the chief of the military police that "the black Capoeiras and other individuals of the same inclination carry spears and other kinds of weapons concealed inside marimbas, pieces of sugarcane, and the handles of small black whips made in our country."[50] He demanded that the patrol apprehend suspects and search them in order to find these weapons and bring the culprits to justice. It is noteworthy that cold arms were not exclusively used by Capoeiras but were widespread among the general enslaved population, who used some of them for their daily work as well as for personal protection.

Rebellions and Capoeiras

The fear of slave uprisings was constant among slave owners, especially after they occurred in Haiti, the United States, and Brazil itself (Bahia and Pará), among other places.[51] Wherever there were more slaves than owners, fear and suspicion increased, and more stringent prohibitions were imposed on any crowd, meeting, or association that might, in the authorities' view, facilitate plotting.

Was there a special attitude toward Capoeira in the early decades of the nineteenth century, and was there a system for putting down possible insurrection? These questions are still applicable today in the context of the attempts of contemporary Capoeiras and modern research to depict capoeira as a crucial element in suppressing the mercenaries' revolt in 1828, or as a major cause of rioting, and good reason for the authorities' apprehension.

The first recorded mutiny in Rio de Janeiro arose from the grievances of German and Irish mercenaries in regard to their conditions of service. It began early in June 1828, in the wake of a punishment of 250 lashes on a mercenary soldier accused of dereliction of duty by his officers. The soldier protested the severity of the punishment, raised his voice, and demanded a fair trial. This show of insubordination was futile, tempers flared, the mercenaries began advancing on the palace of King Pedro I, but they were not given a hearing. Their commander was arrested for fanning the flames of hatred. The mutiny spread rapidly, and by June 10 the riots had already swept through large sections of the city, in areas of São Cristovão, Lagoa, and Praia Vermelha. By the following day hostilities had reached as far as Santana and included raids, robberies, and arson, as well as assault, maiming, and murder of blacks and mercenaries alike. The rebellion was quashed on June 12, with grievous results. The number of wounded and dead was high, the damage was great, and the city was in a state of panic. Elísio de Araújo, who investigated the police between 1808 and 1831, wrote, in 1898, in connection with this rebellion:

> Many of the Germans of São Cristovão managed to gather in one place.
> Those who did not were attacked by a mass of blacks known as Capoeiras
> and engaged them in deadly combat. Even at their posts, and armed with
> rifles, the rebels could not resist the fists, stones, and sticks [of the blacks].
> They fell in the streets and public squares, wounded or dead.[52]

This vivid description of "blacks known as Capoeiras" fighting the mutinous mercenaries generated a different approach to them among twentieth-century scholars: it was the blacks who had saved helpless whites from the cruel mercenaries and hooligans. Jair Moura, a Capoeirista himself and a capoeira researcher, describes the Capoeiras' role in repelling the street fighters and restoring the peace.[53] The anthropologist Leticia Reis depicted the Capoeiras who risked their lives and saved the city.[54] The anthropologist Lewis Lowell stated, "Major Vidigal contacted the Capoeiras of Rio and told them to take care of the

situation, whereupon the latter harried the mercenaries back to their barracks."
According to Lowell, "this story shows that, even though the practice of capoeira
was generally looked down upon by members of the Brazilian elite in the 19th
century, there was also some ambivalence toward the players, based on their
undeniable prowess at fighting."[55] Other scholars, including Paulo Coelho de
Araújo, Antônio Liberac Pires, and Mathias Röhrig Assunção, support Lowell.[56]
In his recent book, *A capoeira escrava*, Carlos Eugênio Líbano Soares presents
various documents proving that Capoeiras never participated in the riots. But
he also makes a direct connection between the "blacks" in the written sources
and capoeira: "The negro insurrection . . . allows us to consider an important
aspect of capoeira and slavery in Rio de Janeiro—the slaves' and liberated blacks'
participation in the politically most dynamic movements of the first half of the
nineteenth century."[57] During this era, neither slave nor black organizations en-
dangered the social order of Rio by rebelling. Soares concludes, "It seems that
the likelihood of such a rebellion was more feared by the rulers than intended by
the Africans and Creoles of the city."[58]

Thus contemporary myths linking capoeira with rebellion are inaccurate, to
say the least. Although the authorities were alarmed at the possibility of a slave
rebellion, this had no direct connection to capoeira.

Six days after the mutiny was crushed, Police Commissioner Nicolāu de
Queirós published an edict in the name of King Pedro I, in the newspaper *Diário
do Rio de Janeiro* and throughout the city, forbidding all blacks, especially slaves,
to use any kind of weapon.[59] This edict was issued in the wake of a rebellion
that was initiated, not by blacks, but by mercenaries, even though there already
existed edicts to the same effect from the eighteenth century. Apparently the
edict was neither observed nor enforced as slaves did carry weapons and were
not averse to using them. The traveler Robert Walsh, who witnessed some incidents occurring in the course of the rebellion, described the following case in
point:

> Several Irish craftsmen worked in Rio and made a very good living. One
> of them, a tailor, returned to his quarter with a bundle of clothes under his
> arm, unaware of the mutiny that had just started, when he was stopped by
> two good-for-nothing *moleques* in one of the streets leading to Campo da
> Aclamação (better known as Campo de Santana). They assaulted him with
> their knives, kicked him in different parts of the body, then ripped his belly
> open and left him to die on the ground with his guts spilling out.[60]

Walsh's interpretation of the situation was as follows: "Imagine that there are
fifty or sixty thousand slaves in this big, unruly city, and that they constitute the

great majority of its inhabitants. It is frightening to think of what may occur at any moment if there is large-scale incitement."[61] But did the slaves really initiate the rebellion?

On June 12, 1828, the day the mutiny was put down, the justice minister sent a letter to the police commissioner demanding that all necessary measures be taken to prevent the recurrence of the events that had taken place a few days before:

> I have already dispatched, through the War Department, edicts concerning the recent disturbances perpetrated by the *Irish soldiers*, and I am willing to take all necessary precautions that such events do not occur again. His Royal Highness recommends that the Commissioner should also take the appropriate measures in regard to the *blacks*, so that they do not insult or provoke the Irish, as has already happened, and that they are arrested immediately at your discretion, so that peace and quiet, which we are trying so hard to maintain in our capital city, will be completely restored. The street patrols should be instructed both to maintain peace and order, and to prevent blacks from using vulgar language that is offensive to the public sense of modesty and morality.[62]

What is apparent here is that the authorities used the term "disturbance" rather than "rebellion," which has much more severe implications. Moreover, mentioning the Irish mercenaries' and the blacks' provocation of the soldiers in the same context suggests a connection between them. It seems that the authorities considered both groups dangerous and guilty. The Irish mercenaries incited the rioters, while the blacks were accused of insulting and provoking the soldiers, thereby instigating brawls and street fighting. It is far from clear whether the references to blacks in the edict, as in other documents, refer to slaves, to free men, or to liberated men of a certain origin. Robert Walsh accused the authorities of using blacks to sow the seeds of hatred of foreigners, and no distinction was made between Irishmen, Germans, or others. His observations suggest that the tension was purely the blacks' fault, because they taunted the mercenaries, called them names such as "white slaves," and made fun of their clothes. He also criticized the biased policies of the police:

> In these brawls, if an Irishman happened to intervene and catch a few slaves—those who had obviously begun the fighting—in order to hand them over to the police—the slaves would be detained for several hours and then released to return and attack again. Conversely, if there was a complaint against a foreigner, he would be incarcerated in the citadel, or sent to work in the galleys.[63]

Walsh expressed deep frustration at the government's policy of freeing guilty slaves while severely punishing foreigners, who seem to have been the scapegoats whom the authorities conspired to oppress by using blacks. This may not have been the whole truth, but there are documents attesting to the fact that tension did exist between white foreigners and blacks, perhaps because of the tough competition for employment. The definitions in the edicts are not unequivocal. In most cases the word "blacks" was used, but accusations may have been made against liberated or free men competing with poor white immigrants who were also seeking employment. Certainly the authorities were very concerned about the increasing number of slaves and were always on the alert. According to the 1834 census, white immigrants numbered 6,727; free blacks, 5,908; and slaves, 43,349. Some researchers claim that there were many more, because the census only included slaves who were twelve years of age and older.[64] Despite attempts by historians, folklorists, sociologists, and anthropologists to depict Capoeiras as having saved the citizens of Rio de Janeiro from the rebel mercenaries in 1828, the reality was perceived quite differently at the time. All the documents concerning those who fought against the mercenaries indicate that blacks were involved. Sometimes slaves were mentioned specifically, though not Capoeiras. Indeed, many viewed blacks as having fanned the flames of violence and conflict. During the fighting people were killed and wounded, so that possession of weapons constituted a serious threat to public peace. Fear of an uprising was inseparable from the system of slavery but had no direct connection with the Capoeiras. This attitude was in evidence for several years after the rebellion in Salvador, Bahia, which broke out on the night of January 24, 1835, and lasted for several hours. This time, the groups that led the rebellion were known as Malês, a term referring to Moslems from West Africa.[65] News about the uprising quickly reached Rio via the newspapers, but the authorities were very cautious in dealing with it, especially in view of the flourishing slave trade between Bahia and Rio. All those concerned received recommendations and edicts regarding the steps that should be taken. One such edict from March 17, 1835, states:

> The Governor . . . hopes that all necessary measures will be taken and that everything essential will be done to calm the citizens of the capital, who fear a repetition of the horrific scenes that occurred in Bahia during the African uprising. I recommend that all precautionary measures be taken in regard to the black Minas who may have settled in these areas . . . in case there are suspicious associations . . . and that anyone who looks suspicious should be searched, in accordance with the law, as and when determined by Your Honor.[66]

This document confirms the apprehension felt by many citizens about the slaves transported from Bahia to Rio and specifically requests an investigation of slaves from Mina.

The precautions taken by the authorities were not only against residents who had already settled in various sections of the city but also against slaves transported to Rio from Bahia. A day later the following instructions were issued:

> It has come to my attention that numerous Ladinos [slaves from the coasts of Mina, West Africa] have arrived in the Province of Rio de Janeiro from the Province of Bahia. The Governor orders Your Highness in the name of the Emperor that investigations should be conducted, and that Your Highness should not approve the disembarkation of anybody unless they establish their innocence and carry no suspicion of involvement in the recent rebellion in that city.[67]

One month later, on April 4, another slave ship arrived at Rio from Bahia, with eighty-nine slaves on board. Most of them were from West Africa.[68] The police commissioner denied their disembarkation until an investigation had been conducted and they were cleared of any crime.[69]

The city at the time was rife with fear and suspicion, with rumors and denunciations. Today it is hard to establish whether these suspicions had any basis or were merely a figment of the imagination of panicky masters. In any case, instructions were again issued about precautions to be taken against potential rebellion, such as this document dated May 13, 1835:

> The government continues to receive allegations about clandestine meetings of colored men. . . . In the name of the Emperor, I recommend that investigations by inspectors, patrols, and lookouts be constantly carried out. . . . A survey of the colored men in the various areas should be dispatched as soon as possible to the secretariat of the Ministry of Justice, listing their names, condition, status, lifestyle, origin, religious affiliations, when and where they meet, and whether they are inclined to mutiny, or preach seditious political ideas.[70]

These fears and apprehensions were an excuse for brutal treatment. For example, on December 28, 1836, a slave named Graciano Mina was apprehended. His previous convictions included disrespect to the authorities, illegal possession of arms, and participation in capoeira. After Graciano tried to escape three times, his owner, Jacomo Rombo, tied him up and beat him mercilessly. The severe punishment and its devastating consequences to the slave's health were widely publicized. Luis da Costa Franco e Almeida, the justice of the peace who was in charge of the Sacramento police force, was appointed to investigate whether such brutal punishment of a slave constituted a crime. After two doctors had examined the unfortunate man, the judge decided that he should remain with his owner and granted him thirty days of convalescence before being reexamined by the doctors. Judge Almeida stated that though this specific case constituted a criminal offense, the slave in question—an infamous and dangerous Capoeirista of Mina origin—might well become a rebel like those in Bahia and Minas Gerais.[71]

In oral history Capoeiras figure conspicuously in the Bahia rebellions.[72] This may be yet another attempt to rewrite history and link capoeira to the struggle to abolish slavery. In reality, not every breach of the peace was automatically attributed to Capoeira, nor were those arrested for playing capoeira automatically accused of plotting a rebellion. However, ethnic origin was considered grounds for suspicion. Most Capoeiras at that time were slaves from West Central Africa, but it was the Malês who instigated the rebellion in Bahia.

Thus it is quite clear that from the authorities' standpoint in the nineteenth century, capoeira was a game played by African slaves who might become aggressive and dangerous but was not significantly different from other activities such as dancing, gatherings, funerals, ceremonies, or rituals. On the other hand, it was used by Capoeiras to undermine public order and threaten the lives of peaceful citizens, though not as an organized movement. In either case, Capoeiras were severely punished when caught, though this is only one aspect of the problem, evident in documents written mainly by Europeans. I want to turn now to what capoeira meant to the Capoeiras themselves.

PART 2. THE VARIOUS MEANINGS OF CAPOEIRA

Unfortunately, the slaves left no written records to shed light on their beliefs and ideas. We know that for the authorities, there were aspects of capoeira that they did not wish or try to understand. They knew what the Capoeiras wore and about their symbols, slang, whistles, and other habitual characteristics, but the authorities quite often preferred to ignore these details, perceiving them either as dangerous and unacceptable or as meaningless and of no interest. This lacuna was filled, to some extent, by tourists and travelers who recorded their impressions of Brazil. In most cases these narratives depicted regions, natural phenomena, events, and incidents that conveyed the special flavor of the place. Unlike the authorities, these authors focused their attention on the unfamiliar, although certainly there were financial considerations. Authors who wanted their books to be published obviously had to produce work that would attract readers, so they selected and described things that they perceived as particularly exotic. Their descriptions also had to be authentic. A travelogue must be analyzed judiciously, and the reader must take into account the interests and motives of its author, which doubtless influenced the interpretation of his or her observations and descriptions.

Dance or Game?

In nineteenth-century documents—police records, newspapers, and travelogues—there are various references to capoeira, sometimes as a game and sometimes as a war dance. For example, police records describe the culprits as "playing" (*jogando*) capoeira; whereas in his travelogue Rugendas describes it as a war dance that might become aggressive.[73] Today it is also defined as a Brazilian battle dance, though Capoeiras use the term "game" and invite each other to "play capoeira." Some use the word *brincar*, used to refer to playing a children's game.

In the course of fieldwork in Rio and Bahia, I interviewed Capoeiras from different groups and asked why past and present Capoeiras use the word "game" rather than "fight" or "dance." The most common response was surprise, not at the question, but because they have no definitive answer, never having considered the matter. After some thought, many of them said that by calling it a game, the slaves concealed their activities from their owners or strangers. Modern-day Capoeiras seem to believe that it was the Capoeiras themselves who called this pastime a game in order to allay, or not to arouse, their masters' suspicions. Hence the authorities also called it a game.[74]

This explanation is hard to accept because "play" does not necessarily signify today what it did in the early nineteenth century. Some activities, including capoeira, gambling, and certain dances, were classified as play at that time but were severely punished by law. The slaves supposedly playing capoeira were subjected to flogging and imprisonment, although many Capoeiras insist that they had managed to deceive their masters into believing that they were playing a game.

Another reason, which I term the spatial dimension, is much more complex and central to this discussion. It relates to the understanding and perception of the term "play" deriving from the cultural differences between rulers and subjects, masters and slaves. "Play" in early-nineteenth-century Brazil had quite different connotations for whites and for blacks.

Blacks' Games and Dances

Among Christian Europeans, dancing was regarded as a debased physical activity, the antithesis of spirituality. The needs of the body and those of the soul were therefore to be kept as separate, as was dancing from religion. The Christian church was adamant in its objections to any form of dancing, having tried to suppress it for hundreds of years by enacting various decrees beginning in A.D. 465 and up until the Trent Convention.[75] Centuries of suppression have mutated into the modern perception of dance as a medium expressing joy, a popular social activity, and a pleasurable diversion.[76] When whites saw blacks dancing, they concluded that they were demonstrating satisfaction and happiness. The seventeenth-century Dutch slave trader William Bosman described the nature of the people on the Gold Coast:

> These degenerate vices are accompanied with their sisters, sloth and idleness, to which they are so prone that nothing but the utmost necessity can force them to labor. They are, besides, so incredibly careless and stupid, and are so little concerned at their misfortune that it is hardly to be observed by any change in them whether they have met with any good or ill success. An instance of which is, that when they have obtained a victory over their enemies, they return home diverting themselves with leaping and dancing. But if, on their side they are beaten out of the field, and utterly routed, they still feast and are merry, and dance, and can cheerfully sport around a grave. In short, prosperity and adversity are not otherwise distinguishable in them. . . . [T]hey feast at graves and, should they see their country in flames, would cry out, "Let it burn," and not suffer it in the least to interrupt their singing, dancing and drinking. They are equally insensible to grief or necessity, sing till they die, and dance into the grave.[77]

These perceptions were also common in nineteenth-century Brazil, as demonstrated by Rugendas in his analysis of the conditions of slaves:

> It seems that the blacks' state is not as bad as the European believes it to be. The slaves are like children, they enjoy the moment and are not concerned with the past or the future. They can get excited about any small event that brings them happiness. People say that at the end of their long working day, the noisiest pleasures have the same effect as resting. It is rare not to see blacks assembled, dancing and singing, at night.[78]

Dancers appeared to be carefree, enjoying the moment and apparently untroubled by their harsh circumstances and enslavement. Europeans did not associate grief, pain, anger, frustration, or hope with dancing. Furthermore, their deep-rooted Christian aversion to blacks' sensuous movements, blatant sexuality, and partial nudity make it understandable that these dancers were perceived as inferior, uncivilized, childlike creatures. To the Western mind, play, being unproductive (and therefore inferior), was the antithesis of work, an insignificant leisure activity.

In the diverse cultures of West Central Africa, the word "dance" has several meanings. Dancing is an inseparable part of daily life. People worked, played, prayed, mourned, and came of age dancing.[79] In Congo-Angola dance included song, music, and ritual. In the past it was customary to train and prepare for war by dancing to the accompaniment of music and song. In some regions it was actually customary to dance during battle, to raise the morale of the warriors and improve their performance.[80] This also applies to dances performed during graduation rituals, rites of passage, healing, death, or merely for fun and entertainment, as can be seen in West and West Central Africa to this day.[81] This, I contend, is why Capoeiras never regarded capoeira as a dance. For them, dancing was not, as for the Europeans, restricted to making stylized movements to music for enjoyment. For them, it was "play" in the African sense. In the Kongo, play is integral to a philosophy of life, a way to understand life, to prepare for it. Through play one can progress in Dingo-Dingo, which is, according to the Zairian researcher Kia Bunseki Fu-Kiau, "the process of living." Play contains all the necessary ingredients for living well, both physically and spiritually. It accustoms the body, muscles, and limbs to move flexibly, steadily, and harmoniously. Joy and laughter generate positive energy. Music synchronizes the dancers' movements and motivates others to join in. Movement, fun, communal singing, dancing, a sense of affinity between individual and community constitute play, which is part of the great process called life.[82] Play in these cultures includes music, singing, and movement that reacts to, affects, and is affected by the rhythms and the response of the audience. Desch-Obi argues that capoeira originated in the Imbangala tribe of southern Angola, where boys practiced the *engolo* to improve their physical fitness, to prepare for battle, and to acquire high status among men, as well as in courtship. In his words, "The point of engolo is to develop in its practitioners the ability to defend themselves against all odds, by ducking, twisting, and leaping."[83] Fu-Kiau's comprehensive study revealed that the word "capoeira" derives from the root *kupura*—"to play"—in the Ki-Kongo language. *Pula* or *pura* means waving, flying from place to place, wrestling, fighting. *Kipura* in Kongolese means cockfighting. He reports that in the Kongo there was a game called kipura in which the players, imitating fighting cocks, created a technique designed to strengthen the body, control it, and achieve physical and mental health and stability.[84] However, there is still no conclusive evidence as to whether capoeira was in fact imported from Africa or evolved in Brazil. What is clear is that African slaves brought with them their traditions and customs, including dance and play. In early-nineteenth-century Rio de Janeiro slaves played their familiar games. Those who watched the game and heard the music described what they saw as both dance and play. The authorities, observing this harmless hopping and clapping, these animal-like movements, arrested and accused the slaves of playing capoeira. Thus while the authorities of that time believed the slaves were playing the game of capoeira, they were in fact preparing themselves for the trials and tribulations of slavery according to the Bantu tradition.

Music and Power in Capoeira

Capoeira in the early and mid-nineteenth century was depicted by travelers as a war dance accompanied by drumbeats or hand clapping. Later the music and the musical instruments disappeared. Police records do not mention musical instruments. Consequently, in the early twentieth century it was assumed that capoeira originally lacked the element of music and was a martial art that the slaves tried to disguise with music, dancing, and singing. The idea of music as concealment was encouraged by two teachers of modern capoeira, Manuel dos Reis Machado, better known as Mestre Bimba, and Vicente Ferreira Pastinha (Mestre Pastinha), creators of Capoeira Regional (1932) and Capoeira Angola (1941), respectively, who believed that the music and the African dance movements were intended to deceive slave owners.[85] Other scholars have supported this assumption. Iria D'aquino, for example, described capoeira as a martial art that African slaves created and developed in Brazil in order to stand up to their better-armed adversaries:

> Because it developed and was practiced under the watchful eye of white masters and plantation supervisors, capoeira was disguised as a diversion, as an innocuous dance performed for their own as well as their masters' enjoyment.[86]

Waldeloir Rego contends:

> After considering the facts I have to conclude that the musical accompaniment did not formerly exist and that the rhythms were introduced later and are so closely synchronized with the kicks that some kicks today are named after their rhythms, and vice versa.[87]

These scholars and others, including many Capoeiras, believe that the role of music has changed over time. At first it was not needed and therefore non-existent. Later it was meant to deceive and was not an integral part of capoeira. Today it has become an organic part of the activity, an accompaniment that, according to Capoeiras, infuses them with energy and reassurance.

Is it plausible that capoeira, originating in West Central Africa where music is an inherent part of every social event, could have existed without music?

In the Bantu traditions there is no distinction between sacred and secular ceremonies. Every activity includes spiritual elements, of which music is one. The Bantu believe that music can communicate between the various spheres and penetrate from the physical world to the consciousness of the other world.[88] Music transmits nonverbal messages and instructions, creating a colloquy by responding to the reactions and behavior of participants, onlookers, and others. Each instrument has a specific role with a spiritual meaning and is an insepa-rable part of an event. The musicians, the dancers, and the audience use music, a nonverbal language with which they are familiar but which is incomprehensible to strangers.

I claim that music was integral to capoeira and played an important part in stimulating, encouraging, and fortifying the participants as well as in instructing and warning them when necessary.

From the few available sources on musical instruments associated with ca-poeira, it appears that at least until the mid-nineteenth century, it was the drum. On December 16, 1818, João Angola, José Pedro de Silva's slave, was arrested "for being at a capoeira gathering with a small drum in his possession."[89] Rugendas's illustration *Capoeira Game* (1824) shows a seated onlooker holding a drum be-tween his legs (see Figure 1.1). Maria Dundas Graham's description of March 3, 1821, probably relates to the same instrument: "The drums are made of hollow tree-trunks, four or five feet long, closed at one end with wood, and covered with skin at the other. To play these, the drummer lays his instrument on the ground and gets astride on it, and beats time with his hand."[90] The French tourist Ri-beyrolles associated capoeira with a drum he identified as "the Congo drum."[91] Fu-Kiau explains that travelers, slave owners, and the authorities often referred to certain drums as "Congo drums." He contends that this was a typographi-cal error, that the word should be "Konga," meaning "to call, to converge on a certain place for a specific purpose." The Konga drum literally means "the call-ing drum."[92] The ethnomusicologist Gerhard Kubik claims that the drum was indeed the instrument associated with capoeira and explains its function:

They [the Capoeiras] assembled in the plantations, often in the night, to practice various positions and techniques of attack and defense, usually

FIGURE 1.3. Ngoma Drum, n.d.
© ROYAL MUSEUM FOR CENTRAL
AFRICA, TERVUREN, BELGIUM.

without arms, but sometimes with knives. . . . The meetings were held
together muscially by a drum, capable of talking and so able to to direct and
control the movements of the trainers.[93]

Kubik regards capoeira as a martial art in which the drum guides and controls
the actions of the participants rather than being a mere accompaniment or a
means of deception. The talking drum is a mentor—a teacher—who instructs
the students. In the Congo, this drum, known as *ngoma*, was and still is of great
importance (see Figures 1.3, 1.4). They transmitted messages to individual soldiers and to entire units, in a language that was familiar to the warriors.[94]

The Italian historian and traveler Filippo Pigafetta, who published a book
titled *Relatione del reame di Congo* in 1591, explained the role of the musical instruments as follows:

On hearing the kettle-drums, or the cornet, or the third instrument, every
part of the army responds with its own instruments to show the signs were
understood, the under officers doing the same. And not only were these
sounds used as a general thing, but also in the act of fighting; for, during the
skirmishes, brave men went with the instruments in front of soldiers, dancing and beating drums to encourage them, at the same time giving warning
of any danger which threatened by the various sounds.[95]

The player uses both hands, one to create the sound and the other to moderate it. Messages are transmitted not only through the sound but also by means of bodily postures and gestures. A player bending his head to one side (*kebuka*) indicated that he was listening to the voices of the dancers or to secret signs or reprimands from the master of ceremonies (*mfumu makinu*) (Figures 1.5, 1.6}.

Turning in one direction the drummer could see blinking (*wabula*), indicating "beat louder," or winking (*bweta meeso*), meaning "be careful." Clearing the throat indicated "you are going too deep, you are revealing secrets, take care, there are strangers among us." The player could answer "bwidi! bwidi!" indicating that he heard and understood the message.[96]

The ability to talk and communicate with other worlds transforms the drum into a living entity, which was why nobody except the drummer was allowed

FIGURE 1.4. *Ngoma Drummer*, 1692. By kind permission of Robert Farris Thompson, *Four Moments of the Sun: Kongo Art in Two Worlds* (Washington, D.C.: National Gallery of Art, 1981), p. 107.

FIGURE 1.5. Ngoma Drummer in Head-Averted Pose of Concentration. By kind permission of Robert Farris Thompson, *Four Moments of the Sun: Kongo Art in Two Worlds* (Washington, D.C.: National Gallery of Art, 1981), p. 107.

FIGURE 1.6. Ngoma Drummer in Head-Averted Pose of Concentration. © ROYAL MUSEUM FOR CENTRAL AFRICA, TERVUREN, BELGIUM.

to touch the drum during the playing. Fu-Kiau says, "'ngoma' is alive when he speaks. You are forbidden to walk across his body and touch his heart."[97] Drums, especially the "talking drums," played an important part in the lives of the Yoruba of West Africa, in particular, in religious ceremonies and in times of distress, danger, and war. They encouraged and urged the soldiers on, scared off adversaries, and communicated with each other. They could alert the neighboring villages when an enemy attack was in the offing, and in the course of a battle they could fool the enemy. In the battle between the Ijaye and the Ibadan, drummers from the Ijaye succeeded in deceiving the enemy leader into thinking that they were reinforcements that had come to help.[98] The drum thus played a key role in the life of the slaves, calling them to gatherings, encouraging them, transmitting messages, accompanying social and religious events, or conveying and receiving messages from the deities and the spirits of the slaves' ancestors.

The Brazilian elite looked on the slaves' performances with great suspicion. Luís dos Santos Vilhena, a teacher of Greek in Salvador, complained in 1802:

> It does not seem very prudent, politically speaking, to tolerate crowds of Negroes of both sexes performing their barbarous batuques through the city streets and squares to the beat of many horrible atabaques [a sort of drum] indecently dancing to pagan songs, speaking various languages, and all with such frightful and discordant clamor as to cause fear and astonishment.[99]

The authorities soon realized the power of the drum. Although, or possibly because, they could not understand its meaning and significance, they were suspicious. The sound of the drum covered great distances, disquieting the authorities and the public at large. A person caught playing a drum might be punished very severely, as happened on December 5, 1820, when the slave Mathias Benguela was arrested and punished for "beating a drum—200 lashes."[100] However, punishment did not stop the drumming, and in 1833 a law was passed forbidding the use of drums in Rio de Janeiro. A relatively large instrument with a powerful sound and deep resonance, the drum could not be hidden under clothing or in a basket, so drumming was apparently restricted to nocturnal events in remote places. To avoid arrest and punishment, slaves and later free and liberated men resorted to improvised percussion instruments, such as pieces of clay or metal utensils, shells, or stones.[101]

The prohibitions, especially of drumming, were also enforced against capoeira. The drumming that accompanied capoeira in Rio de Janeiro in the early nineteenth century had disappeared by midcentury, according to available sources. But the music and the drum were so important to them that the Capoeiras could not give them up.

Capoeira and the Appeal to Supernatural Powers

In African cultures, including those of the Congo and Angola, there was no real dichotomy between sacred and profane, religion and diversion, and no activity was perceived as specifically secular. Every event—recreation, competition, or sheer fun—included elements of religious ritual. Success depended first of all on placating the gods and the ancestors, and on "medicine" and the invocation of supernatural powers. Every event was accompanied by singing, playing musical instruments, and other activities that facilitated contact with the spirit world.[102] Slaves brought these traditions and customs to Brazil and continued to perform rituals and ceremonies, to play and dance at their social events. To survive their enslavement and because their movements and social contacts were restricted, they resorted to their traditional remedies—amulets, incantations, and curses. Most of the documentation from that period was written by whites—lawyers, travelers, and officials—members of the ruling class who were ignorant of African traditions. Many of them saw the slaves as uncivilized illiterates and took no interest in them. Others adamantly objected to any cultural expression by blacks, which they construed as depraved or as a cover-up for conspiracy to rebel. Many activities were either covert or disguised, and what was observed was sometimes colored by vested interests, bias, or ignorance. Some details may have been considered unimportant or irrelevant and omitted by those who wrote about them. Because of these inadequacies, we must turn to more modern sources. Anthropological analysis of the beliefs, customs, and rituals among the Capoeiras may at last shed light on their symbols and rituals in early-nineteenth-century Brazil and reveal their meaning.

CAPOEIRA CLOTHING AND COLORS

From police reports of the period, it seems that typical capoeira garments included a hat and colored ribbons. On December 13, 1814, "José Cabinda, slave of Joaquim José Portela, and Antônio, slave of the monk Manuel da Natividade, were arrested for playing capoeira and wearing colored ribbons."[103] The slave Bernardo Moçambique was arrested on March 14, 1815, for "playing capoeira, possessing a razor, and tying a red ribbon to a pole in Santa Rita Square."[104] Three days later, João Congo, a slave belonging to Francisco Reis de Lima Pinto, was arrested for playing capoeira and for possessing a knife, a cane, and ribbons.[105] In 1818 José Rebolo, Alexandre Pinho's slave, was arrested for playing capoeira and for "wearing a white straw hat with a big yellow and red ribbon tied to its crown [*copa*]."[106] According to other records, on February 28, 1820, Francisco Rebolo, slave of José Pereira Guimarães, and José Ganguela, slave of

Table 1.4. Hats and Ribbons Worn by the Capoeiras, 1810–1821

Nationality	Status	Hat	Color	Ribbon
Angola	Slave	—	—	Yellow
Cabinda	Slave	—	—	Colorful
Creole	Slave	—	—	Colorful
Cassanga	Slave	—	—	Colorful
Cassanga	Slave	—	—	Yellow and red
Mozambique	Slave	—	—	Red
Mozambique	Slave	Bonnet (*bone*)	—	With ribbons
Angola	Slave	Brim (*barrete*)	—	With ribbons
Kongo	Slave	Capoeira brim	—	Red
Revolo	Slave	Hat (*chapéu*)	—	Yellow and red
Cabinda	Slave	Brim	—	—
Cassange	Slave	With pins (*alfinetes*)	White	—
Angola	Slave	Brim	—	—
Congo	Slave	Brim	—	—
Angola	Slave	Capoeira brim hat	—	—
Rebolo	Slave	Bonnet	Red	—
Benguela	Slave	Bonnet	Red	—
Kalabar	Slave	White feather (*pena*)	—	—
Mozambique	Slave	—	—	Capoeira

Source: Soares, *A capoeira escrava*, p. 76.

Manuel de Sousa Bastos, were arrested "for being in a gathering of Capoeiras and wearing red hats—*a capoeira symbol*."[107]

Soares listed all the police records mentioning hats and ribbons in the two volumes of Códice 403 (1810–1821) (Table 1.4).

Four of these slaves were from Angola, three from the Congo, three from Cassange, two from Mozambique, two from Cabinda, two from Rebolo, one from Calabar, one from Benguela, and one of unknown origin. Thus, of twenty arrests of Capoeiras who wore hats or ribbons, fifteen were from West Central Africa, two from East Africa, one from West Africa, one born in Brazil, and one of unknown origin. A hat and ribbons are mentioned in five of the twenty cases. In three cases the color of the ribbons is not mentioned, in one case the ribbons were yellow and red, and in one case the ribbons were red. In seven of the twenty cases, the Capoeiras were wearing ribbons but no hat. Eight Capoeiras were arrested for wearing hats—six with brims, six bonnets, and one hat with pins in it.

The colors of the hats and ribbons varied, though the authorities tended to classify both as symbols of capoeira.

In two cases the hats were quite different. On November 19, 1818, Cristovão Cassanga, slave of Francisco Pires, was arrested for playing capoeira with two others who fled. In prison he hurled a sharp knife and then denied having done so. "He brought with him two hats with pins sticking out of them," the authorities reported.[108] These hats did not mark their wearers as Capoeiras. On the contrary, it was because they were different that they merited this relatively detailed description, and it is difficult to decide the hats' purposes. The case of the slave José Calabar, arrested on August 9, 1821, for playing capoeira with a white feather stuck in his hair is interesting, as it involves a different item from those normally associated with capoeira.[109] The record makes no connection between the feather and capoeira. Moreover, the only Capoeirista caught with a white feather came from West Africa, and it stands to reason that he would use familiar symbols and objects. In another case, not connected to capoeira, on December 22, 1820, Matias Mozambique was seen with feathers in his hair. When the patrol spotted him, he whistled, tried to flee, and resisted arrest.[110]

Returning to the more typical cases, it seems that in the first two decades of the nineteenth century Capoeiras mainly used yellow and red ribbons and hats, which the authorities recognized as their characteristic colors. What did the ribbons and their colors mean, and why did Capoeiras tie ribbons to their hats or to poles?

In the Congo, colors have complex cosmological meanings. The world is perceived as an egg divided into four sections by five points joined by lines (see Figure 1.7). Four points on the circumference of the circle on the south-north and east-west axes form a cross. The fifth point is at the intersection of the two lines inside the circle. The points symbolize all the processes in the world—the movement of the sun, the life cycle, and so on. The lowest point (south), which is the beginning of everything, is *musoni*. The point to the east is life, being (*kala*). The north point, *tukula*, meaning "let us go," symbolizes leadership, authority, and divine power. *Luvemba* to the west symbolizes death, mutability. The vertical north-south line of power connects the deities with the dead. The horizontal line, *kalunga*, or huge ocean, symbolizes the water that divides the living from the dead. Kalunga divides the circle into two arcs, the upper arc symbolizing the physical world and the lower one representing the spiritual world, the supernatural.[111]

According to the Kongolese perception of the world, each point has a specific color that has power and significance through its ability to communicate with our world and the world of the gods and the dead. The lowest point, *musoni*, is

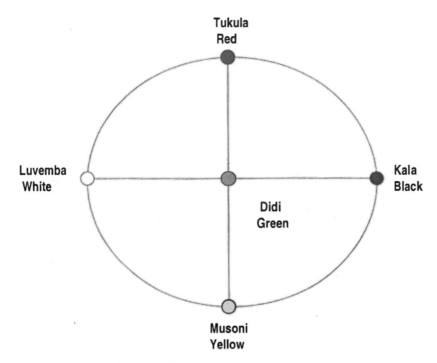

FIGURE 1.7. The Kongolese Cosmology

yellow, the beginning of everything. Its position, south, means that it belongs to the world of the dead. *Kala*, life, is black. *Tukula*, embodying leadership, authority, and power, is red. Its position on the circle, in the north, connects it with the gods. *Luvemba*, designating death and mutability, is white. The fifth point, in the center of the circle, *didi*, is green. This is the center of life and of the earth. Because of its central position, it is the most important point and is the key to healing and discovery, among other things.

Red and yellow are highly significant. Red symbolizes power, charisma, and leadership; yellow embodies knowledge. Because of their position in the circle, red is connected with the gods while yellow is associated with the dead. The ribbons adorning hats, held in the hands, or tied to staffs, enable Capoeiras to communicate with their gods (red ribbons) or with the power linking the gods with the dead (red and yellow ribbons) for protection or help or to intimidate an enemy.

Olfert Dapper's seventeenth-century painting depicts warriors in Luango holding flags and wearing feathered hats and garments that flutter in the wind (Figures 1.8, 1.9).[112] The fluttering robes symbolize strength. The flags, according

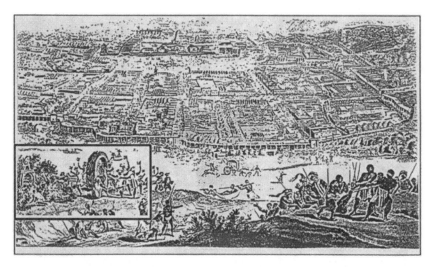

FIGURE 1.8. Warriors Prepare for a Battle—Luango (1668). From Olfert Dapper, *Description de l'Afrique* (Paris: Fondation Dapper, 1990).

FIGURE 1.9. Warriors Prepare for a Battle—Luango (1668). From Olfert Dapper, *Description de l'Afrique* (Paris: Fondation Dapper, 1990).

to Robert Farris Thompson, are associated with the old pygmy tradition of waving leaves to entreat the forest to help them. This was a ceremony purporting to transmit messages between two worlds. The BaKongo adapted this tradition, using a white cloth flag to communicate with the primeval world. The ribbons at the end of the staff are "words" (*mambu*) through which the living communicated with their ancestors. To attract attention in the other world, they "waved the words" (*minika mambu*), a Congolese metaphor for a spiritual warning.[113] The ribbon fluttering in the wind was a "traffic signal" mediating between the two worlds—the physical and the spiritual. It was also used in social events and funerals, and on altars.

In 1707 Dirk Valkenburg depicted slaves playing in the Dombi plantations in Suriname (Figure 1.10). The picture shows men, women, and children participating in activities during a social event. A narrow white ribbon flutters from a wooden pole rising above the roof of a hut.

The same kind of ribbon is described in a scene in Debret's book of the funeral procession of a black king's son in Rio de Janeiro (Figure 1.11):

> The deceased receives delegations from various black nations, each represented by three dignitaries. The diplomat, dressed in a vest, black trousers, a pointed hat [*chapéu de bicos*]. . . . [T]he flag bearer holds a long pole with a colorful cloth fluttering up high, and the guard commander, carrying a stick, either with a narrow ribbon wrapped around it or simply adorned with a lariat.[114]

Elsewhere, Debret describes Café transport: "Usually the first carrier is the flagbearer and is distinguished by a kerchief tied to a staff. The column is led by a headman armed with the horn of a bull or a ram. This emblem is for him a talisman against all misfortunes that might befall the group."[115]

We can assume that, apart from the horn, the fluttering red ribbon evidently also had great symbolic significance.

Thompson's study of altars in the Congo and the New World indicates that slaves used to place white ribbons on them in order to communicate with supernatural powers.[116] An altar of this kind was documented in 1885 in Suriname (Figure 1.12).

The hat also had considerable importance and incorporated much power. Pigafetta reported that at the court of the king of Kongo, "they wore very small yellow and red caps, square at the top, which scarcely covered the head, and were used more for show than as a protection from sun or atmosphere."[117] But each hat had a very different meaning. The *mpu* (cap) was a symbol of authority.[118] In 1885 in the Congo, for example, the king attended official meetings wearing a hat decorated with leopard's teeth, the latter sometimes arranged in such a way as to symbolize the universe (Figure 1.13).[119] He held an embellished staff called *nkawa* or *mvwala* that signified a bridge across the water ("a ferry of the ancestral fathers") connecting the worlds of the living and the dead. He wore a chain around his neck made of leopard's teeth or of ivory and sat on a leopard-skin rug. All these objects, and many others, were symbols of occult power. The king,

FIGURE 1.10. "'Play' on Dombi Plantation" (1707). By kind permission of Robert Farris Thompson, *Face of the Gods: Art and Altars of Africa and the African Americas* (New York: Museum for African Art, 1993), p. 127.

FIGURE 1.11. "Funeral for the Son of a Black King in Rio de Janeiro." From Jean-Baptiste Debret, *Viagem pitoresca e histórica ao Brasil* (São Paulo: Livraria Martins Editôra, 1954), vol. 2, pl. 16, p. 152. Reproduced by kind permission of the British Library.

FIGURE 1.12. Saamakan Vessel-on-Column Altar, Suriname (1885). By kind permission of Robert Farris Thompson, *Face of the Gods: Art and Altars of Africa and the African Americas* (New York: Museum for African Art, 1993), p. 128.

surrounded and ordained by supernatural powers, became a *nkisi*, a powerful medicine man. With these powers he could judge people and even sentence them to death.[120]

Wyatt MacGaffey stresses that these symbolic objects still had political and spiritual meanings in mid-twentieth-century West Central Africa. According to the Mbangala tribe, "The first chief to rule over them took the name Me Mbangala Ngoma. He ruled with great force, and when he was consecrated (*yaala*), he assumed the tufted cap (*mpu ya mbondo*), the *n'kisi nsi*, the baton (*mvwala*) of

FIGURE 1.13. *Court of a Congolese King* (1884). By kind permission of Robert Farris Thompson, *Four Moments of the Sun: Kongo Art in Two Worlds* (Washington, D.C.: National Gallery of Art, 1981), p. 35.

chieftainship, the iron bells (*bimpambu*), the *lubukulu*, and the wildcat skin, and he sat on the skin of the leopard."[121]

This relatively recent scene, evocative of an illustration from Dapper's *King Luango's Court* (1668) (Figure 1.14), shows the king wearing a hat and adorned with a leopard skin on his shoulders and chest. The leopard skin embodies the ruler's power to take life when necessary and his ability to mediate between the two worlds.

This book also contains a description of another ceremony, in which soldiers dressed in white robes and wearing feathered hats wave flags that they hold in their hands (see Figures 1.8, 1.9). In this case, since the purpose of the hats is different, they are made of different material. Soldiers need strength for the battle: they must defeat their enemies and overcome the obstacles and dangers that lie ahead. This is why the feathers in their hats point skyward, embodying the warriors' strength and vigor: "Our power is soaring, nothing will stop us."[122]

The hat's significance was widely known among Africa's many cultures. A nineteenth-century Ketu Yoruba sculpture depicts an Egba Yoruba warrior from Abeokuta leading an Ijebu soldier into captivity. The act of shaving his head "shows that he is no longer free, that he can no longer wear a cap."[123] The perception of the hat did not change with the forced transfer of the slaves to Brazil.

Augustus Earle's painting *Slaves Fighting* (ca. 1822) shows two men using bodily movements similar to Capoeira. One of them uses a hat as a means of protection (Figure 1.15).

Jean-Baptiste Debret (1816–1831) described the function and the attire of a person he referred to as "a black surgeon" (Figure 1.16): "He has the knack of turning his hat (*bone*) into a surgeon's cap (*chapéu*)."[124]

There is no reference to the Capoeiras' clothing in the sources of the period. Apart from the hats and ribbons there is no mention of characteristic items of clothing. In Rugendas's "Capoeira Game" the player on the left wears red trousers and a yellow shirt, and the one on the right has yellow trousers and a red belt (no shirt). Luíz Edmundo (1878–1961), in his *Rio de Janeiro during the Reign of the Viceroy*, described (in a picturesque style) the period from when Rio became Brazil's capital city until the arrival of the Portuguese court, 1763–1808. It contains a depiction of Capoeiras' attire: "A long, generously pleated robe . . . and a

FIGURE 1.14. *Court of the King of Luango* (1668). By kind permission of Robert Farris Thompson, *Four Moments of the Sun: Kongo Art in Two Worlds* (Washington, D.C.: National Gallery of Art, 1981), p. 36.

FIGURE 1.15. *Slaves Fighting* (ca. 1822). Watercolor by Earle Augustus. Reproduced by kind permission of the National Library of Australia.

FIGURE 1.16. *A Black Surgeon* (1834). From Jean-Baptiste Debret, *Viagem pitoresca e histórica ao Brasil* (São Paulo: Livraria Martins Editôra, 1954), vol. 2, pl. 46. Reproduced by kind permission of the British Library.

FIGURE 1.17. *A Capoeira in the Time of the Vice-Regent* (1932). From Luíz Edmundo, *O Rio de Janeiro do meu tempo* (Rio de Janeiro: Imprensa Nacional, 1938). Reproduced by kind permission of Biblioteca Nacional, Rio de Janeiro.

Spanish felt hat on their thick, curly hair."[125] An illustration in the book shows a Capoeirista holding a knife in his mouth and a hat in his hand (Figure 1.17). The hat is a plain Spanish hat with no ribbons. The man is wearing breeches, a shirt, a coat, and sandals.

Luis Edmundo purports to describe an event that occurred a hundred years before his time, but it appears that he was not familiar with the Capoeira characteristics of that period as he depicts items and accessories that were common in his lifetime. In the early nineteenth century most Capoeiras were enslaved and had very little choice as to the style of their clothing. At that time clothes were an indicator of social status. Slaves newly arrived in Brazil wore the short tunics given to them by slave traders, as described by the German officer Carl Schlichthorst: "On arrival at the port, each slave, men and women alike, was given a piece of blue cloth and a red hat, because they had sailed in a garment of paradise [i.e., naked]."[126] Dressed in this minimal attire, they were displayed in the slave market. Other slaves usually wore cotton trousers and shirts. On special occasions, men wore a jacket and vest, and women wore a skirt and blouse, if they possessed these items. Men and children usually wore long shirts, short knee-length pants, or skirtlike lengths of cloth tied around their waists. Schlichthorst reported, "The strongest slaves work in the streets as porters. They are naked except for a short apron tied around their waist that barely covers their thighs."[127] Many were partially dressed or completely naked, which resulted in complaints to the authorities about "indecency." The edicts that followed forbade walking around naked in the city streets and warned about the penalties awaiting owners and slaves who broke the law. George Gardner, a traveler in Brazil in 1838, was happy to point out the improvement in the modesty of the slaves' clothing as compared to what he had seen during his previous visit in 1814.[128] Schlichthorst explains why the slaves were not allowed to wear shoes: "An ancient law forbids slaves, male and female, to wear shoes or any other footwear so that they can be distinguished from free blacks."[129] However, the slaves of the rich were dressed in good clothes, shoes, and boots, to display the status of their owners.[130]

Even at this early stage, when the majority of Capoeiras were West Central Africans, some of those from different ethnic backgrounds, traditions, and customs used other symbols and accessories. A Capoeirista from Calabar in West Africa, for example, wore a white hat with a feather. This was the first indication of what would come later. Changes in the Capoeiras' status, origin, and skin color over the course of the nineteenth century inevitably gave rise to changes in their customs and symbols, as well as in their attire.

The Battle and the Game (1840s–1870s)

PART 1. AUTHORITY AND THE CAPOEIRAS: ENCOUNTER AND COLLISION

Status and Origin of the Capoeiras

FROM WRITTEN DOCUMENTS of the 1840s it is evident that Capoeiras were no longer primarily black slaves from West Central Africa. In the 1840s and 1850s Creoles (persons born in Brazil), persons of mixed race (usually a white father and a black mother), and freedmen joined the ranks of the Capoeiras.[1] This brought about significant changes, not only in the status of Capoeiras, but also in their behavior and attitudes toward the rest of society.

Thomas Holloway found that in 1850, 63 people were arrested for participating in capoeira out of 290 cases in which the reason for arrest was cited (just over 21 percent). In three cases there was no mention of the Capoeiras' origins. Other records reveal that 42 cases (70 percent) were of African origin, and the other 18 cases (30 percent) were born in Brazil.[2] This shows a steep rise in the number of Creoles introduced to the secrets of capoeira, a tendency that continued eight years later (see Table 2.1). These data are interesting, because they

Table 2.1. Origin of Arrested Slaves Accused of Capoeira, 1850 and 1857/8

Origin	Arrests 1850	Imprisonment 1857/8
Brazil (Creole, Pardo)	18	27
Africa (unspecified)	2	0
West Africa	3	6
West Central Africa	31	34
Congo	9	16
Angola	22	18
East Africa	6	14
Total	60	81

Source: Holloway, "A Healthy Terror," p. 661.

resemble the relative percentage of Creoles among the enslaved and liberated of Rio in the population census of 1849 (see Table 2.2).

However, the census figures are unreliable as the authorities used them for various purposes, such as to levy taxes or to achieve political ends. Nevertheless, they provide a general estimate of the size of the urban population at the time. Among the 78,855 slaves, there were 26,514 Creoles (33.5 percent), and the African-born numbered 52,341 (66.5 percent). This proportion is approximately the same for the freedmen: 3,143 were Brazilian born (about 30 percent), and 7,589 were of African origin (about 70 percent).[3]

This was a result of a law enacted in 1850 prohibiting transatlantic slave trading. Despite the gradual increase in the number of Brazilians among the Capoeiras, the number of arrested Capoeiras of West Central African origin in 1850 was still high—close to 52 percent. Another interesting fact is the gradual increase in the number of Capoeiras from East and West Africa. By 1858 Creoles already constituted more than 33 percent. And in the police records of 1863 from the Casa de Detenção (prison), Creoles constituted 65.7 percent, whereas the African born constituted just 34.3 percent.

These changes in the origins of the Capoeiras are significant. These people were born into a set reality, unlike their predecessors, who were torn from their families and countries of origin and brought to a totally foreign milieu. Portuguese was the first language of native Capoeiras, their social status was well defined, and their affinity was with friends rather than a distant African birthplace. Moreover, they absorbed the influences of people from a variety of other cultures, traditions, and customs.

Table 2.2. Population Census, Rio de Janeiro, 1849

Social Status	Brazilians	Foreigners
Free men	79,999	36,320
Liberated	3,143	7,589
Enslaved	26,514	52,341
Total	109,656	96,250

Source: Karasch, *Slave Life*, p. 66.

In the early nineteenth century most Capoeiras were slaves, but official records indicate that liberation at that time also applied to the Capoeiras. Between 1850 and 1880 there was a sharp decline in the number of slaves. While the number of slaves in 1848 was the highest in the history of Rio—approximately 40 percent (according to Chalhoub, it was 41 percent; slightly below 40 percent, according to Karasch)—in 1870 the city's population, 274,972, included 48,939 slaves—less than 18 percent (according to Karasch, about 21 percent). By the beginning of 1888, that is, on the eve of the abolition of slavery, there were no more than 7,488 slaves in the city.[4] There were several reasons for this decline. The first was the cessation of the transatlantic slave trade. The second was the yellow fever and cholera epidemics of 1850 and 1853, which caused fatalities especially among the slave population. The birthrate among slaves was still low, and the decreasing supply soon drove prices up. There was a great demand for laborers in the rural hinterland, such as the Vale de Paraíba, center of the coffee industry, and many slaves were sold to the farmers. Ultimately, especially during the 1860s, emancipation of slaves increased significantly. Between 1860 and 1869, 13,246 slaves were freed, an average increase of more than 1,300 per year. The numbers increased, especially between 1867 and 1868—the years of the war with Paraguay, when the government acquired slaves and liberated them to serve in the army. Many slave owners took their freedmen with them to serve as arms bearers. In the 1870s there was a sharp upsurge in emancipation in response to the demands of movements supporting the abolition of slavery.[5]

The available sources show a gradual change in the status of Capoeiras. In 1836 a black man named Firmino, who was wounded in the head during a *capoeiragem* (capoeira activity), was captured. He claimed to be a free man working as a sailor on the warship *Itaparica*. The regional commander ordered that he be given medical treatment and released, although his written report expressed his doubts as to Firmino's credibility. His ruling was that if it transpired that Firmino was not a freedman, he should be brought to trial and a proper investigation carried out.[6] Firmino's case suggests that there were other, similar cases of liberated or free Capoeiras. The doubts about the veracity of his statement derived from a system in which every black person was thought to be a slave, and the onus of proving the contrary was on him. In the past slaves had pretended to be free or liberated men in order to escape from their owners or the law. The slave Izaias, for example, ran away from his owner, who published an announcement in *Diário do Rio de Janeiro* on January 29, 1849, asking the public's help in finding the fugitive. The published description included particulars of the man's appearance and the warning, "Pretends to be free, and sometimes wears boots to look like a free man. Arrived from the city Iguape. . . . Is a Capoeira. Well known to the police, as he has been arrested by this department in the past."[7] In another case, a justice of the peace from the Sacramento region reported that on March 24, 1840, he ordered the arrest of a man "who claims to be a liberated Creole" on the charge of playing capoeira.[8] The skepticism about the detainees changed with time, and gradually people who were born free joined the Capoeiras. On December 22, 1849, a group of Capoeiras was arrested: João Angola, Paulo Congo, Miguel Benguela, Domingo Cassanga, Lázaro Congo, and Lúcio Estevão Veloso. With the exception of Veloso, all were slaves from West Central Africa. Judging from Veloso's full name, he must have been a free man.[9] Of the 69 Capoeiras arrested in 1850, 63 were slaves (just over 91 percent), 3 were free, 2 were liberated men, and 1 was a "liberated African," the epithet for all those enslaved by illegal slave traders and who had apparently been freed. As of 1808 Britain brought great pressure to bear on Portugal to ban the inhuman transatlantic slave trade. Portugal, having become Britain's ally against French expansionism, had to sign agreements to put a stop to slave trading, initially only north of the equator. In 1817 Portugal agreed to put a complete stop to slave trading within twenty years, and in 1830 a law banning transatlantic slave trading was passed, though in effect it continued to thrive.[10] Boats smuggling slaves that were captured by the authorities had to free their human cargo, who were afterward known as "liberated Africans," though they were in fact nationalized and made to serve high-ranking government officials.

As early as 1850 a little less than 9 percent of those arrested on charges of capoeira were not slaves, while in 1878 the percentage of free Capoeiras who were arrested was even higher than that of the enslaved. Holloway claims that in 1878, 645 people were arrested on charges of capoeira, including 507 free men (78.6 percent), and 138 enslaved (21.4 percent).[11] Soares's figures are different: he found that in the police records of 1881 40 percent were slaves and 60 percent were free men.[12]

In 1862 the police arrested 7,290 people, 404 of whom were detained on charges of capoeira (slightly less than 5.5 percent). The military police made 2,945 arrests, 138 on charges of capoeira (about 4.7 percent). This was a significant decline in the number of Capoeiras arrested. In 1868, at the climax of the war with Paraguay, only 12 such arrests were registered at the Casa de Detenção in the four months from January 16 to May 8. Three years later the number had again increased. Between December 1871 and May 1872 the military police made 171 arrests, including 22 Capoeiras (almost 13 percent). This was a direct result of the end of the Paraguay war and the return of many Capoeiras to the streets.

Social stability in the years that followed is evident in the paucity of information relating to Capoeiras. Some modifications in the Capoeiras' clothing may reflect the social changes mentioned above. In January 1849 the newspaper *Jornal do Commercio* advertised the escape of five slaves who used to play capoeira outside the Casa de Angu (a house serving Angu, a popular dish) at Beco do Carmo in the Candelária region. Five of these men were dark skinned (Pardos), and one was African. All their particulars were listed, including what they wore. Nineteen-year-old João, a Creole, wore colorful cashmere trousers and a striped jacket; José, a coachman, had a bandana tied around his head. Manuel, who was often drunk, wore white trousers, a short green jacket, and a white hat. Joaquim, a cook, wore a frayed navy jacket and black-and-white trousers. Meira, a cigar maker from Angola, wore white trousers and a tight black jacket. In police reports recorded fourteen years later, on July 13, 1863, we find further descriptions of Capoeiras' clothing. It appears that the Capoeiras who were arrested on that date were released two days later, apparently under pressure from their owners who needed them for work. The cook Manuel Cabinda, thirty-eight years old, wore a white shirt, black trousers, and a straw hat. Tomas Benguela, thirty-two, also a cook, wore a dark shirt and trousers. A dark-skinned man named Anastácio wore a white shirt and trousers and a rabbitskin hat.[13] All these Capoeiras were slaves. In his book *Memórias de um Sargento de Milícia*, published in 1853–1854, Manuel Antônio de Almeida, born in Rio in 1831 (he drowned in 1861), describes the clothing of a free Capoeirista: "Chico Juca was brown-skinned, tall. He had red eyes, a long beard, and cropped hair. He always wore a white coat, bell-bottom pants, black clogs, and a white hat with ribbons."[14]

Whereas the Capoeiras of the early nineteenth century usually wore tight pants and rarely a shirt, as shown in Rugendas's illustrations, by midcentury a jacket or a coat and hat had become popular, even among the enslaved Capoeiras. Evidently, the hat or headgear was more varied in shape and color. A white hat with ribbons is mentioned only in Chico Juca's case, but a hat still appears to be an important item of clothing. Mary Karasch contends that the hat was a status symbol. Slaves tended to imitate their owners, for whom the hat signified status, wealth, and distinction. In addition, in the African homeland, kings, noblemen, and other dignitaries wore hats to indicate their rank.[15] In the African cultures, the hat also had mystical significance. As of the 1850s, felt and straw hats of different colors, with brims, served to differentiate between the ethnic groups of Capoeiras.

Capoeiras in Public Agencies

The change in the Capoeiras' status was more strikingly evident in their occupations and organizations. Some Capoeiras were employed in public agencies such as the police, the fire brigade, the National Guard, and the army, all of which were established to safeguard citizens. On the face of it there seems to be a contradiction here. If the Capoeiras were considered a public nuisance, disturbers of the peace, and a threat to security, how could they serve in organizations that were supposed to keep them in order? To cope with this contradiction, the authorities fired Capoeiras from organizations that provided legal and organizational protection. At the same time, they were punished for their crimes by being drafted into the army and the navy for backbreaking and dangerous jobs, with the intention of keeping them away from the city and subjecting them to iron discipline. On October 15, 1853, the National Guard was ordered to release one José Antônio da Silva who had been arrested on July 14 on suspicion of participating in capoeira. He had a previous police record and had been reported by Fulão Cavalcante for wounding several people and being a public menace.[16] Da Silva's was not the only request of this kind. In 1859 the police commissioner requested the dismissal of Felisberto do Amaral from the National Guard on the following grounds: "The man is very dangerous, and is known as the head of the Capoeiras who meet in the Santa Rita neighborhood. It was he who threw a stone and wounded policeman Lúcio Feliciano da Costa in the head in the course of pursuing a capoeira group."[17] The National Guard was founded in 1831 as a civil militia to keep the peace. Membership in the organization was conditional on civil status, which meant that only free men, but not liberated men or foreigners, were accepted. In Rio de Janeiro in 1849, of 51,037 free men, 6,544 (almost 13 percent) were members of the National Guard. Of these, 9.5 percent were in the cavalry, and all belonged to the ruling class (624 men). All the others, more than 90 percent, were from the lower classes. This organization had become ineffective by midcentury. Other special units, such as the Pedestres (infantry), founded in 1841, dealt with specific problems related to slaves and to disturbances.

The newspaper *Correio Mercantil*, dated December 1855, wrote that a fire-fighter from Carioca Station, a member of a capoeira group, threw a pointed file that fortunately missed the cashier of a tavern on Guarda Velha Street.[18] In December 1869 the military police caught a group of Capoeiras in civilian clothes near the king's palace. A brief inquiry revealed that four of them were military policemen.[19] The authorities now had to contend with the problem of free and liberated men participating in capoeira. These men were not slaves whose owners were responsible for them but free, independent men who were answerable to nobody. A letter sent from the police secretary to the admiral on January 4, 1848, states, "I bring to Your Lordship's attention the liberated Creole José de Oliveira, and request that he be transferred to service in the navy."[20] Three months later the secretary wrote again, with the same request, in regard to the Creole Patrício Augusto Barata. He asked that Barata should not be allowed to disembark "before fulfilling his duty to the public in the capital city and serving in warships anchoring in other ports, because he is a dangerous Capoeira leader".[21]

The same policy prevailed during Antônio Simões da Silva's term of office (1849). Sixty Capoeiras had to sign a promise to obey the law, maintain public peace, and behave properly. Breaking this commitment would lead to arrest and punishment. Forty other Capoeiras were removed from Rio by recruiting them into the army.[22] This policy changed when Minister of Justice José Thomas Nabuco d'Araújo noted, with growing displeasure, that capoeira had taken root even among the soldiers. On January 19, 1859, the minister complained that in their spare time many Capoeiras among the soldiers took off their uniforms and trained in capoeira and caused disturbances. He demanded that off-duty soldiers be forbidden to leave the barracks. That year the soldiers were ordered to stay in camp after duty hours.[23]

The policy of drafting criminals into the army was in force for ten more years. The minister of justice ordered the transfer of four men to active military service, claiming that "although they are members of the Civil Guard, they were arrested as members of a Capoeira gang who stirred up a riot in Lapa Square on August 29, 1869."[24] This coincided with the need for more soldiers during the war with Paraguay (1865–1871) when the easiest, cheapest, and fastest way to augment the military was to recruit Capoeiras and other criminals as auxiliary forces. It is noteworthy that the Capoeiras' punishments in this period were adjusted to their social status. In the mid-nineteenth century many Capoeiras were still enslaved, and their owners were opposed to the authorities sentencing and punishing their workforce. In April 1845 a new police commissioner was appointed who viewed the rampant Capoeira rioting as a threat to society and concluded that even harsher punishments were required. Any slave arrested for capoeira was sent to a reformatory where he received 100 lashes and a sentence of one month's hard labor. The slave owners protested vehemently. In August, four months after the amendment, the penalty was changed to 150 lashes and the slaves' immediate return to their owners. This punishment was in force for a number of years, and a prison supervisor, reporting in 1852, stated that every slave arrested on charges of capoeira was flogged 150 times.[25]

Punishments were inflicted according to the criminals' status. Slaves were flogged or ordered to do public works so long as this did not conflict with their owners' interests. Others were incarcerated or drafted into the army or the navy, as required. In the 1840s and 1850s most offenders were sent to the navy; in the 1860s and 1870s they went to the army.

Capoeira as a Public Menace

In the 1830s and 1840s the authorities were already aware of the changes taking place among the Capoeiras. These changes were made explicit in orders issued by the authorities that used new terms. "Capoeira slaves" and "black Capoeiras" were replaced by "Capoeiras" and "Capoeira groups."[26] These groups were well organized in a hierarchy accepted by their members. It was found that the Capoeira leaders constituted the greatest danger, because they incited the ordinary members to cause disturbances. A letter to the admiral of the fleet in January 1848 contains the following: "I bring to Your Lordship's attention the liberated Creole José de Oliveira . . . who in addition to being a drifter is a capoeira leader and has been identified as such by many people."[27] We do not know who these "many people" were, but identifying the detainee as a capoeira leader indicates that the term was familiar both to the public and to the authorities. The Creole Patrício Augusto Barata was also arrested on the same charge, and a recommendation was issued to find him proper work, "because, as a capoeira leader, he is dangerous."[28]

Disturbances by the Capoeiras, the ensuing damage to property, and the murder of innocent passersby created panic. Police Commissioner Matoso Câmara Eusébio de Quiroz Coutinho complained to the general officer in 1841 that Capoeiras were inflicting damage on the city and that "they audaciously appeared in great numbers when the Corpo de Artifícios conducted its maneuvers." "I beg Your Lordship," he continued, "to be so kind as to apprise me prior to the day, time and place when such maneuvers are held, so that the infantry can be alerted to stop Capoeiras from gathering and practicing their usual nonsense."[29] On April 25, 1849, the deputy commander of the Sacramento neighborhood described the activities of the Capoeiras as "one of the greatest problems in our fair city."[30] On June 16 the police commissioner emphasized the continuing need for extreme vigilance in various sections of the city. He wrote that he had learned from a report by an assistant representative of the Sacramento neighborhood that groups of Capoeiras had gathered in Capim Square. Despite repeated requests to reinforce the patrols and the guards, the request was not granted "due to lack of funds."[31] On July 7, 1849, the *Diário do Rio de Janeiro* reported that the commander in chief of the Corpo de Permanentes had requested a patrol of "the four quarters of the São José precinct, from 10:00 in the morning until 1:00 at night, because of widespread disturbances by Capoeiras."[32] The police were apparently unable to cope with the groups of Capoeiras who were wreaking havoc on public order. In the mid-nineteenth century there were 800 policemen in a city whose population was 206,000. The city was divided into 8 districts and 195 quarters, each with a commander and six deputy commanders.[33] The military and police forces consisted of about 400 men—10 officers, 116 cavalrymen, and 274 infantry, who patroled the streets at night. The police commissioner was directly accountable to the minister of justice. Until 1831 the Guarda Real (Royal Guard) was responsible for maintaining law and order. It was superseded by the Corpo Municipal Permanente (Permanent Municipal Corps), which was authorized to patrol and to make arrests. In 1858 its name was changed again, this time to Corpo Militar de Polícia da Corte (Military Corps of the Court Police). Of the arrests made by this organization, only 4 percent were on charges of capoeira during this period. The Corpo de Artifícios, a special army unit, was occupied with maintaining order and arresting Capoeiras.[34] The written sources of the time increasingly refer to Capoeiras as "good-for-nothings" and "drifters" who mocked the authorities, created disturbances, and murdered innocent citizens just for fun.

In the daily *Correio da Tarde* of November 3, 1849, Capoeiras were described as follows:

> Capoeiras, capoeiras! With a blow to the head they make more noise than half a dozen Hebrew Gideons. With a small knife in one hand and a glass in another they offend the bravest men and fool the police, making them take to their heels with the greatest impudence. Eloquent and provocative, pretending to be just watching the streets and squares, they sometimes disguise themselves in an old coat and wield their short clubs. This is what the Capoeiras are like.[35]

Four years later the police commissioner wrote the following letter to the minister of justice:

The most common street crimes are murder and various degrees of wounding. It is interesting that the reason for these crimes is not revenge or robbery but the pleasure of seeing blood flow. The perpetrators say that "the wish to try the metal" makes them commit these acts of violence. They are commonly known as Capoeiras. In the course of one afternoon in February these scoundrels murdered seven people in the Santa Ana district.[36]

The Capoeiras' notoriety was corroborated by two travelers, D. P. Kidder and J. C. Fletcher, who quoted an article published in the newspaper *Correio Mercantil* about Capoeiras attacking an innocent citizen. According to this report, a gang of Capoeiras attacked a man named Mauricio after eight o'clock in the evening and beat him with a club, wounding him in the forehead and thigh and injuring one of his arteries. The bleeding victim was treated by Dr. Thomas Antunes de Abreu, who came to the poor man's rescue.[37] Other newspaper reports, official letters, and police records attest that capoeira gangs molested innocent passersby, leaving them beaten and wounded and sometimes dead. This is a grim picture of lawlessness, of a city where gangs of hooligans acted without restraint or mercy.

It seems that only strangers visiting Brazil understood the real causes for the violence. In 1857 Kidder and Fletcher described Capoeiras as "members of some sort of secret society . . . where all the glory goes to whoever destroys the most lives."[38] Karasch perceives the Capoeira groups as fraternities "filling an institutional need—that of protecting their people—the maltas (groups) enrolled male slaves into fraternal paramilitary organizations that defended the other slaves in their neighborhoods."[39] Karasch thus presents a completely different interpretation of the Capoeiras' activities, suggesting that they were not barbarous bandits but teams that protected their neighborhoods against their enemies. Moraes Filho, whose book was published in 1878, supported this view in his explanation of the Capoeiras' motives forty years earlier: "They took a solemn vow. . . . They were not detached from problems of parishioners or neighborhoods if circumstances required united action. For example, when, because of capoeira, an owner sold a slave affiliated to one of the maltas to another plantation, they had a meeting to decide how to retaliate."[40] But according to Kidder and Fletcher, apart from belonging to these secret, tight-knit groups, Capoeiras mainly directed their activities against other blacks. This is corroborated by other testimonies. On Sunday, May 14, 1847, during the Espírito Santo festivities, the commander of the Campo de Santana quarter, Pedro Luíz da Cunha, took a walk with the court clerk Manoel José Moreira Otaviano. Around eight o'clock in the evening four Capoeiras suddenly came running, waving knives and chasing a black man who was fleeing and whistling with all his might. According to the two officials, the chase stopped when the pursued man reached the First Quarter and his pursuers turned back to the Second Quarter.[41] Whistling, very common in the early nineteenth century, was a means of communication among Capoeiras. The man may have been trying to warn his friends about the approach of his pursuers, and it may also have been why the latter did not continue the chase, for fear of retribution outside their precinct, where other Capoeiras might have been waiting to strike back. In another case, on May 2, 1838, a police commissioner wrote that he had found out from "a justice of the peace that between seven and nine o'clock in the evening, in the Santa Ana district of Catumbi, in a place called Coqueiros, groups of black Capoeiras show up in small bands, armed with clubs. These groups often go as far as Conde Street, where they commit murder."[42] He asked for patrols to scout the area frequently. He specified in his letter that groups of capoeiras showed up at certain ranches and went as far as a specific place—Conde Street—where they murdered their victims. The letter offers no explanation or motive for these crimes, but the following may provide a clue. On March 3, 1842, the police commissioner wrote to the admiral:

> I send Your Lordship the following men, and request that they be drafted for service in the navy: Feliciano Francisco, laborer; Inácio Viegas Tourinho, chicken peddler; Francisco Peçanha, chicken peddler; Emigídio Marcus, laborer; and Domingos Antônio Pereira, daily laborer—all black Minas—who live in a densely populated area. This may have triggered a sudden very large gathering of Capoeiras, which necessitated police intervention. I believe it would be best to separate these men and offer them a different future. Assuming that some of them would benefit from service in the navy, I hope Your Lordship will approve this step.[43]

This letter refers to a group of free or liberated men, all employed, all of West African origin, all living in the same crowded neighborhood, probably with many of their own kind. Knowing that in this period the percentage of Capoeiras from West Africa was negligible, it can be assumed that the group in question may have originated from West Central Africa. The rivalry and tension between the various tribes is evident in Kidder and Fletcher's descriptions: "In Rio de Janeiro the blacks originate from many tribes, and some are hostile to one another."[44] The great number of ethnicities in Rio was conducive to brawls among enslaved and even liberated men. Perhaps the source of this antagonism is attributable to their history, to ancient rivalries among enemy tribes, or to the conflicts between

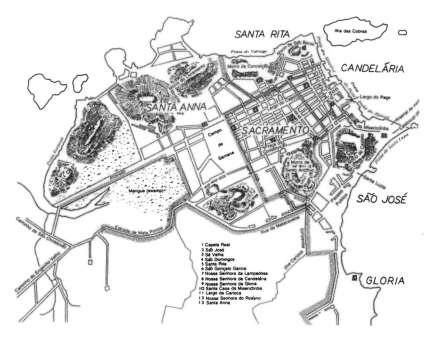

MAP 2.1. The Neighborhoods of Rio de Janeiro, 1831. From Mary C. Karasch, *Slave Life in Rio de Janeiro, 1808–1850*, p. 56. © 1987 Princeton University Press. Reprinted by permission of Princeton University Press.

these ethnic minorities over respect and prestige. On the other hand, it may have arisen from local disputes over status and employment or struggles for control and power.

Available sources suggest that in the 1830s and 1840s Capoeira activities were usually restricted to rioting and disturbances in the Gloria, Sacramento, Santa Rita, and São José neighborhoods of Rio (Map 2.1).

By midcentury murder and injuries became more prevalent in the struggle for control of the urban space. Soares found that at this time there were seven major Capoeira groups, known to the authorities by the name of the district under their domination. In 1872 the police commissioner explained the phenomenon of capoeira in the following terms: "They form organizations of sorts according to neighborhoods, each with a specific leader. Not only do they struggle among themselves to gain control, but they also kill and maim other innocent citizens."[45] In the third quarter of the nineteenth century these groups melded into two major groups, the Guayamos and the Nagoas.

PART 2. THE SECRECY AND THE ONGOING "GAME"

It is evident that as of the mid-nineteenth century the municipal authorities, journalists, and scholars regarded Capoeiras as violent and disruptive bandits. Holidays, Sundays, and parades gave ample opportunity for conduct that created chaos and terrified the population.[46] Furthermore, these sources indicate that capoeira was increasingly detached from its original music and dancing and was essentially a criminal activity. Capoeiras were observed at public festivals and mass celebrations, dancing, leaping, and hopping in front of military parades and religious processions, displaying the kind of disturbing behavior expected of them. But this is only one side of the coin, that which was influenced by prejudice, political interests, and the authorities' values. The other side was repressed, concealed, and unrecognized by the whites. As far as the Capoeiras were concerned, they continued to play capoeira. Indeed, the changing reality compelled them to play not only with their fellows, as they had previously, but also to develop new games, in public squares, in front of military parades, religious processions, and other social events. They began to mock the authorities and challenge the social order. As James Scott notes in *Weapons of the Weak*:

> Those in power . . . are not, however, in total control of the stage. They may write the basic script for a play but, within its confines, truculent or disaffected actors find sufficient room for maneuver to suggest subtly their disdain for the proceedings.[47]

Apart from criminal acts by rival capoeira gangs vying for control of neighborhoods, capoeira as a "game" continued in Rio de Janeiro, maintaining its character as play that represented the "game of life" as comprehended by the descendants of West Central African slaves, even though their ethnic and racial backgrounds became more diverse. They organized public contests and diverted themselves with competitions. They played capoeira in front of military and religious processions and mocked and derided public officials. Their performances included music, dancing, and interaction with spectators. Although public officials tried to brand the Capoeiras as dangerous and violent hoodlums, the masses admired them and enjoyed their performances.

A Martial Art

Many Capoeiras had been sent, reluctantly or willingly, to fight in the Paraguayan war (1865–1870) and were promised freedom and privileges on their return. Indeed, some Capoeiras received citations and decorations from the government for their heroic deeds in the war, and tales were told of their physical prowess hand-to-hand combat.[48] After the war capoeira was redefined, characterized as a martial art associated with self-defense and battle. Moraes Filho described the Capoeiras' activities as "dangerous, difficult physical training that required practice and agility. Only after long training do these fighters make a name for themselves."[49] In 1872 a police commissioner had reported, "[Capoeiras] not only fight among themselves but also injure and murder innocent passersby."[50] Five years later, oficial documents described Capoeiras as "usually fighting among themselves, with tragic consequences."[51] Based on the Brazilian government's documentation, many scholars concur with this statement. Gilberto Freyre, For example, remarked that the "ancient" art of capoeira had lost its multidimensionality as a result of official policy:

> To protect themselves from harassment by the police, these idlers organized themselves . . . and this is really the reason why the art of *capoeira-gem* among us ceased to be a typically Afro-Brazilian diversion to sink into crime and sexual aberration, into gangs armed with daggers or razors, who "in endless forays sow terror and panic among the peaceable, bourgeois inhabitants."[52]

When other social groups—native Brazilians, persons of mixed descent, even white immigrants or local aristocrats—learned capoeira, many of them viewed it as a martial art for acquiring physical fitness and agility. How is it possible that capoeira could become a martial art deriving from the agility of criminals who were a menace to public security, as the authorities insisted?

The Game of Life

Although written sources have emphasized the violent and aggressive nature of capoeira while intentionally disregarding its other, covert aspects, the latter have appeared between the lines. For example, on January 17, 1872, Antônio, a young slave belonging to Antônio Soares de Araújo, learned capoeira in a public square, "entertained . . . with acrobatic and agile exercises which the crowd calls *capoeiragem*."[53] This note published in *Diário do Rio de Janeiro* shows that capoeira was obviously enjoyed by the young man, and he was not the only one amused. According to another article in the same journal of March 5, 1872, capoeira "attracted attention to the curious spectacle, also known as capoeira, just as moths are attracted to light."[54] Though the authorities and the press viewed this activity as threatening to the "public peace," the masses thoroughly enjoyed it. The police, in this instance, were apparently more concerned by the gathering crowds than by Francisco Ferreira da Silva and Afonso Talange's demonstration of "their abilities in the art of capoeira."[55] The participants were evidently *not* engaged in personal conflict or in violent activity but were demonstrating their agility and skill in the game of capoeira for spectators' enjoyment. This match in the public square of São Francisco de Paula was a social event, probably accompanied by shouts, clapping, and even music, dance, and song. In the 1870s Capoeiras had regular meeting places for teaching and practicing capoeira, as can be seen from Moraes Filho's explanation: "The . . . Capoeirista also had his district, the meeting place of the capoeira gangs. His schools were the squares, the streets, the alleyways."[56] Plácido de Abreu gives more precise details. The famous Capoeiras gave lessons to beginners on Sundays. At first, training was conducted without weapons, but as the novices improved they received first wooden and then metal staves. Russel Beach was frequented by the São José and Lapa groups, and the Santana group practiced in the Pinto favela.[57] But there were other motives for practicing capoeira, and for many people, mainly of the lower classes, it had a much deeper meaning. The public square of Sé, for example, was "the area selected for exercising recruits to the art."[58] The authorities were informed of these "dangerous gatherings . . . of Capoeiras who frequently assemble and create disorder."[59] On March 11, 1872, José Leandro Franklin introduced Álbano to the elements of capoeira: "This one teaches and that one learns the . . . art of *capoeiragem*. . . . [T]he lecture helped many comrades and potential aspirants, but they unfortunately ran away."[60] The police broke up this gathering, arrested the participants, and accused them of causing disorder. This scene was not simply a physical training course, as the journalist suggested, but a game in the broader sense of the word. People met, demonstrated their abilities, learned from each other, and enjoyed themselves despite the authorities' disapproval.

Capoeira continued to be practiced at social events—holiday celebrations, religious processions, military parades, and so on. On January 19, 1859, for example, Minister of Justice José Thomaz Nabuco d'Araújo noted, "The Capoeiras use the festival days for their 'runs,' commit crimes, and intentionally frighten peaceful citizens."[61] According to Kidder and Fletcher, "During a holiday they [Capoeiras] will rush out at night and rip up any other black they chance to meet."[62] In March 1874 the *Jornal do Commercio* reported in regard to Capoeiras, "On Sundays and festival days, gangs of murderers roam the streets, some of them full of evil intentions, others quite unaware of their crimes."[63] In 1878 Moraes Filho wrote, "The Capoeiras form up in groups of 20 to 100 in front of troops and carnival processions . . . provoking disorder, running, [and] wounding."[64] Carlos Líbano Soares explained, "The Capoeirista was a common figure in the city's underworld. While most of the suspicious figures tried to maintain their anonymity in the crowd, the Capoeiras looked for notoriety and fame."[65] These assumptions arise from ignorance and misunderstanding. I suggest a different approach. Not only were the Capoeiras not feared by the masses, but they were admired for their skill and for their courage in confronting the authorities.

According to Moraes Filho, "When there were funerals in the churches and during religious festivals . . . the church steeples were crowded with Capoeiras . . . who greeted their admirers from above."[66]

On January 29, 1878, two women, Isabel and Ana, were arrested for "showing their expertise in *capoeiragem*. The inhabitants of the tenth district know them and are the first to say that they deserve a badge of honor."[67] According to Plácido de Abreu (1890), "When two groups were fighting and the police appeared, the rival forces would unite in order to elude the public force."[68] Moreover, Capoeiras often managed to elude the police thanks to the crowd who helped them to get away. For instance, on January 29, 1878, the *Jornal do Commercio* reported that "as a result of the police presence, a crowd assembled, and in the confusion the Capoeirista F. Dias managed to escape."[69] In some cases, Capoeiras' trials were dismissed because the witnesses did not show up in court. On April 2, 1874, Isidoro da Conceição was arrested for threatening the merchant Bernardino Monteiro Varela. The plaintiff described how the accused entered his bakery "swaying (*gingando*) with capoeira movements," and after being asked not to dance, he ran off, promising to return and avenge the insult. A short while later, Isidoro returned with a razor but was stopped by a small crowd that demanded he drop his weapon, which was then taken to the police station as evidence. The defendant claimed that the police had not brought witnesses or evidence to prove there was a quarrel between him and the plaintiff, even though, as previously alleged, the public was present and apparently hauled him off to the authorities. Isidoro was released for lack of testimony.[70]

Some claim that these types of responses indicate the masses feared the Capoeiras. I would argue to the contrary, that the common people were sympathetic to them. Ordinary people frequently helped them to escape by creating confusion in the streets or by not testifying against them in court and thus preventing any legal proceedings against them. The difference of interests between rulers and subjects, masters and slaves, generated contradictory opinions, such as the desire on the part of the authorities to abolish any nonwhite cultural expression versus the slaves' desire to preserve and maintain their heritage.

Many documents give explicit details of the Capoeiras' presence during processions and parades. A German mercenary, Carl von Koseritz, described "the notorious Capociras who are only seen when the military bands are marching in the streets, when they place themselves in front of the troops and often become unpleasant."[71] Koseritz did not explain how the Capoeiras made an nuisance of themselves, but we do know that the authorities tried to prevent it. Sometimes they succeeded, as on January 27, 1878, when "the police arrested a large gang of Capoeiras who were walking in front of the band of the 10th Infantry battalion."[72]

How did the Capoeiras behave in the military and religious parades? What motivated them to lead these processions? Why did the authorities disapprove of this activity? Marcílio Dias was arrested in the mid-1860s because he "*capoeirava* (played capoeira) in front of a band of musicians."[73] He did not walk or run ahead of the troops. He performed the movements specific to capoeira, and as a result he was sentenced to fight in the Paraguayan war and was killed at the front.[74] However, the authorities did not succeed in eliminating this practice. The journal *O Mosquito* reported on August 26, 1871, that "while a band was crossing Rossio Square on Sunday, a townsman in a dandified costume . . . was shamefully jumping and playing capoeira in front of it, and an astonished crowd gathered."[75]

Seven years later the journal *Gazeta de Notícias* complained, "There is no way to eliminate the Capoeiras. As the number of those who go to jail increases, so does the number of those who are left outside to create work for the police. The day before yesterday, one of these 'artists' walked in front of a band of musicians and performed various movements that were worth a few hours in prison."[76]

Thus it seems that the Capoeiras' antics both pleased the crowd and humiliated the authorities. Nonetheless, much remains unknown; for example, the character of the musical bands, the events in which the Capoeiras participated, and why their activities so provoked the authorities. Hence it is necessary to examine the status and role of these processions and parades.

The anthropologist Roberto da Matta points out that the religious processions were very different from the military parades:

> In [religious] processions, everyone is united by fraternal ties with the saint, and through this relation . . . they are linked to all the other believers who also follow the saint. . . . A military parade is an obvious and revealing demonstration of force since the contingents of armed men, ready for war and in uniform march in perfect order, are seen and applauded. Whereas in the religious processions the movements are less rigid and more emotional, in military parades they are kept under strictly control.[77]

During the nineteenth century, the division between state and church was not so marked. The civil and religious elite participated in all events, as did the police and soldiers. The French traveler Jean-Baptiste Debret, who lived in Brazil during the 1820s and 1830s, described eight different types of processions in Rio de Janeiro. The feast of São Sebastião, for example, was celebrated each year on January 28. A cavalry unit led the parade, followed by the brotherhoods' flags, court officials, members of the Legislative Council, and the statue of the saint, which was carried by local council workers. These were followed by the clergy— members of the Imperial Chapel and their musicians first, then the city's dignitaries and ministers, and an infantry unit with their band.[78] It was also customary for both secular and religious leaders to participate in the procession of Nosso Senhor dos Passos:

> A few mounted police head the march. Then comes the standard of the brotherhood of Nosso Senhor dos Passos, followed by the members of the fraternity and various staff members from the imperial palace. . . . The unveiled statue is carried by the choristers of the Imperial Chapel, who are followed by the ecclesiastical, civil, and military elite of the court. All this to the accompaniment of liturgical music, the priest, the canopy bearers, local parliament members, ministers and distinguished people, and preceded by two rows of infantry and the military band.[79]

According to the Portuguese traveler Luíz Agassis, this tradition continued for many years, and during the parade of São Jorge in 1865, the emperor and his son-in-law, the duke of Saxe, supported the canopy while the ecclesiastical elite marched in front of them.[80] The troops and musicians accompanying the processions certainly added grandeur and formality and probably contributed to the participants' security. The processions continued for several hours, halting frequently to allow the bearers of the heavy canopy "to catch their breath and give the crowd a chance to observe and admire."[81] The intention of these parades was to reinforce support for their sovereign, which was why they had to adhere to certain rules and maintain order. Debret described the Santo Antônio procession, which lasted for about four hours. In the beginning, as he wrote, "everything was carried out in perfect order," but "when the procession returned, fatigue and darkness justified some degree of disorder."[82] He explained that this was due to groups of people who took the easy route to the church, through the side streets, while the priest and two other groups kept to the more difficult main route.[83] Debret gives us a very different picture of a parade that was "opened by the master of ceremonies, . . . then three or four black acrobats turned somersaults and performed a thousand other antics to animate the scene" (see Figure 1.11).[84] Debret describes this funeral procession for the son of a black king as a

FIGURE 2.1. Ceremony for Our Lady of the Rosary (1835). From João Maurício Rugendas, *Viagem pitoresca através do Brasil* (São Paulo: Livraria Martins Editôra, 1954), fig. 4/19.

"turbulent spectacle": when "the ceremony ends, the military police disperse the last idlers with whips so that everything should end according to the Brazilian norms."[85] Rugendas made a similar observation about the ceremony for Nossa Senhora do Rosário (Figure 2.1): "A black crowd arrived with drums and flags waving. . . . The blacks who participated joined discussions and loud arguments with very comic gestures that were totally inappropriate to the sanctity of the place."[86]

These processions did not comport with Brazilian standards. They included African music, clapping, somersaults, songs, and rituals that, according to Debret, created "noise" and "disharmony." Fifty years later, Kidder and Fletcher called the blacks' music "noisy provocation."[87] They also noted, "No other class participates with more devotion than the masses in these religious processions and other events," though "only a few people observed the procession with elevated emotions." Many others "derived much pleasure from seeing their masters undertake such hard work for a change."[88] They were also entertained by the Capoeiras who interfered with these processions by running, jumping, and performing their special capers in front of the soldiers and the bands, thus demonstrating their scorn and disrespect in the midst of the "perfect order." All these activities, for which the Capoeiras might well be imprisoned, aroused the admiration of the crowds.

The Capoeiras continued to participate in such events until the fall of the monarchy in 1889. The authorities tried to diminish their significance, insisting that those who performed capoeira in the processions were not "real" Capoeiras but mere children who posed no danger to anyone. For example, according to the records of the House of Deputies for September 1887:

> The brutal, dangerous, incorrigible Capoeirista is not he who walks in front of the musicians at public festivities, performing capers and agile movements. He is the one who hides the dagger, sneaks about in the crowd, hides behind the mask during carnival, and treacherously injures others. Those who precede the bands in public streets . . . are innocent lads, harmless, perhaps novices, who carry no deadly weapons.[89]

To sum up, when other social groups—native Brazilians, persons of mixed descent, white immigrants, and even local aristocrats—began practicing capoeira many of them considered it a martial art. Conversely, for many Capoeiras, perhaps even some of those who used it to commit crimes, capoeira embodied values and rituals and had other goals. It was a game in the broader sense of the word. There was an obvious clash of interests between the authorities and the lower classes, who were not only trying to preserve their traditions but also had found a unique way to express their criticisms of their rulers. As the reality changed, the Capoeiras were no longer isolated. Their patterns, customs, and rituals were infiltrated by other mores, and they soon became an influential factor in local politics.

THREE

Patrons and Oppressors (1870s–1930s)

PART 1. THE FEAR OF CAPOEIRA

IN THE 1870s there was a noticeable expansion of capoeira activities and an improvement in their social status, conducive to a change of attitude toward them. After the Paraguayan War the Capoeiras became increasingly involved in politics. Indeed, the war brought about far-reaching changes that would lead to the fall of the monarchy and the establishment of a republic. The war began in 1865 and lasted for five years, during which time many people were killed or wounded. Scathing criticism was leveled at the government, which had for so many years neglected to deal with Brazil's problems, her primitive technology, the vast uninhabited western regions, an antiquated work system, and an incompetent bureaucracy based on favoritism and corruption, among others. Industrialization and the economic growth resulting from accelerated war production led to contacts between Brazil and other South American states with a republican ideology. This influenced many young Brazilians who lashed out against the officials of the old monarchy, demanding that they be punished for their crimes and injustices. Young officers and others who had borne most of the economic burden of the war as well as liberated men who had participated in the war effort

were looking for solutions to the ongoing economic and political problems. This
social unrest resulted in the reestablishment of the Liberal Party and the publication in 1869 of a manifesto demanding that ministers assume responsibility
for enforcing the proposed changes, grant citizens more civil rights, and take
steps to effect the desired economic changes. The changes took place not only in
the political sphere but also in economic reforms that involved modernization
and industrialization.[1]

During this period three social groups were striving to bring about the desired change: young officers eager to climb the social ladder, engineers who used
their technical expertise to establish close connections with the military, and
industrialists who had profited during the long war years and after. Liberal pro-
fessionals—lawyers and doctors who despite their conservative upbringing subscribed to and supported the new reforms imported from Europe—had similar aspirations. Rejecting the obsolete views of the degenerate landed oligarchy,
they took up residence in the cities. They believed in treating people according
to achievement rather than social class and supported and encouraged new economic initiatives and attempts to emulate Europe. These social, political, and
economic changes were also reflected in Capoeiras' activities, organization, and
hierarchy.

The authorities had used the war as a pretext for removing from the cities
the young men who threatened social order. After the war the problems resur-
faced, however, and the government had to wrestle with a complex new situation. War veterans, mostly free men who just a few months earlier had been
national heroes and great patriots suddenly became a dangerous nuisance as far
as the authorities were concerned. All these attitudes are reflected in a report
published in the *Jornal do Commercio* on April 22, 1870:

> When the people of Rio de Janeiro welcomed the courageous volunteers
> with applause, flowers, and cheers on their successful return from Santa
> Cruz, in that joyous time when the monarchy received those who had vol-
> unteered to shed their blood in the fields and copses of Paraguay with open
> arms, tears of joy were mixed with smiles of gladness, the blood of innocent
> people flowed like water at the hands of the murderous, heartless, and soul-
> less rascals known as Capoeiras. From Campo da Aclamação to Cardume,
> the place where the brave defenders and the martyrs of our country walked
> around, the blood of the innocent flowed. . . . At the entrance to the estate
> on 77 São Cristóvão Street, adults and children were mowed down, and a
> black man who was peacefully cheering with the crowd was stabbed twelve
> times. . . . Many lives would have been lost if the local inspector of police
> had not appeared.[2]

In 1871 the police commissioner also elaborated on the difficulties of dealing with this problem:

> Capoeira as such is not considered unlawful. Only causing physical injury, beating or murder by Capoeiras, in groups or individually, are classified as crimes. This explains the authorities' difficulties when they initiate legal proceedings against them, especially because, as members of the National Guard, they cannot be defined as drifters. . . . They are army and navy veterans . . . and as such they file complaints through their commanders.[3]

A year later, in the 1872 annual report, the police commissioner was still writing about the difficulties of trying to suppress capoeira since there was no specific law forbidding it and suggesting that the rioters should be charged with offenses such as assault and murder.[4] Three years later he again recommended outlawing capoeira and harsh punishments for those who practiced it. Foreigners should be deported, and Brazilians should be jailed in an isolated prison such as the one on the island of Fernando de Noronha in the southern Atlantic Ocean.[5] These recommendations were ignored. Repeated complaints in the press were also to no avail. The *Diário do Rio de Janeiro* of March 1874 reported, under the headline "Injuries":

> Last night, between 8:00 and 9:00, a black man of about twenty was badly injured in the chest on Ourives Street, corner of São José. He staggered as far as Ajuda Street where he fell next to No. 17 and died. The commander of the Fourth Precinct and the Deputy Commander investigated the incident and ultimately found the murderers. We discovered that groups of Capoeiras were spotted in the vicinity of Ourives and São José Streets last night.[6]

The *Jornal do Commercio* reported the same incident:

> Capoeiras—another bloody story concerning the murderers who are overrunning our city. At eight o'clock on the night before last, a large group of them gathered on Ourives Street, corner of São José, a favorite capoeira meeting place. . . . The press screams its indignation, but the following Sunday, the following holiday, the same scene recurs. It's sad. Moreover, it's absurd. If the police do not have enough manpower at their disposal, then this should be remedied.[7]

On January 28, 1878, the *Jornal do Commercio* reported, under the headline "Capoeiras":

- Yesterday afternoon the Pardo slave João was arrested on Ouvidor Street on charges of capoeira . . .

- José Ribeiro was arrested at four o'clock in the afternoon on Hospício Street for practicing capoeira . . .
- at 4:30 in the afternoon, the police arrested, in the São Francisco de Paola area, a large group of Capoeiras marching in front of the band of the 10th Infantry Battalion. They arrested José Albino da Silva, alias Juca Rosa. The townsmen surrounded these Capoeiras in another section of the São José neighborhood. When they reached the barracks they captured thirty-odd men, some of whom were armed with razors and sticks.[8]

A day later the same newspaper reported about Capoeiras who resisted arrest and managed to escape during the ensuing commotion.[9] The German tourist Carl von Koseritz, whose *Imagens ao Brasil* was published in 1883, described Rio as follows:

> Yesterday, *moleques* (ruffians), shoeshine boys, newspaper vendors, and the like fomented riots and deliberate provocation. . . . One group met in São Francisco Square, rolled two barrels into the middle, and their loud shouts in Ouvidor Street created panic and provoked more calls of "Close! Close!" Ruffians, drifters, and Capoeiras then converged, and when the police arrived, they were greeted with a hail of stones. During the confrontation, as is always the case, bystanders were injured by stones, kicks, knives, and gunshots. The police appeared on horseback and cleared the streets with drawn swords.[10]

From the authorities' perspective, it was the Capoeiras who always caused trouble. They might appear at any time, armed with all sorts of weapons.

Characteristics of the Capoeiras

ORIGIN

Statistics clearly indicate that there were more free men than slaves in the late 1870s and early 1880s. In 1881 Soares found that among the enslaved Capoeiras, 40 percent were domestic servants, 26.7 percent were unskilled, 20 percent were craftsmen, and 13.3 percent worked in the streets as porters, water carriers, and the like. Among the free men, 61 percent were craftsmen, 14.3 percent were unskilled, 10 percent were laborers, peddlers, porters, water carriers, and so on, and only 4.8 percent worked as domestics.[11]

An English botanist, Hasting Charles Dent, noted the paler skin color of the new generation of Capoeiras.[12] The admission of persons of mixed ancestry into the ranks of the Capoeiras that began in the mid-nineteenth century

Table 3.1. Skin Color of Capoeiras and Record of Arrests

Skin	Arrested 1885	Percent 1885	Arrested 1889	Percent 1889
White	23	21.9	36	32.7
Black	38	36.2	33	30
Other	44	41.9	41	37.3
Total	105	100	110	100

Source: Bretas, "A queda do Império," p. 242.

was gaining impetus. Marcos Luíz Bretas, quoting French records of the 1880s, states, "The great majority of Capoeiras are mulattos. There are also a number of whites, and some foreigners (Italians, Greeks, Portuguese, but no Spaniards)."[13] According to Soares, among the enslaved Capoeiras in 1881, 13.3 percent were brown skinned, and the rest were black. Among the free Capoeiras, the picture was different. One-third were black, 38.1 percent were brown, and 28.6 percent were white. Bretas's data indicate that of the free men in 1885, 20 percent were white, which increased to 33 percent five years later.[14] (See Table 3.1.)

Police records clearly show these changes. On November 26, 1860, a seventeen-year-old Porto-born Portuguese shoemaker was arrested on charges of capoeira and was incarcerated for five months.[15] On July 2, 1871, the *Jornal do Commercio* reported that José Crosel, a French citizen arrested on charges of capoeira in the Lapa region, was accused of resisting the authorities, a breach of paragraph 16 of the penal code, implemented because capoeira had not yet been outlawed.[16] In 1879 ten Capoeiras from a group in the Santo Antonio region were arrested. Five were blacks whose ages ranged from twenty-five to thirty-two, most of them born in Rio. Five were whites, three of whom were Portuguese, born in Porto. Plácido de Abreu, for example, was born in Portugal in 1857. He immigrated to Brazil as a poor boy, joined a Capoeira group, and was arrested in 1872 and accused of manslaughter. After his release, Abreu worked as a cashier and devoted his free time to writing novels, plays, and poems. It is his novel, *The Capoeiras*, that I quote from extensively in this work. His introduction to the book offers invaluable data on the customs and characteristics of the groups that he obviously gained firsthand. He was murdered in February 1894.[17]

Rio was expanding fast in this period. In 1872 the population was 266,000; within two decades it doubled to 522,000. In the last decade of the nineteenth century the city's population increased by a further 200,000. Among the immigrants who poured into Rio in 1890 there were twice as many men as women,

constituting 56 percent of the population. There were relatively few families and
married couples and a high percentage of poor bachelors who came to find employment in the big city and were willing to accept any work. Wages were low due
to this vast supply of labor. After the abolition of slavery in 1888, thousands of
freedmen joined the ranks of the unemployed, living at subsistence level in the
no-man's-land between decency and crime. They were thieves, prostitutes, swin-
dlers, army and navy deserters, drifters, domestics, and children who worked for
thieves for a pittance.[18] Many of them learned capoeira and joined the groups
that controlled the various sections of the city.

Gradually, capoeira infiltrated the ranks of the social and economic elite.
Restless young aristocrats looking for ways to prove their manhood trained in
capoeira, which was also considered a martial art. On January 10, 1890, when
the suppression of capoeira was at its height, Pedro Murat Pilar, brother of Luis
Murat, general secretary to Rio de Janeiro's governor, was arrested on charges of
capoeira. This may have been the reason for the bitter argument between Murat
and Police Commissioner Sampaio Ferraz about the latter's policy concerning
the Capoeiras. They tried to settle the dispute in a showdown at Café Inglês. Ferraz managed to show his great capoeira skills, but Murat eventually succeeded
in throwing him onto one of the tables.[19] The journal *Vida Policial* of 1926 revealed that Ferraz was rumored to have found a Capoeirista who was willing to
work for him and inform on his friends. All the people who were betrayed were
arrested and sent to Fernando de Noronha Island. After the first big wave of arrests, the informer said to Ferraz:

> "There are no more Capoeiras in Rio de Janeiro!" Senhor Sampaio Ferraz
> looked at him sharply and said, "You are a liar! . . . There are two more Ca-
> poeiras in the city—you and me! . . . I can't leave because I am the police
> commissioner and have lots of things to do here, in the capital! Nothing
> however prevents you from going away and keeping your friends company."
> And so it was.[20]

It appears that young men of good breeding enjoyed being Capoeiras. The most
famous of these was José Elísio dos Reis, better known as Juca Reis, son of Count
São Salvador de Matosinhos, one of the richest men of his time. He was known
for his escapades, disturbances, escapes, and attacks, for example, his attack on
the French actress Suzanne Castera on March 19, 1877, and on Senator Gaspar
de Silveira in 1879. To protect him from the consequences of his misdeeds, his
family sent him abroad. But on April 18, 1890, several hours after he returned
home to Rio, he was arrested and sentenced to be sent to Fernando de Noronha
Island with many other Capoeiras. The minister of justice, Quintino Bocaiúva, a

close family friend, tried to use his influence to save the young man from the humiliating punishment, claiming that a man should not be arrested for crimes he had stopped committing. The provisional government was asked to deal with the issue. The considerable deliberation ended in deadlock, and the minister threatened to resign if his motion was not adopted. The ministers who rejected his appeal claimed that all criminals were sentenced for their past felonies, not for their present or future ones. The majority ruled that even a count's son should be duly punished. The provisional government's prime minister, Manuel Deodoro da Fonseca, asked Bocaiuva to stay in office. The latter eventually came around, and that was the end of the crisis.[21] Juca Reis remained in custody until May 1, 1891, and was sent with the other Capoeiras to Pernambuco and from there to the prison on Fernando de Noronha Island. On his release after a few months, he sailed for Europe and never returned to Brazil.

PHYSICAL SKILLS

The *Diário do Rio de Janeiro* of February 17, 1872, reported, under the headline "Capoeiras": "When the very existence of a race is threatened the training courses begin, probably for the purpose of forming a new organization. . . . We call the authorities' attention to the aim of these schools."[22] This excerpt represents a new approach to capoeira, referring to it as a special course, and suggests that it is a response to racial threat. In fact, capoeira was perceived as war on racial grounds. At the turn of the century capoeira exercises had become a routine practice at certain times and places, as described by Plácido de Abreu:

> Until recently, the Guaiamus [a Capoeira group] still taught new arrivals at the Livramento favela, at a place called Mangueira. The practice sessions always take place on Sunday morning and include head and leg exercises, kicks, and razor and knife practice. . . . The Nagoas [a rival group] have the same training sessions, except that theirs are held on Russel Beach for the residents of S. José and Lapa, and at the Pinto favela for those of Santa Anna.[23]

Plácido de Abreu explained, "The famous Capoeiras teach the novices, first without weapons. Then, after some basic training, they let them practice with wooden arms, then with metal ones."[24] The term "capoeira games" is not used and is replaced by the euphemisms "training" and "acrobatic exercises."

Acquisition of capoeira skills demanded perseverance. Arduous training exercises and a great deal of effort gave the new Capoeiras proficiency in and command of the swift, flexible movements, as well as absolute physical control. Mello Moraes Filho was amazed at their fitness and coordination: "A Capoeirista performing in front of his rival leaps, vaults, attacks, evades, hops, feints. He uses his legs, head, hands, knife, and razor almost simultaneously. It is quite usual for one of them to defeat ten or twenty adversaries."[25] Luíz Edmundo also described the Capoeirista's astonishing agility: "He runs, retreats, advances, turns around—fast, wary, and decisive. He is fast, volatile like liquid, and as elusive as a thought, as lightning. He advances and retreats, reappears and disappears in a split second. All his power lies in his amazing coordination."[26]

All this explains the fear Capoeira gangs aroused in the hearts of peaceful citizens. In his article "Poesia popular no Brasil," published in 1879, Sílvio Romero noted, "Every group has a leader who is accountable to a higher leader."[27] According to Aluízio Azevedo, there was a clear hierarchy, with every member of a group occupying a position according to his skills:

> Firmo soon gained sympathy and consolidated his leadership. He evoked the admiration and affection of the group, and his friends were inspired by his agility and courage. They knew by heart the numerous legends about his heroic deeds and victories. Porfiro was his second in command, without challenging his primacy. Both commanded the respect of the small fry.[28]

Moraes Filho wrote that "the only ones fit to be capoeira leaders were those who, owing to their courage, were indomitable. The leader of leaders was the bravest, the most intelligent, and the most cautious of all."[29]

CAPOEIRA GANGS: NAGOAS AND GUAIAMUS

In the third quarter of the nineteenth century Capoeira groups were identified by neighborhood. For example, in the Glória region a group was known as Flor da Gente (Flower of the People); in the Lapa neighborhood, Espada (Sword); in Santa Luzia, Monturo (Dunghill); in São José, Velho Carpinteiro (Old Carpenter); in Santana, Cadeira da Senhora (Lady's Chair) (Map 3.1).[30]

These and other groups coalesced into two major groups, the Nagoas and the Guaiamus. The Guaiamus subgroups were São Francisco, Santa Rita, Ouro Preto, Marinha, São Domingos de Gusmão, and some smaller groups. The Nagoas subgroups were Santa Luzia, São José, Lapa, Santa Anna, Moura, Bolinha de Prata, and several smaller groups.[31]

They competed against each other for supremacy in the various districts of the city. Historians have characterized this rivalry as a struggle for control over urban space, a political conflict between social classes. While the Nagoas ruled mainly in the peripheral areas and the poor neighborhoods whose population consisted mainly of Africans and their descendants, the Guaiamus dominated

MAP 3.1. The Capoeira Bands and Their Neighborhoods, 1874. Reproduced with the kind permission of Carlos Eugênio Líbano Soares, *A negregada instituição: Os Capoeiras no Rio de Janeiro*, p. 62.

the more respectable neighborhoods in the city center, and, according to documents of the period, their members were mainly mixed-race (Map 3.2).[32]

The origins of the names of the two major Capoeira groups are unknown. Some claim that Guaiamus is the name of a crab indigenous to the swampy area in the new neighborhood where the group members lived. The crab's dark color is similar to the skin color of the group members.[33] The term "Nago" refers to all slaves who spoke the Yoruba language. *Nago, anago,* and *anagonu* are still used in Benin and Nigeria to refer to Yoruba speakers. Some claim that "Nago" derives from *nago* or *anago,* the term of disrespect the Fon people gave their Yoruba neighbors. A study conducted in 1963 in Benin found that *nago* or *anago* means "dirty" or "lice-infected." In the wake of tribal wars, many of the Yoruba fled to the border of Dahomey, where they arrived exhausted, sick, filthy, and covered with lice, but the word lost its derogatory connotations with time and became common among the Yoruba themselves in Nigeria, Dahomey, and Brazil.[34]

The first writer to delve into the causes of the strife between Capoeira groups was Abreu. He contends that the rivalries seemed to have changed in his time:

MAP 3.2. Nagoa and Guaiamu
Bands in the City of Rio de
Janeiro, 1874. Reproduced
with the kind permission of
Carlos Eugênio Líbano Soares,
*A negregada instituição: Os
Capoeiras no Rio de Janeiro*,
p. 51.

"In the past, when two capoeira groups were fighting and the police appeared,
the adversaries joined forces to retaliate."[35] In Abreu's days, then, even when
they were in deep trouble, Capoeiras from rival groups no longer joined forces.
Was this a result of the bitter competition between them, or were the authorities
no longer so threatening? The answer to both questions is most likely yes. The
rivalry between the groups was so intense that there was no room for dialogue
or collaboration, and Capoeiras became involved in local politics and enjoyed
the protection of political leaders. Their differences were increasingly based on
social, racial, and political grounds. Soares suggests that while the Guaiamus
were mixed-race and admitted European immigrants living in the better sections of the city, the Nagoas were mostly blacks of African origin and their off-
spring from the poorer neighborhoods of Rio.[36] Assunção finds this assumption
problematic as Africans and Creoles were present in all the city parishes. He argues that the composition of the gangs did not follow strict ethnic lines and cannot be explained as a binary opposition of Africans versus Creoles: "No simple
dichotomy can explain the boundaries between Nagoas and Guaiamus."[37] This
claim reflects the gradual evolution of Capoeira membership. Moreover, people
tend to affiliate with peers, those with whom they have something in common,
such as social background, religious beliefs, or race. According to Moraes Filho,

Capoeira groups were divided into two major ethnic groups: Africans and Mes-tiços.[38] Furthermore, in March 1906 *Revista Kosmos* published a representa-tion of the "typical" Guaiamu and Nagoa that showed clearly that the latter was darker skinned than the former (Figure 3.1).

Abreu reports:

> When, in a capoeira encounter, one of the participants is killed and he hap-pens to belong to one of the Guaiamus groups, they will not rest until they avenge his death.
>
> A case in point is the death of the famous Françez [Frenchman], mur-derer of sixteen people and leader of the S. Domingo de Gusmão. It hap-pened after the end of the Paraguay War, when one of the battalions arrived near here. Gigante [Giant], leader of the group Bolinha de Prata, killed him with a threshing machine at S. Cristóvão, in retaliation for the death of a no less famous Capoeirista, Jorge Marinha, who himself had killed a Nagoa on Ourives Street. . . . The death of Françez was revenge for the death of Pinta

A CAPOEIRA

TYPOS E UNIFORMES DOS ANTIGOS NAGOAS E GUAYAMÚS,
SENDO OS PRINCIPAES DISTINCTIVOS DOS PRI-
MEIROS CINTA COM CORES BRANCA SOBRE A ENCARNADA
E CHAPÉO DE ABA BATIDA PARA A FRENTE E
DOS SEGUNDOS COM CORES ENCARNADAS SOBRE A BRANCA
E CHAPÉO DE ABA ELEVADA NA FRENTI.

FIGURE 3.1. Dress of the Old Nagoas and Guaiamus (1906). From *Revista Kosmos*, Mar. 10, 1906, BN. Courtesy of Biblioteca Nacional, Rio de Janeiro.

Prata [Silver Birthmark] from Lapa. . . . The *caboclo* Jacob's death came next, . . . followed by the death of Allemãozinho [Small German].[39]

This list, abbreviated here, represents a vendetta that, to quote Abreu, "exists up to this day."[40] Although he does not refer directly to the status of the various Capoeiras, their names and nicknames suggest that racial and social rivalries were rife among them. The Guaiamu Jacob who was killed is referred to as "caboclo" (a half-caste of mixed white and Indian parentage); nicknames such as Little German and Frenchman signify origin, all of them Guaiamus; and the Nagoas' nicknames (Giant, Silver Birthmark) represent personal traits.

In the annual report for 1875, the police commissioner discussed the intense rivalries between the Capoeira groups in terms of religion. He was of the opinion that "they are either bloodthirsty sects that worship Shiva or murderous Druze."[41] They were thus presented as members of dangerous religious sects participating in bloody rituals. It is hard to fathom why he mentioned precisely the Indian deity Shiva or the Druze, and what he knew about these religions and their rituals, but he obviously cast aspersions on religions other than Christianity. During this period, Capoeiras were recognized as religious devotees who used superstitious and Christian symbols and amulets to endow themselves with supernatural powers. Distinct colors, cloth, and other accessories are discussed at length in the second part of this chapter.

Relations among the Capoeira groups and between them and the authorities derived from the social and political realities of that period and from the Capoeiras' newly acquired social and political status.

LOCAL POLITICS

Well organized and ensconced in their particular strongholds, the two large groups enjoyed the protection of political leaders, the success of whose candidates was assured by the Capoeiras.[42]

The major change in Capoeira status in the third quarter of the nineteenth century was their involvement in politics. Politicians were aware of the power of the Capoeira gangs, of their command of the streets and their intimidating effect on the citizens, and took advantage of this to further their own political aspirations. As early as 1872, Capoeiras were involved in the August elections. In the Brazilian electoral system of that period, very few people had the right to vote. Women, slaves, men under the age of twenty-five, criminals, foreigners, and workers were excluded. Illiterates—that is, most adult males—were also not allowed to vote because they were, theoretically, ignorant of the political system and incapable of making an intelligent choice. A basic income level was also mandatory, and this too excluded many potential voters. Furthermore, only those with considerable means and property were eligible for senatorial positions. Emilia Viotti da Costa indicates that until the fall of the monarchy in 1889, the electorate was estimated at only 1.5 to 2 percent of the population,[43] justified on the pretext of preventing ballot rigging by irresponsible and ignorant voters. Ironically, it was actually the government, the politicians, and the elite who manipulated elections to advance their own interests.[44] There were clashes and controversies in parliamentary debates and protocols. The liberal congressman Martinho Campos lashed out against the Conservatives who had won the elections six months before: "The truth is that the worthy ministers have been delivering the crown and the capital of the Empire to the razors of the Flor da Gente for so long . . . and the Government's bayonets have intervened everywhere to help the Capoeiras' razors against defenseless Brazilians. This is the truth."[45] The March 1906 issue of Kosmos explained, "In its golden age, the Glória group, the worst of them all, was like a real political organization. A member of parliament, now deceased, called it Flor da Minha Gente [Flower of My People], and with their help achieved formidable power in the election."[46] As bodyguards, the Capoeiras had great influence, especially during elections, guarding the polls and encouraging or deterring voters. Opponents were savagely beaten, whereas supporters were given an armed escort to the polling stations. The local press aired these grievances after the 1872 elections: "Let the government stay friendly with Glória, with the São José murderers, and with their bayonets, swords, and bloody razors. Let us praise ourselves, the innocent, intelligent, and pureminded, who look with hope to the future and are disgusted with all this blood, filth, and rottenness."[47]

Until that time there had been no significant difference between Conservatives and Liberals. De Costa suggests that major issues such as the abolition of slavery and religious questions had supporters and opponents in both parties. Considerations were personal and self-interested rather than ideological or value oriented. Martino de Campos, Liberal leader of the cabinet in 1882, summed up the situation: "Today we can say that Liberals and Conservatives are very much alike and, may I add, so are the Republicans. We all seem to belong to the same family, are certainly in the same boat, and have no ideological differences of opinion."[48]

The Paraguayan war, however, had altered the social fabric of Rio. New groups, mainly from the middle and upper classes, including manufacturers, engineers, and young officers, who had begun to amass money, power, and influence, tried to change the existing political system by rebelling against the old oligarchy, especially the landed aristocracy. They were not necessarily committed to social reform. On the contrary: they steered clear of granting the masses authority, rights, or privileges. It was under the Conservative government that the Law of the Free Womb (September 28, 1871) was enacted.[49] The Conservative duke of Estrada-Teixeira subscribed to improving the standard of living of the lower classes in order to gain support, especially from the Capoeiras. For instance, on August 22, 1872, during the election period, the newspaper *A Reforma* reported that a card signed by the duke was found near a church. It was addressed to the Glória justice of the peace, Judge Eleoni de Almeida, and his delegate, Correia de Melo: "Here is the rest of the support you requested. This one is lawful; and belongs to the Flower of My People. Wishing you success and happiness. Your grateful friend Dr. Duke Estrada-Teixeira."[50] The duke was a close friend of the journalist Ferreira de Meneses, founder of the *Gazeta de Tarde*, who initiated support for the abolition of slavery. On September 19, 1872, the newspaper *A República* published an item about the connection between the duke and abolition:

> Liberation. We found out yesterday that a female mulatto slave approached the Duke of Estrada-Teixeira and congratulated him on his success in the elections. She pleaded with him to help in liberating her. The duke was not indifferent to her appeal and set her free.[51]

Undoubtedly there were mutual interests underlying the dubious connections between some respected Conservative politicians and the Capoeiras. The politicians had won impressive victories in the polls, and the Capoeiras had received substantial payoffs, as well as protection by the establishment for their criminal activities (Figure 3.2).

It seems that even after having been arrested Capoeiras were hired by the police. The newspaper *Cidade do Rio* noted on December 10, 1889:

> Capoeira is the greatest evil the empire has bequeathed us. When the monarch's police decided to suppress capoeira and imprison those who practiced it, the measures were always limited to signing a "promise of good behavior" and two or three days in jail. After their release, the Capoeiras were often recruited by the secret police.[52]

The *Gazeta de Notícias* confirmed this assertion in an article published on December 16, 1889: "In the past, these villains [i.e., Capoeiras] were employed by the police ."[53] A prominent Capoeirista of the time is a case in point:

> Manduca da Praia is, apparently, a supporter of the government's party in the electorate . . . when the knives, razors and ballot papers are invariably

FIGURE 3.2. *An Electorate Bully* (1878). From Mello Moraes Filho, *Festas e tradições populares do Brasil* (São Paulo: Livraria Itatiaia Editôra, 1979), p. 262.

in evidence. He breaks the jaws of the insolent, shakes his fist at the head-quarters of Petrópolis, has powerful connections and pulls strings. . . . He safeguards our national sovereignty, and makes money on every election campaign.[54]

Manduca da Praia's status also afforded him police protection, according to Moraes Filho: "There were twenty-seven legal proceedings against him on account of injuries, both light and severe injuries that he had inflicted. He was exonerated on all counts thanks to his own and his friends' influence."[55] The press made frequent allegations about ballot rigging, but the Capoeiras could exert tremendous political leverage and escape punishment. Complaints were soon voiced, for example, in *A República* in March 1873:

This is a reign of terror: we are under the thumb of gangsters. The fears we expressed when we saw the voters caving in to these abusive attacks have been fully and sadly confirmed. The Flor da Gente's power is accepted and is now openly in command, making plans, . . . while the police have gone bankrupt and formed an alliance with them.[56]

The Liberals did not remain idle. They took retaliatory action in 1878, after their leader had the king's approval to form the new government. Campaigns against the Capoeiras and other opponents were launched. A new police commissioner, the Liberal Tito Augusto Pereira de Matoso, and a new minister of justice, Lafayette Rodrigues, were elected. They issued a writ forbidding prisoners to confer with their lawyers prior to investigation. The first to be affected by this step were the Capoeiras who had previously contacted their patrons (including police commissioners and investigators), who would then use their influence to release them. Steps were later taken to deny the vote to Conservative supporters, that is, marginal elements opposing the Liberals. On January 28, 1878, *A Comédia Popular* published a photograph of the duke of Estrada-Teixeira negotiating with the "Flower of His People." The caption read: "The Dr. Duke Estrada-Teixeira nominated by the "Flower of His People" asking for entry to the Liberal Party! They exchanged condolences, discussions, and mutual sentiments; but there was no change in the public order."[57] (See Figure 3.3.)

The *Gazeta de Notícias* published the following poem in 1878:

> In January
> The sun was so bright and hot
> That it immediately caused
> The Flor da Gente to wither.[58]

On the night of January 27, 1878, one hundred Capoeiras were arrested.[59]

The Republicans gradually pushed the Capoeiras off the political stage. On May 13, 1888, slavery was abolished under the supervision of Princess Isabel.[60] At the same time, a new military unit, the Guarda Negra (Black Guard) was established, composed of free blacks whose job it was to protect the monarchy and replace the Flor da Gente. Its members swore an oath of allegiance to Princess Isabel. This stormy period in Brazilian history, of ceaseless conflict between Republicans and Monarchists, also had its influence on the Capoeiras. Those in support of Princess Isabel opposed those who wanted to undermine her rule and openly defied the Republicans, who tried to deny any connection with them.

On December 30, 1888, a confrontation between the Republicans and the Guarda Negra erupted into violence in Rossio Square, leaving a large number of dead and wounded, as described by José Mariano Carneiro de Cunha:

> The group called Guarda Negra clashed with the Republicans on Sunday. The Republicans speak openly about killing the blacks, as they did over

FIGURE 3.3. "Duke Estrada-Teixeira negotiates with the Flower of His People." From
A Comédia Popular, Jan. 28, 1878, in Carlos Eugênio Líbano Soares, *A negregada
instituição: Os Capoeiras no Rio de Janeiro* (Rio de Janeiro: Prefeitura da Cidade do
Rio de Janeiro, 1994), p. 330. Courtesy of Biblioteca Nacional, Rio de Janeiro.

there [in the clash]. I never thought that civil war was possible in Brazil
after the abolition of slavery, but it is inevitable. What they want today is the
extinction of a race, and because the blacks are very courageous, the result
will be a bloodbath.[61]

On July 15, 1889, the newspaper *Novidades* also described one of these clashes:

The Capoeiras went as far as pelting the Republicans with stones in front of
the Brazilian Congress. This stopped after a commander asked the Capoeiras to desist. The chosen spot was Ouvidor Street. . . . The plan was to attack the Republicans from the front and the rear simultaneously. . . . [C]lubs
were raised, razors swung, and stones flew in the air. . . . Many were injured.
Panic spread in the city. The cavalry arrived.[62]

When the monarchy fell on November 15, 1889, the Republicans launched a relentless retaliatory war against the hated Capoeiras. Immediately after the de-
thronement, the political situation was tense, and the new regime faced the very
difficult task of defusing the volatile situation and restoring order among all op-

ponents of the republic. There were great expectations for improvement under the new regime, but in fact, the standard of living and wages deteriorated, generating disillusionment and rioting. The government issued more banknotes, and people began speculating. Prices doubled and tripled. Wages were doubled, but inflation rocketed to 300 percent. The situation deteriorated even further because of massive waves of immigration, flooding Brazil with thousands of young people desperately seeking employment. The country entered a period of recession that continued until early in the twentieth century, when order was finally restored under the government of Campos Sales. Attempts to contend with the situation began with the resolute suppression of capoeira initiated by Police Commissioner João Batista Sampaio Ferraz, a sworn Republican, who was determined to root out violence and crime from the city, with the Capoeiras as his prime target.[63] He prepared a detailed list of all prominent Capoeiras and of the rank and file and began making massive arrests. In one week, December 12–18, 1889, 111 Capoeiras were arrested.[64] These arrests and the harsh punishments imposed raised the hopes of the middle classes and the Republican elite. As the *Gazeta de Notícias* reported on December 16, 1889:

> In the past these villains were employed by the police, but today we believe that they will serve time on Fernando de Noronha Island, where hard labor should arouse remorse for all their wrongdoings and teach them the right path to follow when they are released. Continue your honorable task, dear Police Commissioner, set aside your scruples, so that there will be no more innocent victims. Work vigorously, until there is not a single razor-bearing Capoeirista at large.[65]

On October 11, 1890, capoeira was officially outlawed. José Murilo de Carvalho estimates that at the outset of the Republican regime, there were approximately twenty thousand Capoeiras. A year later, in 1890, 6 percent of all prisoners were Capoeiras.[66] The numerous arrests had the desired effect, and according to the press at least, capoeira had disappeared from the streets. Some researchers insist that the Capoeiras were the scapegoats of the regime,[67] and in 1902 the monarchist Eduardo Prado, crying out against the contemptible ways of the new government, wrote:

> A dictatorship that does not recognize the law and silences the press, has expelled, whether justly or unjustly, a great number of trained Capoeiras, many of whom oppose the authorities. On this pretext they were exiled to Fernando de Noronha Island without allowing them to utter a word in their own defense.[68]

This policy undoubtedly succeeded, and the powerful Capoeira gangs were dismantled. They lost their power and political influence, but the numerous records of arrests in the 1890s and the early twentieth century indicate that the phenomenon did not vanish altogether. In the legal proceedings against Otávio Carlos in 1893, for example, it says: "In Campo de São Cristóvão . . . the accused, armed with a razor, practiced exercises of agility and flexibility known as capoeira."[69] On July 27, 1902, Tomas do Régio was arrested for practicing capoeira and carrying arms.[70] Two years later "Frederico José de Freitas was arrested for practicing capoeira and physical training in the company of other drifters who managed to escape."[71]

PART 2. IN SYMBOLS WE TRUST

In the late nineteenth and early twentieth century, in an effort to maintain their traditions, the Capoeiras turned to the supernatural, borrowing rituals, customs, and symbols from the cultures around them in order to compensate for their marginality in society. Ancient spiritual symbols lost their original meaning and became physical, or were replaced by new symbols, especially from the Yoruban cultures and from Catholicism.

Symbols and Colors

On March 10, 1906, *Kosmos* described the Capoeiras wearing "types and costumes of the ancient Nagoas and Guaiamus: the main characteristics of the former—a belt with the white color on top of the red, and a beret pulled forward, and the latter with the color red on top of the white and a beret raised in front" (see Figure 3.1).[72] These items, unique to the Capoeiras, merit fuller attention.

THE HAT

In *Festas e tradições populares do Brasil* (1878), Mello Moraes Filho states that the Capoeiras were divided into two major ethnic groups: "Africans, whose symbols were the colors and the style of wearing the hat [*carapuca*], and the Mestiços, who can be recognized by their straw or felt hats, both of which have become the latest fad."[73] These distinguishing features were described in the press even fifty years later. An article written in March 1925 about the Capoeiras terrorizing the public describes a black Capoeirista wearing his hat tilted back and his relatively paler adversary wearing his hat pulled down (Figures 3.4, 3.5).

The hat also had a symbolic function, which Moraes Filho described as

FIGURE 3.4.
A Fight between Two
Capoeiras (1925).
From *Vida Policial*,
Mar. 21, 1925, p. 2, BN.
Courtesy of Biblioteca
Nacional, Rio de
Janeiro.

FIGURE 3.5.
A Fight between Two
Capoeiras (1925).
From *Vida Policial*,
Mar. 21, 1925, p. 2, BN.
Courtesy of Biblioteca
Nacional, Rio de
Janeiro.

follows: "If you are threatened and unarmed, grasp hold of your hat, and then you will be able to strike accurate blows with it."[74] Abreu wrote, "Coruja [owl, a Capoeirista's nickname] came closer holding his hat in his left hand in front of him like a shield."[75] Augustus Earle's painting *Slaves Fighting* demonstrates the hat's important role as protection (see Figure 1.15).

In the early nineteenth century the hat signified its owner's status. A ribbon attached to it endowed the wearer with strength and support from other worlds and from supernatural powers. By late in the century, according to our sources, the ribbons had disappeared, but the hat retained its magical powers, providing protection in the physical rather than spiritual sense, so that essentially it was a distinguishing trait of a particular group. Then hats became fashionable. Moraes Filhho explains, "The evidence that capoeira had come to stay is that there wasn't a kid that didn't wear the group hat or know how to *gingar* [make the basic capoeira movement]."[76]

THE MEANING OF COLORS

In the early nineteenth century Capoeiras wore red and/or yellow, which had spiritual meanings. At the end of the century, red and white predominated. Abreu mentions that the Nagoas' color was white and the Guaiamus were recognized by the red.[77] In the various cultures—Catholicism, Yoruba, Bantu, and so on—color had numerous and diverse symbolic meanings that changed over time.

The adoption of red and white among the Yoruba was widespread in the rituals of the Candomblé Ketu-Nago, deriving mainly from the cultures of West Africa. The customs of the Capoeiras were also influenced by this. The folklorist Cascudo, for example, analyzed the meaning of white and red for capoeira:

> White [is] purity, joy, dedication to saints who were not martyrs, and to
> Holy Mary. Red is blood, blood of the martyred saints, the flames of Pente-
> cost. . . . The African holy ones (the spirits of jeje-nagos) have their colors:
> Oxalá (the creator of man) is white; Xango (the god of fire and thunder) is
> red.[78]

These are what the colors signified for the Candomblé and the Catholics. Oxalá and Xango are Afro-Brazilian gods borrowed from the Yoruba; Mary and the martyrs belong to the Christian traditions. For the Nagoas white signifies purity, creation, and joy, whereas for the Guaiamus it indicated belligerence and sacrifice. However, these interpretations do not take into account the ethnic makeup of the rival Capoeira groups. The Nagoas, mainly of West Central African origin, were influenced by those customs and traditions. The Guaiamus included members of mixed blood, many of them of Indian descent. To the Bantu, white signified justice, initiation into secret religious societies, healing powers, protection against the evil eye, and success in battle and in the hunt. In Kongolese cosmology, white is also associated with death.[79]

Red had the greatest significance for native Brazilians. Indian tribes smeared their bodies with the red juice of the urucu fruit. Freyre believes this was intended to prevent sunburn and insect bites, in addition to warding off evil spirits.[80] The symbolism of red and white in Christianity and local cultures facilitated its adoption as a symbol, and in the late nineteenth century, color acquired other functions and meanings apart from distinguishing between the groups. Coelho Neto, in *O Bazar*, described the terrifying encounters between the Nagoas and the Guaiamus. He explained that when the leaders decided that a dispute could be settled by a fight, each group sent a representative bearing the group's color, red or white. During the fight, both gangs kept their distance, and whoever won was applauded by both groups.[81]

Colors also taunted adversaries. Abreu wrote that a group's color was zealously protected, and any sign of disrespect was casus belli:

> When rival Capoeiras meet in a bar, the Guaiamu orders wine (red) and gin (white). He pours the latter on the floor and shakes his hips over it and then pours the wine on the gin. This is a pretext for starting a fight, because the Capoeiras resent their color being trampled, and even more if their adversaries pour their colors on top of it.[82]

Kosmos reported on March 10, 1906, that the Nagoas wore a white belt over a red one, while the Guaiamus wore a red belt over a white one. The primary significance of color changed over time, with the physical significance of one color overshadowing the other, for example, the Nagoas pouring gin over wine or wearing a white belt over a red one.

FROM *KANGA NITU* TO *CORPO FECHADO*

The Kongolese had a custom called *kanga nitu* (binding the body) to protect it from evil spirits. In the 1670s the Italian monk Cavazzi noticed that mediums tied red taffeta around their waists for several rituals and that they were daubed with white clay (*mpemba*) above their waists and on their limbs (Figures 3.6, 3.7).[83]

Before hunters set out, they took the *nkisi*, a medicine, to protect themselves and their dogs during the hunt. Warriors smeared themselves with special drugs to ward off enemy arrows and protect them from other harm.[84] Porters wore a charm on their bodies that enabled them to carry heavy loads, and entire

FIGURE 3.6. Evangelical Mission in the Reign of Kongo. From António Giovanni Cavazzi, *Descrição histórica dos três reinos do Congo, Matamba e Angola, pelo P. João António Cavazzi de Montecóccolo*, translated by Graciano Maria de Leguzzano (Lisbon: Junta de Investigações do Ultramar, 1965).

FIGURE 3.7. Ceremonial Procession. From António Giovanni Cavazzi, *Descrição histórica dos três reinos do Congo, Matamba e Angola, pelo P. João António Cavazzi de Montecóccolo*, translated by Graciano Maria de Leguzzano (Lisbon: Junta de Investigações do Ultramar, 1965), pl. 23.

FIGURE 3.8. *Scenes of Magic.*
From António Giovanni
Cavazzi, *Descrição histórica dos*
três reinos do Congo, Matamba
e Angola, pelo P. João António
Cavazzi de Montecóccolo,
translated by Graciano Maria
de Leguzzano (Lisbon: Junta
de Investigações do Ultramar,
1965), pl. 33.

communities wishing to retain a monopoly on trade routes used dangerous magic.[85] Infertile women or those who wanted more children tied small ropes and threads on hands and feet, as in the case of Dona Beatriz Kimpa Vita (1684–1706).[86] In Cavazzi's drawing *Scenes of Magic,* the third caption explains the use of a belt hung with sacred relics or objects. Looking carefully at the picture one can see threads on the magician's hand (Figure 3.8).[87]

The Kongolese sometimes put some medicine into a bead or other small container and tied it around their wrist or waist as a way of ensuring that the power was secure. For example, since eleusine (millet) is associated with paternal blessings and domestic prosperity, it was customary to tie a piece of eleusine around a child's waist on a piece of cotton previously worn by the father.[88] The medicines were carefully selected according to their desired purpose. Any medicine could cure or kill, and one had to know exactly how and when to use them:

> The *nkisi* has life. If it did not, how could it help and cure people? But the life of a *nkisi* is different from the life in people. It is such that one can damage its flesh (*koma mbizi*), burn it, break it, or throw it away, but it will not bleed or cry out. . . . *Nkisi* has an inextinguishable life coming from a source.[89]

The *nkisi*'s strength derives from a compound of medicine (*bilongo*) and spirit (*mooyo*) packed into small containers. The medicines themselves are embodiments of the spirits and their guidance.[90] There were few in Kongo who were allowed to prepare and dispense such medicines. These *nganga* underwent many years of training, learning about the plants and other substances they used.[91] These practices continued together with Christianity, which was introduced and accepted by the king of Kongo in the late fifteenth century. Missionaries complained that the natives still used witchcraft and pagan rituals and tried to convince them to change their habits. The Capuchin monk Jerome Merolla da Sorreto explained that mothers of newborn babies should prepare a cord made of palm fronds consecrated on Palm Sunday instead of binding their infants with superstitious cords made by the *nganga* who whispered spells.[92] Another Capuchin monk wrote:

> They wear on their arms and necks, in sign of servitude to the Madonna, little chains that have been blessed, and also Carmelite scapulary. . . . They carry any chaplets and medals that they may possess. At the same time they publicly retain superstitious objects, and sometimes idols and fetishes are sold in the market.[93]

In Brazil throughout the nineteenth century, men and women wore amulets to guarantee their safety. Thomas Ewbank points out that one of the more popular amulets among the enslaved was the *figa*: "The first money a slave receives is spent on a *figa* carved out of a rosemary root."[94] This amulet against the evil eye was shaped like a fist with the thumb sticking out between the forefinger and the middle finger. Debret describes another amulet, "a mysterious cone made of a bull's horn, a valuable piece of jewelry . . . tied to the neck to guard against hemorrhoids and other diseases, cramps, and so on."[95] Debret also describes a black surgeon who wore around his neck "a small sea-horse, a costly amulet" (see Figure 1.16).[96] Travelers were suspicious of the blacks' charms and amulets and were doubtful as to their spiritual and medical efficacy. Debret was surprised at the wide use of the arruda herb: "A popular superstition concerns the arruda herb (herb grace), a kind of amulet which is much in demand and is sold every morning on the streets of Rio de Janeiro. . . . It is believed that this plant, taken as an infusion, will guarantee sterility and cause abortion. . . . In imminent danger they say: 'Take arruda, it is a remedy for everything'" (Figure 3.9).[97]

    Carlos Julião's drawings depict other practices. Julião, an engineer who conducted cartographic surveys for the Portuguese in India, China, and Brazil, published a book titled *The Customs of Whites and Blacks in Rio de Janeiro and Serra do Frio* (Figures 3.10–3.12). In his illustrations it can be seen that men and

FIGURE 3.9. *Vendor of Arruda.* From Jean-Baptiste Debret, *Viagem pitoresca e histórica ao Brasil* (São Paulo: Livraria Martins Editôra, 1954), vol. 3, pl. 11.

women alike wear amulets around the neck and hanging from a sash around the waist. These "bolsas de mandinga" (amulets) were small pouches "that contained powerful natural substances—leaves, hair, teeth, powders, and the like. Each bolsa had distinct powers, but the most common ones were believed to protect the wearer from bodily injury."[98] The slaves transported to Brazil continued to use these medicines, which they carried around the waist, neck and wrist.

With time, however, familiarity with and use of the medicines decreased, and binding the body acquired more significance. Leaving the homeland for a new climate and new vegetation changed the rites and rituals, and knowledge of the medicines remembered from the old country was affected. While the medical lore was known to very few people, the practice of binding the body was widespread. A common expression in Kongo was "kukutudi ko, vo kuzeyi kanga ko," "do not untie if you do not know how to tie"; that is, if you don't know how to protect—to tie—don't try to untie or undo, because this will expose you to danger.[99] Even today the knot retains its significance, evident in a well-known capoeira song:

> Do nó escondo a ponta
> Paraná[100]
> Ninguém sabe desatar
> Paraná

> I hide the end of the knot
> Paraná
> Nobody knows how to untie it
> Paraná

In Kongo, and later in Brazil, binding the body was both physical and spiritual. The spiritual aspect involved rituals of preparing and dispensing medicines to protect the body; physically, the medicine was tied around the waist, neck, or wrist. In the early nineteenth century, Capoeiras, mainly from West Central Africa, where these rituals were well known, had a propensity to "tie up their bodies" to protect themselves not only from other Capoeiras but also from other dangers. In Rugendas's 1824 illustration *Capoeira Game* (see Figure 1.1) both contestants have red ropes tied around their waists, as do the other figures

FIGURE 3.10. *Clothing Style of an Urban Woman*, Rio de Janeiro. From Carlos Julião, *Riscos iluminados de figurinhos de brancos e negros dos Uzos do Rio de Janeiro e Serro do Frio* (Rio de Janeiro, 1960). By kind permission of the British Library.

FIGURE 3.11. Man and Woman Hawkers or Merchants, Rio de Janeiro. From Carlos
Julião, *Riscos illuminados de figurinhos de brancos e negros dos Uzos do Rio de Janeiro
e Serro do Frio* (Rio de Janeiro, 1960). By kind permission of the British Library.

depicted; this can be seen also in Debret's illustration of a palmito (palm heart)
vendor (Figure 3.13) and in Julião's pictures (see Figures 3.10 and 3.12).

Before setting forth to battle, Yoruba warriors tied amulets (*ifunpa*) around
the waist, neck, and arms. Each amulet had its own purpose: Okigbe protected
against cuts and bruises; Egbe made you disappear suddenly in times of danger
or an attack; Aki-ya would strengthen your spirit.[101] Women who danced before
the gods (*orishá*, spelled orixá in Brazil), removed the kerchiefs (*gele*) from their
heads and tied them around their bosoms and backs as a mark of respect (*oja*).[102]
In Brazil, all these traditions were intermingled. In early-twentieth-century religious ceremonies in Bahia and Recife, women danced with yellow ribbons tied
around their necks. When one woman stopped dancing, she handed the yellow
ribbon to another woman, who would, in turn, tie it around her neck and continue dancing. Freyre observed similar ceremonies with red ribbons but commented that he did not understand the mystical significance of the act.[103] Other
customs linked to the ritual of binding to ensure strength and protection, as well
as to show gratitude and respect, included tying kerchiefs around drums, altars,
and trees (Figures 3.14–3.16).

FIGURE 3.12. Enslaved Market Women, Rio de Janeiro (ca. 1776). From Carlos Julião, *Riscos illuminados de figurinhos de brancos e negros dos Uzos do Rio de Janeiro e Serro do Frio* (Rio de Janeiro, 1960). By kind permission of the British Library.

FIGURE 3.13. Palmito Vendor. From Jean-Baptiste Debret, *Viagem pitoresca e histórica ao Brasil* (São Paulo: Livraria Martins Editôra, 1954), vol. 2, pl. 17.

FIGURE 3.14. Atabaque Drum with Ribbons.

Drums and drummers played a very important role in Kongo. The drum received its special powers from the priest (*nganga*) in a ceremony in which glue produced from the *mudimbu* or *n'dimbu* tree and mixed with other substances was spread over its surface. The drummer had to add spit or blood to the mixture to establish his special connection with the drum. This glue was smeared in the center of the drum's membrane before it was played. Without the glue, the drum was "naked" (*nyoma yampene*)—unprotected, unbound. Though knowledge of how to prepare the glue and its use were lost with time, the need to protect and tie the drums remained, hence the custom of tying ribbons around them as was common among the Yoruban cultures. The photographer José Cristiano de Freitas Henriques Junior took a picture of a king and queen during the feast day celebration of the Brotherhood of the Rosary in Rio de Janeiro sometime between 1864 and 1866 (Figure 3.17).[104]

The drums in the photo are not decorated like the drum in Rugendas's *Capoeira Game* (see Figure 1.1). According to Karasch, "The Central African tall drums survived, and they still appear in modern religious rituals. Now known as the atabaque, a name that does not appear in nineteenth-century sources,

FIGURE 3.15. Tree Altar (1982). By kind permission of Robert Farris Thompson, *Face of the Gods: Art and Altars of Africa and the African Americas* (New York: Museum for African Art, 1993), p. 126.

they are central to the process of spirit possession, as they must have been in the nineteenth century."[105] Today these drums are treated with great reverence, in both religious and secular performances. They are "dressed" in cloth and adorned with beads and shells, a sign of honor and respect for the gods.[106] In early-twentieth-century Bahia, the Capoeiras revived the use and ornamentation of drums, probably influenced by the Candomblé (see chapter 4).

Capoeira underwent a similar process. In the third quarter of the nineteenth century, due to the Yoruban influence, a new accessory—a kerchief or a scarf tied around the neck—was added to the Capoeiras' attire. The notion of binding merged with that of protecting the neck, and a new tradition took root.

Moraes Filho called it a kerchief-tie.[107] Aluízio Azevedo (1890) made a distinction between the kerchief-tie and the scarf: "Firmo . . . did not bring a tie . . . but he had a perfumed white kerchief that carefully protected his collar [from dirt]."[108] However, in another part of the story, Firmo is described as having around his neck a tie that fluttered in the wind: "He did not remove the colorful tie that was fluttering with a loose lasso knot on his shirtfront."[109]

In the 1930s, Luíz Edmundo described the famous Capoeirista Manduca da

FIGURE 3.16. Altar in Bahia (1982). By kind permission of Robert Farris Thompson, *Face of the Gods: Art and Altars of Africa and the African Americas* (New York: Museum for African Art, 1993), p. 184.

Praia wearing a "blue silk kerchief around his neck."[110] Mestre Bimba (1900–1974), founder of Capoeira Regional, claimed that the silk kerchief was used to protect the neck against gashes from the razors that were widely used as weapons in the late nineteenth century. He believed that silk would withstand a razor cut and prevent wounding such a sensitive part of the body.[111]

Rego commented:

> The silk scarf to which Mestre Bimba refers was not specific to the Capoeiras. It was a fashionable accessory to protect the collar from dust and perspiration. Even today, when a black man plays, he puts a simple cotton scarf or a small towel between his neck and his collar.[112]

In the course of the nineteenth century *kanga nitu* was replaced by *corpo fechado* (closed body). The goal was the same—to protect the body from bad luck, enemies, and dangers but now by "closing the body" (*fechar o corpo*). Various symbolic objects could grant the wearer supernatural powers and achieve this goal. Sometimes specific movements could achieve the same results. Luíz Edmundo quotes Manduca, who described a fight with another man whom he easily overpowered. At the end of the fight, with his adversary lying vanquished on the floor and bleeding from the mouth, Manduca said, "I was crawling out on my belly, and when the cricket shouted, I opened the arch and fell into the world. In my half hour I go far, because I come from the harp (*lyra*) people and my body is closed."[113]

This vivid description can be translated as follows: "When the crowd began to gather, shouting comments and attracting attention, Manduca da Praia opened the 'arch' [i.e., made his way through] and made a run for it before the police arrived." We know that the Capoeiras, like many of African descent, often employed ambivalent metaphorical expressions. Indeed, Kongolese fighting

FIGURE 3.17. Black King and Queen in Rio de Janeiro (ca. 1865).

rituals were described by means of similar metaphors, including the ability to fly, the symbolic arch, and the closed body. Dapper's *Illustrations from Luango* (1668) (see Figures 1.8, 1.9) depicts groups of warriors holding flags and wearing white garments fluttering in the wind and feathered headdresses. Nearby is an altar surmounted by an arch, on which a figure is arranging or placing an offering. Before going out to fight the warriors passed underneath this arch, and it was this ritual that kept the inner circle intact, thereby imbuing the warriors with strength and power. Fu-Kiau adds that in the past young Bantu men and women warriors, after a long period of training, underwent a ceremonial test. The men had to crawl between the legs of a straddling naked woman—a community healer who knew the martial arts—without touching her. If he failed, he was removed from the ranks of the warriors and not allowed to participate in the battle. This test was called "passing under the arch" and was intended to test the warriors' ability to focus on their task and to resist temptation. After passing this test, they received medicines to protect their bodies in the battle.[114] This test had another symbolic significance that characterized various rites of passage and initiation: a symbolic rebirth. Wyatt MacGaffey explains: "If a man wishes to appeal to his paternal ancestors he must first inform a living female member of the clan of his appeal, to which she will be the 'upper' witness, the dead being 'the witnesses below.' . . . [T]he upper witness . . . steps across a 'child's' body lying on the threshold of her house at dawn, thus "giving birth.""[115] These ceremonies took place secretly, in secluded places, but the ritual of passing underneath a symbolic arch was familiar to many. Apparently the arch was still widely considered in Brazil a symbol guaranteeing strength, protection, control, and power. This may explain why Manduca da Praia "opened an arch," passed under it, was enabled to "fly," and was granted the ability to "close his body." Even today, when Capoeiras enter the *roda* (circle), they turn a cartwheel known as *au*, creating an arch that penetrates the circle and begins the game. Robert Farris Thompson explains, "Turning a cartwheel symbolizes drastic change. Technically you overturn everything while walking on your hands. This means that you are walking in another world."[116]

These practices were used in Kongo in the late eighteenth century by the local priests. Father Cavazzi described them as follows: "In order to augment the reputation of his prowess, he frequently walks upside down on his hands, with his feet in the air, like all prestidigitators, with extravagant movements and shouted obscenities."[117] The Africans brought these beliefs and rituals with them to Brazil. In the early 1780s an inquisition from Rio de Janeiro accused a black freedman of witchcraft. He was accused of walking through the streets "with his head toward the ground and his feet in the air, jumping . . . in the air and speaking the language of his country."[118] Debret's drawing of a funeral procession of a Kongolese king's son (1808) also depicts a man walking on his hands with his legs lifted towards the sky (see Figure 1.11).

A capoeira song that is popular today exemplifies this symbolism:

> Yê
> Menino, quem foi teu mestre?
> Teu mestre foi Salomão
> Que andava com pé pra cima
> A cabeça para o chão
> Ensinava capoeira
> Com a palmatória na mão.[119]

> Yê,
> Boy, who was your teacher?
> Your teacher was Solomon
> Who walked with his feet up
> And his head toward the floor
> Taught capoeira
> Holding his palmer in his hand.

The *palmatória* was a cane used to punish schoolchildren. The palmer has symbolic meanings in many cultures. In the above song, the teacher—King Solomon—represents wisdom, strength, and knowledge. The teacher stands on his hands while instructing his pupils and teaching capoeira. This undoubtedly indicates entry into spiritual worlds directly connected to capoeira.

In the early twentieth century, another symbol associated with King Solomon enabled the Capoeirista to close the body and protect himself, as reported by the Capoeirista Jair Moura: "The prayer 'Solomon's Ark' is well known among the old mestres and was very popular among the Capoeiras. It ended as follows: 'Close your body, brother, take good care of yourself in Solomon's ark.'"[120]

The ark (*arca* in Portuguese) has a long history in the Bible. Noah built one to save his family and the animals from the flood with which God punished the world for man's sins. The Holy Ark housed the sacred tablets of the Decalogue, Aaron's staff, and a pot of manna. It symbolized God's pledge to protect the Israelites in their journey through the Sinai Desert, and they took it with them into battle against various enemy tribes and peoples. Also memorable is King David's leaping and dancing before the Ark on the way to Jerusalem, the new capital he was going to inaugurate. In the course of the journey, one of the wheels of the wagon broke "for the oxen shook it." The person who grasped it "was smitten by

God," evidence of the Ark's formidable power.[121] The ark also has symbolic significance in Christianity: Noah's ark was considered the protector of all animals; the Holy Ark was perceived as God's presence among his chosen people and his commitment to safeguard and protect them. Eventually it became a symbol of the church, which was perceived as an ark filled with God's presence. Thus the capoeira prayer/song describes how to close the body like Solomon's ark and protect oneself. I shall also discuss the symbol known as Solomon's Seal.

The Capoeiras had the ability to disappear suddenly—a feat also known today. There is no explanation for how this is possible, or whether amulets, witchcraft, or incantations are used. The Capoerista vanishes as soon as the police arrive on the scene. Luíz Edmundo gives an example of a Capoeirista's disappearance in Rio de Janeiro: "When the police hurried with drawn bayonets to the scene, the Capoeirista vanished into thin air like a cloud of smoke and was never found."[122] At the same time, in Bahia, another young man made a name for himself as a Capoeirista who also possessed this incredible ability. His name was Manoel Henrique Pereira, known as Besouro (Beetle). He used to fight the police and humiliate them by taking their weapons and returning them to the police station. His nickname derived from the belief that when he found no other means of escape, he would turn himself into a beetle and fly away.[123] Many tales were told about him and his escapades. In one case he was lured into an ambush where forty armed men were waiting to kill him. Their bullets missed him, but then somebody betrayed him, and he received a knife wound that eventually killed him.[124] These stories combine the magical ability to disappear with being bulletproof.

In the late nineteenth and early twentieth century we find other descriptions of Capoeiras who used Christian symbols and amulets to endow themselves with supernatural powers. This is also why, at this period, the Capoeiras' piety was emphasized, even in paintings. Edmundo, for example, points out:

> They were very religious. If they were in a hurry to start the fight, they might leave their knives behind, but they would never leave their *bentinhos* or go without saying a Hail Mary or Holy Father. Quite often, in the dark hour before dawn, one of them could be seen kneeling in front of a lighted niche on a street corner, pounding his chest, kissing the ground, and praying devoutly to the spirit that he had liberated from its earthly shell.[125]

Bentinhos consisted of two pieces of cloth tied with two pieces of string and decorated with the image of Mary and Jesus on one side and one or more images of a saint on the other side. It was stored in a bag and tied to the body. The historian Maria Salvadori identified *bentinhos* as objects like the two square pieces of cloth with prayers written on them that the Benedictines wore around the neck. Capoeiras, she wrote, used these religious items to pay their respects to the dead and when praying to God. The chronicler João do Rio explained how Capoeiras and criminals used various objects to display their religious devotion while at the same time committing dreadful crimes:

> [It is] true crisis in religion. . . . To pray to God for salvation and wear the *bentinhos* around the neck, with the holy saints between its papers, will not necessarily rehabilitate people like Carlito or Cardosinho who cross themselves when they get out of bed and kill a man a few hours later. Serafim Bueno is a despicable criminal with blind faith in miracles and in Jesus. This hangman, this detestable thief, trembles when he talks about punishment from heaven. But none of these men has repented.[126]

Cardosinho was indeed a Capoeirista who terrorized people in 1904–1905. At that time Capoeiras were identified as religious, enacting Christian ceremonies. The higher-class Capoeiras and the spread of Christianity among the lower classes reinforced the adoption of Christian rituals, symbols, and elements. Yet the emphasis on the Capoeiras' piety does not necessarily mean that in earlier times they had been lacking in spiritual devotion but rather perhaps that in the early twentieth century their connection to religion was more evident. It is also possible that whoever wrote about them in previous periods was ignorant of slave traditions and cultures.

In the mid-nineteenth century amulets were typically composed of disparate elements, as described by Fletcher and Kidder:

> In the course of the church celebrations, the believers (and others in this case) may carry several religious objects . . . in the shape of *medidas* or *bentinhos*—pictures, images, medallions of saints or the pope, etc. They are "exchanged"—never bought—in the church. The medidas are ribbons cut the exact length of the statue of Our Lady or of a patron saint. When they are put on the body, they heal any kind of disease and grant the wishes of their happy owners. Certain colors match each of the statues of Our Lady. I was once told the important fact that when a devout Fluminense [native of Rio] makes a vow to Our Lady, he must take great care not to use the wrong color. . . . The bentinhos are two small cushions with the painted image of Our Lady or one of our patron saints. They are also used on the body, tied in pairs by a ribbon, one on the chest and the other on the back. These are the most effective protectors against enemies from outside, whether attacking from the rear or from the front.[127]

Amulets were widely used by slaves, men and women alike, during the nineteenth century. But only toward the end of that century were they connected with Capoeiras. Perhaps it was only then they began using amulets as a result of changes in the ethnic, social, and cultural makeup of the groups, including a strong Christian influence, or perhaps their use of amulets was such a matter of course that the sources had not bothered to mention it earlier. I think that both theories are acceptable. In the early nineteenth century, Capoeiras whose origins were mainly in West Central Africa used amulets unknown to the authorities and other observers. The amulets obviously had to be concealed from the slave owners. With time, as traditions changed, they were replaced or disappeared as a result of encountering other cultures and Capoeiras of different cultural, religious, and racial backgrounds. The Yoruban cultures had profoundly affected capoeira since the mid-nineteenth century, popularizing the use of amulets, as did Christianity. Necklaces, idols, pictures, and images were worn or carried openly. Healers no longer had to concoct their drugs in secret. Amulets were distributed in broad daylight during festivals and holidays. Fletcher and Kidder remarked on a widespread custom that is still popular in Brazil today:

> The pagans are not content with writing their thanks and a description of the affected or sick organs. They also hang in their temples . . . replicas of arms, legs, eyes and other parts of the body. In the Glória Church, wax models of arms, feet, eyes, noses and torsos are on display. . . . A plantation owner from Tijuca . . . told us that he had just returned from visiting a neighbor whose arm was paralyzed. . . . One day a "holy man" told him to find a candle vendor, buy from her a wax model of the paralyzed limb, and present it to the Virgin Mary. Needless to say the arm healed completely.[128]

Moura explains how Capoeiras could "close the body":

> They put around the neck the *patuas* [leather bag] containing powerful prayers to avert bad moments in life and to warn them against evil. The amulet and a rosary, strung on cord and tied around the neck, were hung between the chest and the armpit.[129]

Moura told me that he personally kept his amulet in his armpit. He did not know why. The Yoruba wore necklaces and chains to protect the body. In Kongo, in extreme cases, they tied medicines around the neck.[130] It seems that in Bahia these traditions merged. The amulets themselves were very interesting. According to Moura:

> The patua could be made of any one of twenty holy ingredients, including the *pedra d'ara* [a sacred stone in the middle of an altar]; *agnus dei* [a wax

medallion blessed by the pope] worn around the neck for protection; *sanguinho* [a small piece of cloth used by the priest to wipe the sacramental wine goblet]; *calix-bento* [blessed chalice]; *cera de veia benta* [probably a blessed wax tablet]; *leite de Senhora* [an image of the Virgin Mary carved on each side of a stone].

According to superstition, a Capoeirista who owned a patua consisting of any of these elements was able to liberate himself from all danger and become strong and brave. . . . This is what is known as *corpo fechado* or *fechar o corpo*. . . . A Capoeirista who wore an amulet was known as a sorcerer. It was customary to prepare the patua on Good Friday with a thread from a priest's garment or the *santo lenho* [holy cross], and bless them in the course of a funeral procession of a dead master, to obtain protection from Heaven.[131]

Another example, again from Moura, describes the mixture of traditions in what has become a capoeira symbol:

The amulets were put into cloth or leather bags with powerful prayers and the Cinco Salomão (Solomon's Five). In standard Portuguese this is the Signo de Salomão (Solomon's Sign), and the initials JMJ (Jesus, Maria, Joseph). They were efficacious magic, especially against enemy trickery, death in battle, and the like.[132]

Referring to the term "Cinco Salomão," Moura believed he corrected a linguistic error by saying "Signo de Salomão," which means "Solomon's Sign" or "Solomon's Seal." This sign consists of a pentagram or hexagram with a small cross at the top and the initials JMJ at each of the lower corners (Figure 3.18).

Mestre Noronha wrote a book titled *O ABC da Capoeira Angola* (The ABCs of Capoeira Angola), in which he described their various beliefs (Figure 3.19):

I, Mestre Noronha, declare the following, having often visited this circle of tough guys who always treated me well, thanks to the Holy Ghost, amen [draws three crosses and Solomon's Sign]. I, Mestre Noronha, always went into the Capoeira circles in the hills [the favelas] with my body closed, with my *orishá*, my God, and my prayer, amen. Xango [god of fire and thunder], my God's Father [again draws Solomon's Sign] . . . P.D.N.S. Jesus is the one who takes care of me in time of pain, amen [repeats Solomon's Sign].[133]

Solomon's Star, better known as Solomon's Seal, is a symbol of great significance. Solomon inherited from his father, King David, a large kingdom extending from the Euphrates to the Egyptian border. He expanded it even further and built fortresses and impressive structures, including the Temple and the cities of

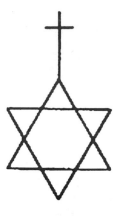

FIGURE 3.18. Solomon's Seal as a Symbol of Capoeira.

/2\

A ARMA DE MAIS VALOR PARA O
CAPOEIRISTA É UM NAFE NONE
PARTICULAL DE UMA NAVALHA PARA SUA
DEFEIZA PESSOAL QUE É UM NAFE
ARMA CORTA E LIGEIRA PARA QUEM
SABA MANOBRAL COM A NVALHA QUE º
CAPOERISTA CHAMA DE NAFE PARA AQUELE
SÃO DIZORDEIRO QUE VIVE ZOYA E MORRO EU
MESTRE NORONHA DOU ESTE DEPUIMENTO PORQUE
ESTA ROSA DE BANBA POREM ELLES
SEMPRE MITRATOU MUITO BEM GRAÇAS O DIVINO
ESPRITO SANTO AMEN ttt. ✝ JMJ✝
EU MESTRE NORONHA SEMPRE FU NASRODAS
DE CAPOEIRA LA DOSMORROS COM MEU CORPOFECHADO
COM MEIOS ORMAR EM DIAS E MINHA
ORAÇÃO AMEN. XANGOU MEU PAI
EM DIAIS ...✝ JMJ✝. PQNSJ-CRISTE
É QUEM MI VALE NA HORA DA MINHA AFRIÇÃO
A MEM ttt. ✝

A DEIFEIZAPARA UMA NAVALHA A
PESSOUA TRAZ COMCIGO MESMO
SEM TER ARMA OCAPOERISTA TEM Sᵐ DEFEIZA
PARTICULAR QUE ADIMRA O
PUBLICO

FIGURE 3.19. Reproduction of a Page from the Manuscript of Mestre Noronha.

Hazor, Megiddo, and Gezer. He made several political marriages in exchange for peace agreements, but his kingdom was divided after his death. The Bible accuses Solomon of idolatry, which led to the downfall of his kingdom. His end was tragic, according to the Bible, but he is perceived in collective memory as the greatest king of all times. The Moslems saw him as a prophet-king, the Christians as the archetype of Jesus. He was also said to have possessed supernatural powers. Midrash Kohelet Raba 2:7 claims that his knowledge of agriculture was learned from demons. Rabbi Abba Bar Cahana contends that "Solomon would send spirits to India, and they brought him water from there to irrigate [his gardens] here and grow fruit." In *The Antiquities of the Jews* Josephus Flavius also wrote about Solomon's extraordinary skills and powers:

> And God gave Solomon such great intelligence and wisdom that he surpassed the ancient ones, even the Egyptians. . . . And God blessed him also with the knowledge of fighting the demons, for man's benefit . . . and he left versions of invocations with which to exorcise evil spirits that possessed people and to ensure that they would never return. This remedy is highly effective until this day. For I saw one Elazar, of my people, who freed people taken over by evil spirits in the presence of Vespasian and his sons and numerous other troops. This is how he wrought this. He put next to the possessed man's nose a ring. Under the ring's stone was a root that Solomon had mentioned. . . . When the patient smelled it, Elazar pulled the evil spirit out of the man's nostrils. The man collapsed then and there, and Elazar exorcised the demon, pronouncing Solomon's name and reciting the incantations he wrote so that the demon would never return to possess that man.[134]

No wonder, then, that the symbol associated with Solomon could accomplish so many supernatural feats. Until the fifteenth century, Solomon's Seal was an indecipherable muddle of hexagrams and pentagrams. Later the pentagram was associated with Solomon's Seal and the hexagram with the Star of David. Many reasons have been suggested as to why the star shape became Solomon's symbol—a star is a light in the sky, which makes it a spiritual symbol; it represents "the war between the forces of light and the forces of darkness." "Stars shine in the dark and are guiding lights in the night of the unknown."[135]

In Babylon the star was a symbol of deity, and in ancient Greece it was thought to possess protective powers. In Hellenistic times the star provided protection against witchcraft. For Christians and Moslems, the pentagram had a dual meaning: it protected against evil (carved or painted on city gates, doors, entrances) and signified abundance and health.[136] The star's symbolism is exemplified in the fourteenth-century poem "Sir Gawain and the Green Knight":[137]

> Then they showed him the shield that was of sheer gules,
> Emblazoned with the pentangle of pure gold hues.
> He pulls it up by the baldric, places it about his neck;
> It splendidly suited the handsome knight.
> Now why the pentangle pertains to that noble prince
> I am intent on telling you, though tarry me it would.

It is a sign that Solomon set some time ago
In betokening of loyalty, by the title that it has,
For it is a figure fashioned on five good points,
And each line overlaps and locks with the other,
And everywhere it is endless, and the English call it
All over, as I hear, the endless knot.

. . .

Now all these five pentads favorably pertained to this knight,
And each one united with the other so that none had an end,
And fixed upon five points that never failed,
Or never settled the same on any side, or severed either,
Without an end at any corner, anywhere to be found,
Wherever the design started or proceeded to a point.
Royally, with red gold upon red gules;
It is proclaimed the perfect pentangle by the people
With lore.

The symbolic elements comprising Solomon's Seal are compatible with the values the Africans brought with them to Brazil and with the ideals of the Capoeiras. Exactly when Solomon's Sign (or Solomon's Five) was adopted as the Capoeiras' symbol is unknown, and evidence is available only from the early twentieth century in Bahia. There the Signo de Salomão was a pentagram or a hexagram with a small cross at the top. Mestre Bimba adopted this shape as the emblem of his school, and many of his pupils continued to use it. One of his pupils, Mestre Decanio, who is still alive, used it as the title of a series of books he wrote about capoeira. When I interviewed veteran teachers and young Capoeiras, they either did not know or refused to say what the pentagram means or when it became the symbol of capoeira.

Each teacher adopts the symbols he prefers, which is why so many different emblems are drawn on the floors of capoeira schools. The floor of Mestre Curió's capoeira school in Pelourinho, Salvador's tourist center, for example, is covered with designs painted by the teacher and his pupils. But this area too has become commercialized, and I was asked to pay for permission to take photographs of the emblems and for receiving a detailed explanation about each design. I conclude that it is hard to know whether these symbols are supposed to help the capoeira circle or a teacher's business.[138] Whatever the case, the various signs initially had a profound spiritual significance for the people who adopted them. Today the diverse beliefs of the young Capoeiras have affected the old traditions and use of symbols, in addition to commercializing the field, thereby accelerating the evolution of their essence and meaning.

FOUR

New Center, New Style

Capoeira Regional and Capoeira Angola
in Twentieth-Century Bahia

PART 1. A NEW CAPOEIRA CENTER

From Crime in Rio de Janeiro to National Sport in Bahia

CAPOEIRA WAS OUTLAWED in 1890, one year after the fall of the monarchy. Since the late nineteenth century ideas of *branqueamento* (whitening) had been circulating in Brazil, influenced by racial "scientific" theories justifying the superiority of whites that spread across Europe and the United States. This Bela Época (Beautiful Epoch) was characterized by the wish to emulate European social and cultural customs and norms and to reject anything associated with cultures perceived as inferior, first and foremost the heritage of blacks.[1] Brazil in the late nineteenth and early twentieth century was undergoing crucial social and political changes. Slavery was abolished in 1888, and a year later the monarchy was replaced by a Republican regime. In the 1890s European immigrants flooded into Rio, and unemployment, poverty, and disease plagued the city. The government now lacked the means to control the masses, unlike the time of slavery when owners were held accountable for their slaves' conduct. The freedmen and the unemployed free men, the lowest and poorest stratum of society, posed a threat to the rest of the citizens. The authorities tried to instigate a work ethic as a major value, a reflection of a stable, civilized, and progressive society opposed to hooliganism, idleness, and vagrancy. In this context the new regime, struggling against social and economic instability, began to wage a relentless war on capoeira and eventually succeeded in stigmatizing the Capoeiras as drifters and criminals, enemies of progress. In 1906 *Kosmos* reported, "Today's Capoeiras are no longer devoted to their art. It would be more accurate to call them masochists, razor-wielders, [and] knife-drawers."[2] And police records depict them as terrorizing the peaceful citizens of Rio.

Yet little by little in the early twentieth century, capoeira gained recognition and tacit approval as a martial art or sport, an admission that in certain social situations and for specific purposes it was acceptable. This was the first time respectable whites recognized the potential advantages of capoeira. The handbook *Guia do Capoeira ou Ginástica Brasiliera* (Guide to Capoeira or Brazilian Gymnastics), published in Rio de Janeiro, bluntly states in the introduction: "This work was written by a high-ranking officer in the Brazilian army, an expert in weaponry, a military instructor, and an authority on defensive gymnastics, the genuine art of capoeira."[3] It adds: "Our efforts are directed at elevating Brazilian gymnastics . . . to a national level, like English football, French Savate, German wrestling, and other national sports."[4]

Capoeira had to be legitimized, to become socially acceptable. First and foremost, it had to be presented as a national activity, integrating the talents and abilities of the three major races in Brazil—the white, the red, and the black. To quote from *Kosmos* of March 1906:

> Why, when and how was capoeira formed? Probably in the transition from the Portuguese monarchy to a free empire. . . . Since capoeira is neither Portuguese nor black, it must be mulatto, a crossbreed between Indian and black, and *mameluco* [a crossbreed between white and Indian]. . . . The razor came from Lisbon's *fadista*; some samba and monkey movements from the Africans; and above all the agility and catlike nimbleness of the Indians in turning swift and unexpected somersaults.[5]

Capoeira's standing was also enhanced by emphasizing the benefits of physical fitness and flexibility—capoeira's advantages as a martial art for self-defense. A booklet published in 1928, titled *Ginástica Nacional (Capoeiragem)*, presented both the history of "the sport called capoeira" and its basic movements. Mário Santos, in the introduction to his booklet written one year earlier, expressed the following opinion:

> It's high time that we freed ourselves from foreign sports and paid attention to what is ours. . . . Brazilian gymnastics are equal in value to all the others

. . . better than boxing that only uses the arms; better than Greco-Roman wrestling based only on strength. It is superior to Japanese close combat that combines all these arts, because it (capoeira) includes the intelligence and vitality characteristic of our hot blood by combining the exercise of arms, legs, head and body![6]

In the same year Coelho Neto published a book emphasizing the need to teach capoeira because it surpassed all popular martial arts worldwide. He repeatedly claimed that "capoeira should be taught in all schools and in all army and navy bases, not only because it is an excellent exercise that develops a harmonious body and sharpens the senses but also because it includes superior self-defense exercises."[7] He also discusses the official appeal he made with Germano Haslocher and Luíz Murat to the Parliament in 1910 proposing compulsory capoeira studies for soldiers and official institutions. The three were disappointed when their initiative was rejected on the grounds that capoeira was Brazilian. Neto leveled scathing criticism at the government for preferring inferior foreign martial arts to those of their own country.[8]

It was imperative to get capoeira off the streets and bring it into organized schools, academies, and other institutions.

In the 1920s and 1930s, official capoeira schools and institutes were opened. An article published in the *Vida Policial* of January–February 1926 reports, "Dr. Sampaio Ferraz took advantage of the temporary Republican dictatorship to suppress capoeira. But as soon as order was restored, the Capoeiras returned to the capital, where they no longer teamed up in bands but reinstated both the game and the schools."[9] A student Capoeirista and a physical education expert in the Brazilian Ministry of Education and Health, Inezil Penna Marinho, wrote in 1936 about capoeira in an elite school: "Here in Rio, Sinhozinho [a capoeira teacher] has established a school in Ipanema [a good neighborhood] for good young men who aspire to courage."[10] He declared that capoeira was brought to Brazil by enslaved Bantus but had become more sophisticated thanks to the mulattos "who are more intelligent than the blacks and more agile than the whites."[11] In 1930 Abranches Dunshee stated, "The art of capoeira has become one of our most popular . . . arts. Its admirers do not come only from the lower classes. Famous public figures, including high-ranking politicians, have acquired excellence in this style."[12] Six years later, Viriato Correia disapproved of how capoeira had penetrated the upper echelons of society:

Rio has become a disorganized city. Brazilian consciousness has clouded to such a degree that high officials occupying public positions, doctors, lawyers, authors, and politicians are not ashamed to brag about their *rasteria*, *cabecada*, and *rabo de arraia* [capoeira movements] skills.[13]

Nevertheless, he also enumerated its advantages: "agility, kicking speed, elasticity, physical coordination and boldness."[14] He considered that "at least ten men armed to the teeth" were required to overpower a Capoeirista.

From Liberac Pires's research we learn that in the 1930s Capoeiras could be arrested for making agile movements and displaying physical skills, or, as defined by law, for "running wild." However, he continued, the number of arrests and especially of convictions on these counts were diminishing gradually. Of all accused of capoeira, 76 percent were acquitted and freed after trial and 22 percent were found guilty and punished according to the severity of their crimes; there is no clear indication of the court's intent with regard to the remaining 2 percent. Of those convicted, 60 percent were charged with using weapons such as razors, bayonets, knives, and clubs. Possessing a weapon was not a punishable offense, and in some cases in which weapons had been used, the accused Capoeiras were exonerated and freed.[15] However, the legal system was not equitable in those days. Foreigners, especially Portuguese, were acquitted in most cases, whereas native Brazilians were usually incarcerated. Moreover, during a trial, the prisoner was required to prove his good intentions by presenting character witnesses, whose testimony would hopefully tip the scales.[16] The authorities perceived capoeira on the one hand as a martial art or sport taught in schools for the privileged and on the other as unruly conduct and hooliganism practiced by the lower classes.

In the 1930s, despite all these efforts to view capoeira in Rio de Janeiro as a popular sport and martial art, it was actually in Bahia that it was esteemed and perceived as "genuine." This is especially interesting in view of the capoeira schools founded in Rio and Niterói as early as the 1910s, though they did not last long. Two great capoeira masters from Bahia—Mestre Bimba, who started Capoeira Regional, and Mestre Pastinha, who continued to develop Capoeira Angola—live in the collective memory. All capoeira teachers like to boast that they were students of these mestres, or of their second-, third-, or fourth-generation students. Hence according to some new traditions, Bahia is not only the source of authentic capoeira but also its place of origin.

To understand this, there are two questions that require answers: Why did the center of capoeira move from Rio to Bahia? And why was capoeira forgotten in Rio to such an extent that Bahia was substituted as its original source?

In the 1930s, when Getúlio Vargas assumed power, there was a turnabout in the attitude of intellectuals and the authorities to capoeira, as well as on the part of the lower classes (mainly blacks). The intention was to integrate blacks into Brazilian society, to legitimize and nationalize their culture, thereby reducing their antagonism toward the privileged classes. As with many other elements in Brazil, the Vargas regime cleverly exploited the popularity of capoeira and applied it to the Brazilian national "project." This also included Candomblé and samba, which received approval on condition that they were performed at officially recognized venues—Terreiros de Candomblé or Escolas de Samba. It goes without saying that this step made financial help and public support important political and social tools. The lower classes also benefited from this policy. The acceptance of their values, traditions, and customs made them feel like participants in Brazilian national identity. Despite the enforced supervision, they could now dance, celebrate, and hold their ceremonies without having to hide from the authorities.[17]

At the same time, influenced by Nazi theories of race prevailing in Europe, physical education in Brazil was increasing in importance. As Inezil Penna Marinho, a physical education expert in the Brazilian Ministry of Education and Health at the time, pointed out, "Physical education has assumed a major role in creating a model for our race."[18]

Capoeira was also an important tool for inculcating the new values. According to Marinho, "More intelligent than the black, more agile than the white, the mulatto is the ideal Capoeirista."[19] This policy was first applied to all Brazilians, and as far as capoeira was concerned, legitimization would apply equally to Rio de Janeiro and to Bahia. Evidently, as mentioned above, the Bahian capoeira was embraced. Vargas himself met with Mestre Bimba, shook his hand, and called his art "the only authentic Brazilian national sport." Several studies have offered only partial explanations for this drastic turnabout. The Capoerista and scholar Luíz Renato Vieira claims that it was Bimba's charisma that gained him recognition.[20] In my interviews with Bimba's students and in the books and newspaper articles written about him, he emerges as a charismatic figure who left his imprint on all who knew him, even after his death.[21] The anthropologist Leticia Reis contends that the authorities and Capoeiras tried to erase the concept of capoeira in Rio de Janeiro as being violent and dangerous.[22] In my opinion, the transfer of capoeira from Rio to Bahia was a complex process affected by two contradictory trends that happened to coincide: the disrepute of capoeira in Rio and the declaration that Bahia was the city that reflected authentic African culture in Brazil.[23]

During my interviews with veteran Capoeiras from Rio de Janeiro, they spoke nostalgically about their capoeira circles of the 1960s and 1970s and about the police officers who dispersed them with clubs or rounded them up and took them to a police station.[24] They confirmed that the stain on the art of capoeira lingered in Rio many years after it was accepted in Bahia. Declaring capoeira a healthy sport made it easier for the authorities, and for Getúlio Vargas as their leader, to welcome famous and charismatic Capoeiras from Bahia and ignore those from Rio. Both Bimba and, to a lesser degree, Pastinha introduced capoeira into the schools, in line with the moral values the authorities desired to encourage.

In the late eighteenth century, in the aftermath of the Islamic wars, numerous African tribesmen were captured and sold to slave traders in exchange for money and arms. Between 1780 and 1830, following the Santo Domingo revolt, there was an increasing demand for workers on the sugarcane plantations in Bahia. The enslaved from West Africa were brought in to the area in great numbers. Many wars were fought after the Oyo Empire fell in 1835, and countless slaves were then sold to Brazil. Most of those arriving in Bahia were from Benin, including ethnic groups such as the Jeje from Dahomey (today Togo and eastern Ghana), Hausa, Tapas, and especially the Yoruba, known as Nago in Bahia. The relatively large number of West Africans who had similar traditions, combined with their virtually simultaneous arrival in Brazil, had a far-reaching effect on Yoruban rituals and language.[25] In the late nineteenth and early twentieth century, studies by intellectuals and scholars—Nina Rodrigues, Piere Verger, Edison Carneiro, Artur Ramos, among others—focused on the more accessible Yoruban cultures. Rodrigues believed that the black race was inferior to the white and that racial intermixture would lead to *fraqueza biológica* (racial weakening) or to *subdesenvolvimento psicológico* (psychological underdevelopment). In his book *The Africans in Brazil* (1890), he contended that Yoruban beliefs, a composite of the interrelationships among the gods, were superior to all other African religions.[26] Manuel Querino, Ramos, Carneiro, and Roger Bastide adopted these ideas and added their own in regard to the authenticity of Candomblé and the superiority of the Yoruban cultures. Freyre, extolling the Mestiço, depicted the Nordeste (Northeast) as the birthplace of the ideal Brazilian:

> The truth is that there is no region in Brazil superior to the Nordeste in
> richness of tradition and brilliance of character. Many of our regional values
> have become national, having surpassed other less Brazilian ones, due to
> the economic supremacy that sugarcane has given Nordeste for more than a
> century . . . and to the extraordinary values of this aesthetic.[27]

The government emphasized the effects of African influence on Brazilian culture but still regarded African culture as inferior in all respects. I assume that it was much more convenient to appease African-Brazilian traditions in a relatively remote area, northeastern Brazil, than having them closer to the Brazilian capital, Rio de Janeiro.

Capoeira in Bahia

In Bahia, throughout the nineteenth century, capoeira was a marginal activity, mentioned in only a few documents, the first of which seems to have been Rugendas's engraving *São Salvador* (see Figure 1.2). There is no text attached to the painting, but the participants' positions and movements bring to mind another engraving by the same artist, *Capoeira Game* (see Figure 1.1). Both scenes present the tranquil atmosphere of a social event, including music and applause, and the spectators are engaged in other activities—watching, eating, and flirting. Thirty years later, James Wetherell, vice-consul in Bahia in the 1840s and 1850s, wrote in his diary under the heading "Blacks":

> Negroes fighting with open hands is a frequent scene in the lower city. They come to blows, or at least not sufficient to cause any serious damage. A kick on the shin is about the most painful knock they give each other. They are full of action, capering and throwing their arms and legs about like monkeys during their quarrels. It is a ludicrous sight.[28]

Without actually using the term "capoeira," Wetherell suggests the characteristics of this activity. The movements resembled a fight but without the intention of hurting one's opponent, making the whole scene a ludicrous and playful game. To date, the first known documents in Bahia in which the term "capoeira" is employed to indicate an activity similar to the capoeira of Rio appeared in the newspaper *Alabama* in the years 1866–1870.

> The *moleques* of Santo Antônio came, wearing blue caps as a mark of identification, with their flag, to attack those from the Sant'Ana neighborhood.... The combat turned serious. The fighters became violent, and this resulted in many head wounds and injuries, and the outcome of the struggle was that the Santo Antônio *moleques* lost their flag.[29]

Neighborhood gangs with different symbols confronted each other, creating disorder that ended in violence. Manuel Querino also described a scene in which rival capoeira groups with identifying flags engaged, and the defeated group lost its flag.[30]

Scholars insist that the main reason for the paucity of references can be attributed to the differences between Rio de Janeiro and Salvador. Rio, they claim, was an urban center, and this compelled the slaves to develop martial arts as a strategy for coping with the daily arduous reality, whereas in the plantations of Salvador, where slaves did not have to compete with each other, capoeira was a form of amusement and activity. Moreover, Rio, then the Brazilian capital, was the political center where Capoeiras gradually became integrated and were recognized, and practitioners from higher echelons of society also participated, whereas Salvador was a backwater where capoeira was an insignificant activity.[31] Indeed, Rio was a lively place, with many slaves, tourists, and nobles, as well as the royal court, whereas in São Paulo there were edicts and orders against capoeira and Capoeiras in the early nineteenth century, as can be seen from the following edict of 1833:

> Anyone found in the streets, public houses or any other public domain, practicing or exercising the game known as capoeira or any other type of fighting will be arrested and will pay 1,000–3,000 Reis if he is a free man. If a slave, he will be arrested, and his master will punish him with 25–50 lashes. If not, he will also have to pay 1,000–3,000 Reis.[32]

Such edicts and orders were also published in São Paulo in the 1850s and 1860s. São Paulo developed slowly throughout the nineteenth century. Its population of 12,000 at the beginning of the century had a little more than doubled by the end of the century to 25,000. Early in the nineteenth century, Salvador already had more than 46,000 inhabitants, and by the end of the century there were more than 108,000. When comparing the three cities, it is evident that Rio de Janeiro and Salvador had much more in common than they had with São Paulo. Salvador was the capital until 1763, when Rio replaced it. Both Rio and Salvador had government institutions such as law courts, military, and other establishments. Both were port cities with commercial centers. São Paulo, on the other hand, was still in its infancy.

How was it, then, that both Rio and São Paulo prohibited capoeira while no such edicts have yet been found in Bahia? I believe that the main factor is the similarity of origin of the majority of the slaves in Rio and São Paulo. In early-nineteenth-century Bahia, most of the slaves arrived from West African ports; in Rio and São Paulo, most slaves came from West Central Africa.[33] The martial arts of West Central Africa crossed the Atlantic to become a popular practice in Rio and São Paulo, even though the authorities tried to suppress them through arrests and edicts. Conversely, Bahia confronted a very different threat in the form of attempted revolts. For example, a few days before the Corpus Christi celebrations on May 28, 1807, a plot was discovered and the organizers were caught before their plans succeeded. On January 5, 1809, 300 slaves attacked the city of Nazaré in search of weapons, ammunition, and food. On February 28, 1814, another revolt erupted in the town of Itapuã, where 250 runaway slaves murdered fishermen and other slaves who refused to join them. They were stopped by the army near the village of Santo Amaro. In May 1822 a revolt by 280 slaves on the island of Itaparica resulted in many deaths and injuries. It was ultimately suppressed by army forces sent from the nearby city of Salvador. On December 16, 1826, another mutiny occurred in Urubu, a suburb of Salvador. Four years later, in 1830, there was an insurrection in the center of Salvador. It was quickly suppressed by the army. The majority of the insurrection leaders in these cases were Hausas, joined by African Jejes and Nagos.[34] The best-known revolt occurred on the night of January 25, 1835 (see chapter 1). According to João Reis, although the Nagos formed only 22.7 percent of the total slave population and of those liberated, very many of them were arrested during the rebellion, including 76.9 percent of the slaves and 46.1 percent of the liberated. Twenty percent of the Hausas were arrested, a relatively high number given that they constituted just 9.1 percent of the population. It is noteworthy that very few of the slaves from West Central Africa—Congo, Angola, Cabinda, Benguela—who comprised 24 percent of the total slave population, participated in this attempt, and only 3 percent of all the arrested slaves came from these regions.[35] In Salvador, West Central African slaves were preferred, as they were good workers, obedient, and quick to learn. The Bahian authorities' major concern was thus to prevent gatherings of blacks. Many edicts banned all dances, *batuques* (drumming), and games. Religious practices other than Christianity were also forbidden.[36] Though no official reference was made to capoeira, by the end of the nineteenth century it was practiced by male blacks mainly during work breaks and on Sundays and holidays.[37] Public squares, the port, and *barracões* (barracks) served as arenas. The *roda* was open to anybody who wanted to play, and recognized *mestres* were responsible for the standards of the music, rhythm, and ritual, as well as for the safety of the participants. The game, also known as *vadiação* (vagrancy, idleness), reflected a defiance from elitist perceptions of acceptable and respectable behavior.

In the 1920s Capoeiras in Bahia were persecuted by the police commissioner, Pedro de Azevedo Gordilho, known as Pedrito. He was deposed from office during the 1930 revolution and sought refuge in the house of Archbishop D. Augusto, where he was captured and taken to prison.[38] Rejoicing at his downfall, the people sang:

> Sexta, Sábado, Domingo é meu
> Cadê Pedrito? O gato comeu.
>
> Friday, Saturday, Sunday are mine
> Where is Pedrito? The cat ate him.

During the 1930s, the African-Brazilian religions were gaining strength both legally and in practice. Land was acquired in the suburbs, and centers of worship that also served as social centers were built. Hierarchical organizations were created and received recognition and respect from the authorities. Celebrations and social events were approved, encouraged, and praised in the press. The 1936 carnival, for example, was described by reporters as the most popular event of the year. In this period, capoeira was still associated with the lower classes, taking place in city squares, esplanades, and public spaces, as described in the *Estado da Bahia* in June 1936:

> The Capoeiras' favorite spots for whiling away the time are in the working-class neighborhoods. On [the festival days] Ano Bom in Boa Viagem, on Monday of Bonfim at Ribeira, during the carnival at Terreiro, and during the Santa Barbara celebrations in the marketplace of the same name ... capoeira circles are inevitable. They are still lacking in other parts of town such as Cidade de Palha, Alto das Pombas, and Massaranduba. . . . The Capoeiras are still invited to play outdoors in Peri-Peri, Candeias, Grande, and so on.[39]

The connection between capoeira and celebration was associated with another black pastime—dancing the samba and the *batuque*. In the 1930s the samba was already popular and spread quickly throughout Brazil. The *batuque* was known in Bahia as a martial game, in which two competitors in a circle tried to knock each other down to the rhythm of beating drums and sometimes *pandeiros* (tambourines).[40] Mestre Bimba's father was an acclaimed *batuqueiro* who passed on his secrets of the art to his talented son. Today many Capoeiras claim that the dynamic aspects of capoeira, especially the incorporation of numerous *batuque* movements, contributed to its gradual disappearance.[41] At that time the Capoeiras of Bahia were mainly lower-class blacks or of mixed blood, for whom capoeira was just a pastime.

CAPOEIRA REGIONAL

The most significant change in the concept of capoeira was introduced by Manuel dos Reis Machado, Mestre Bimba. He turned capoeira into a profession, thereby creating Capoeira Regional, the most popular style today. He was born in Brotas in Salvador in 1900, the youngest of twenty-five children. From the age of thirteen to twenty-seven he worked as a stevedore. He learned capoeira from an Angolan named Bentinho, practicing and gaining experience in capoeira on the docks with the other laborers.

According to Rego, Bimba opened a capoeira school in Bahia in 1932 at Engenho Velho de Brotas. He called it Centro de Cultura Física e Capoeira Regional (Center for Physical Education and Regional Capoeira) and was the first to receive an official license for his institute.[42] The license was signed on July 9, 1937, by Dr. Clemente Guimarães, a technical supervisor in the department of vocational and secondary education in Bahia.[43] However, even before receiving the coveted documents, Bimba's enterprise had received unofficial recognition. The *Tribuna da Bahia* reported that on December 2, 1924, "the first public performance of capoeira was presented without police interference."[44] *A Tarde* reported that in 1927 Mestre Bimba "put on a performance in honor of MP Simoẽs Filho, the newspaper's founder."[45] In the *Estado da Bahia*, the following article was published on June 30, 1936:

> The presentation of capoeira will take place on the evening of July 1 at
> 10:00 in the Praça Municipal [Main Square] in a barrack especially constructed for this purpose. The manager of this interesting fight will be the
> well-known local teacher Manoel dos Reis Machado, accompanied by his
> colleagues: Manoel Rosendo de Sant'Anna, Delfini Telles, José Alves, José
> Avelino, Pedro Braga, José Boi, Francisco Telles, Romão Bispo, Fernando
> Cassiano, José Olympio dos Santos, and Odilon Santos. The demonstration
> will be accompanied with two berimbais, three tambourines, and a ganza [a
> kind of rattle]. They will show Bahia that capoeira is still alive . . . and that it
> is still sought after by people social standing and many schools.[46]

This announcement suggests several things. The statement "a demonstration to prove that capoeira is still alive" suggests that it was no longer merely a social game among friends or a disturbance but a performance to attract new students of the art in a formal framework—in this case, Bimba's school. The article gives the names of all the participants, of the important kicks and defenses, and the musical instruments. Bimba knew how to make the most of presenting capoeira to the general public and to the authorities. He seized the opportunity after extricating himself from a fight by using capoeira kicks and movements. The incident occurred on August 9, 1936, and was reported in *A Tarde* on the following day under the headline "It Is Not Easy to Catch a Capoeirista":

> Today the famous Capoeirista Mestre Bimba showed up in our newsroom
> to report being attacked yesterday at 10:40, when he was going uphill on
> Vila América at Engenho Velho. Mestre Bimba told us that a group of police
> officers . . . led by Barra Preta were fooling around there when, without any
> provocation, they attacked a young man. Mestre Bimba tried to extricate the
> young man from the hands of his assailants. He was attacked with a sword
> but was not wounded because he used the capoeira techniques and managed to get the young man out of there.[47]

This description is especially interesting in that it attributes to the police all the crimes previously ascribed to the Capoeiras. Moreover, capoeira is presented here as an efficacious and noble martial art.

In 1937 Bimba was officially invited by the governor of Bahia, Juracy Montenegro Magalhães, to perform capoeira for his guests. Magalhães's letter to Rego, written twenty-nine years later, says in part:

> True, as the governor of Bahia I did invite the Capoeirista Manoel dos Reis Machado, known as Mestre Bimba, to perform at the palace, and there were occasions when important guests watched the performance. . . . I rather think that performances of this kind had become customary in Bahia.[48]

Previously, blacks had entered the palace as employees and, very rarely, as academics. It was thus a precedent for an uneducated black man to be invited to the palace to display his skills.

Bimba's greatness lies in his realization that capoeira must be recognized, officially detached from its connotations as a pastime, and integrated into physical education and self-defense. He also added elements from other martial arts such as karate, judo, and jujitsu and introduced all this into the curricula of special schools. In other words, he devoted all his energy and time to professionalizing capoeira. Jorge Amado wrote in 1944, "The only professional Bahian Capoeirista is Mestre Bimba, the most famous man in town. All the others are amateurs, which does not mean that they are inferior to him, or do not take their craft seriously, or that they could not topple each of you with a single energetic kick."[49]

Capoeira courses were highly structured and included a warm-up, exercises, regular rehearsals, and training. The lessons were conducted with military discipline. The course entailed lessons one hour three times a week and lasted six to twelve months. Previously, at least in Bahia, capoeira was learned by imitation and there was no organized instruction, so that Bimba's method was quite innovative. His courses were divided into stages. The first stage, preliminary training, included learning the *ginga*, the basic movement from which the Capoeirista attacks or defends and to which he returns, and the various kicks and movements of defense and evasion. At the end of the first stage there were graduation ceremonies, at which initiates received medals and kerchiefs. The ceremony consisted of a formal opening speech in which Bimba explained the purpose of the event. Then the new and more experienced students demonstrated capoeira movements with and against each other. The highlight of the gathering was when the graduates' godmothers were invited to pin the medals to their chests and tie the kerchiefs around their necks. Finally, there was the *tira-medalha* (removal of medals), when the new graduates underwent a baptism of fire—entering the capoeira circle with a trained Capoeirista who had to remove the medal from the chest of the novice with a single kick. Different colors of kerchiefs and belts denoted the students' levels: blue kerchief for the lowest level, red for the second, and yellow for the advanced level. Bimba also introduced the ideas of graduation and best student from education, baptism and godparents from Catholicism, and medals from the army and competitive sports.[50] The official teaching of capoeira then spread to other institutions. From 1941 to 1943 Bimba taught capoeira to soldiers at the Barbalho Fortress. He recounted that at first he refused to do this, for fear that the soldiers would want to compete against Capoeiras, but he eventually decided that there was much to be gained from the acceptance of capoeira as a martial art and concentrated on its technical rather than spiritual and ritual aspects.[51] He also insisted that all his students wear trousers, a shirt, and shoes, because it was understood that people who did not wear this clothing belonged to the lower classes, like the spontaneous capoeira circles of the streets. On June 23, 1953, Vargas watched a performance by Bimba and his students, thus giving capoeira his stamp of approval and designating it the Brazilian national sport. Among Bimba's esteemed students were former Governor Guapore, Dr. Joaquim de Araújo Lima, Judge Décio Seabra, Alberto Barreto, Rui Gouvêia, and Jaime Tavares.[52]

His numerous paid performances in Salvador, Rio de Janeiro, and São Paulo, his capoeira academy, and his teaching at other official organizations proved it was possible to make a good living as a professional Capoeirista.

In the 1960s more capoeira schools were opened, and an increasing number of students came from the upper classes. After the military coup in 1964 capoeira and other sports received a great boost, among other reasons to take the public's mind off politics, so that physical education became part of the regime's policy, and sport became a public and national interest. Physical education was compulsory from kindergarten up to university, and sports, including capoeira, became the masses' favorite pastime. But first capoeira—its instruction, rules, standards, and costumes—had to be unified. At the end of the 1960s the military regime convened famous Capoeiras from all over Brazil for the Programa Nacional de Capoeira. It was decided to work on three aspects: (1) internal organization, including the election of delegates from different sectors—women, capoeira teachers, capoeira lecturers, owners of capoeira schools, street Capoeiras, representatives of sports clubs and physical education, as well as folklore capoeira groups; (2) politically, to deal with all requests, complaints, and problems related to capoeira on a national level; (3) technically, to present capoeira in an organized fashion throughout the country, including public conventions for all strata of society.[53]

In 1972 the Federação Brasileira de Pugilismo (Brazilian Federation of Boxing) founded the Departamento Especial de Capoeira, to be responsible for establishing an international standard for capoeira. All capoeira schools had to apply for and receive certification from the federation and comply with its codes and regulations. The curriculum included civics and mores, law, organization, refereeing capoeira contests, and Brazilian folklore and music. Capoeiras were classified into ten levels, distinguished by their belt colors, which corresponded to those of the national flag. Level 1 was green; level 2, green and yellow; level 3, yellow; level 4, yellow and blue; level 5, blue; level 6, green, yellow, and blue; level 7, white and green; level 8, white and yellow; level 9, white and blue; and the highest level, 10, white. At level 5 the Capoeirista became a graduate. Prior to level 5 it was the teacher who determined a student's progress, and a year of training and a test were required for each belt. Some schools also required a written examination in theory. At level 6, the Capoeira became an assistant instructor (*contra mestre*) but only after a practical and theoretical examination and acceptance by the Technical Division of the State Federation of Capoeira. To achieve the rank of teacher, the student had to be at least twenty-one years old, have at least two years of experience as an assistant instructor and ten years of capoeira experience. At level 7 and up, a man was allowed to open his own capoeira school and be formally recognized as a *mestre* throughout Brazil. Advancement from this level depended on a teacher's personal dedication and contribution, public involvement, compliance with the rules of morality and of capoeira, and at least ten years of experience between levels.[54] It is strange that just when the government was endorsing capoeira throughout Brazil, Bimba's status declined. He ran into financial difficulties, was out of favor with the authorities, and complained bitterly about the lack of support and assistance he received. He left Salvador in 1973 and moved to Goiania, where he was invited by a former student to teach at the university. Soon after this, quarrels flared up between him and the establishment, and he became consumed by bitterness and criticism. He died there, penniless, on April 5, 1974. Mestre Bimba is still recognized as the founding father of Capoeira Regional, though the authorities took over its organized supervision.

The first official capoeira contests were held in 1975, and national championships were arranged in classes according to weight (as in boxing). These contests aroused controversy over what determined victory. The importance of speed, technique, and other elements were heatedly debated and are still problematic today. In the 1970s many of Bimba's students moved to large cities such as Rio de Janeiro and São Paulo, hoping to make a living by teaching capoeira, as is reflected in the following song:[55]

Vou m'imbora p'ra São Paulo
Vou ve se dinheiro corre,
Se dinheiro num corre
Ai meu Deus de fome,
Ninguém num morre
Iê, vamos imbora
Iê é hora é hora.

I'll take myself to São Paulo
See if the money runs
If the money does not run
Oh God of hunger
Nobody dies
Iê, let's go
Iê, it's time it's time.

White upper-class Capoeiras gradually opened their own schools, adopting a variety of techniques and emphasizing various aspects of capoeira. The process of sanctioning capoeira the introduction of new values continued, and today Capoeira Regional is taught throughout the world, including the United States, Europe, Australia, and Israel. It is accepted as a Brazilian battle dance and as Brazil's national sport.

CAPOEIRA ANGOLA

Vicente Ferreira Pastinha was born on April 5, 1889, in Salvador. He reminisced that as a child he suffered a lot from the bullying of an older child. A black man noticed his distress and offered to teach him capoeira so that he could deal with his aggressor. At the age of eight he took his first lessons with Angola-born Benedito. At the age of twelve he entered the naval college, where he taught capoeira informally to his classmates. When he was twenty, he says, he opened his own unofficial "school" in Campo de Pólvora, which he operated from 1910 until 1922, supplementing his income by working as a carpenter, newspaper vendor, gambling house bouncer, shoeshine boy, gold miner, and other trades.[56] On February 23, 1941, his life took a different turn. At Jingibirra fim de Liberdade, Amorsinho, a famous Capoeirista of the older generation and owner of the place, asked him to teach capoeira there. With Amorsinho's recommendation, he opened a capoeira school and named it Centro Esportivo de Capoeira Angola (Capoeira Angola Sports Center). Nobody knows when the term "Capoeira Angola" was first used. In early-twentieth-century records of Rio de Janeiro and Bahia it was simply "capoeira," and Bimba had added "Regional" to the name of his school. Pastinha must have wanted to distinguish his version of capoeira from Bimba's. As he wrote in *Esportivo de Capoeira Angola* (The Sport of Capoeira Angola):

> I, Mestre Pastinha, hereby declare to all Capoeiras, students, friends and ad-
> mirers, that I own a Capoeira Angola academy, one of the best in Salvador,
> capital of Bahia. It provides first of all physical training in Capoeira Angola
> and it also provides defense against the misguided philosophy. To sum up,
> this is what we designate as the Capoeira Angola style.[57]

Although Capoeira Regional was not actually specified as "the misguided philosophy," the intention was obvious. In fact, when Bimba opened his school and
taught Capoeira Regional or won outright victories in capoeira contests, other
Capoeiras strongly objected to his methods, claiming that he did not compete
fairly because he did not set rules as to what was allowed or forbidden and fought
to win at all costs.[58] Others claimed that his instruction methods and his division
into levels and stages were not compatible with the spirit of the game. He was accused of introducing methods and movements from other martial arts that un-
dermined capoeira's cultural-philosophical basis and hence its authenticity and
purity. As Amado described it:

> Mestre Bimba came to show the Cariocas [people from Rio] from Lapa how
> to play capoeira. He mixed techniques of jujitsu and boxing with Capoeira
> Angola, which is an offshoot of an Afro-Brazilian dance, and returned
> home with the new capoeira, Capoeira Regional.[59]

Despite the numerous critics of Bimba's methods and devotees of the pure Capoeira Angola, Pastinha did not attract enough students and eventually had to
close his academy. In February 1944 he made another attempt to open a school
with previous students and friends but failed again. In 1949 he finally managed
to establish a center for Capoeira Angola, which was officially recognized in
1952.[60] His public performances attracted the attention of tourists and intellectuals, including the writer Jorge Amado and the painter Carybé (Hector Júlio
Paride Bernabó). He soon became the cultural representative of Salvador. In
April 1966 he was a member of the Brazilian delegation to the First International
Festival of Black Cultures (FESTAC) in Senegal. But despite winning universal
acclaim, his school building was closed in 1971 for renovation and replaced by a
restaurant. In 1979, at the age of ninety, and after incessant pleas, the director of
Fundação de Patrimônio (Heritage Foundation), Mario Mendonça de Oliveira,
signed a contract with Pastinha allowing him to open a capoeira school on Gregorio de Matos Street. Pastinha's devoted and famous students João Pequeno

(João Pereira dos Santos), João Grande (João Oliveira dos Santos), and Ângelo Romero gave practical demonstrations while Pastinha sat on a chair and directed them. The contract included a clause obliging Pastinha to teach a number of students free of charge. Students who could afford to pay preferred other schools. Some months later, Pastinha had a stroke and was hospitalized, and the school was closed. He died in 1981 at the age of ninety-two, destitute and forgotten except by a few students. At the time of his death and especially afterward, there was a revival of Capoeira Angola, probably as a result of press coverage of his poor health and the deprivation that may have led to his miserable death. There was also public debate about the state of capoeira, in particular Capoeira Angola. Despite political issues, tourism was gaining momentum in Salvador, arousing great interest and a desire to encourage capoeira as integral to Bahian folklore. So capoeira was presented for tourists and guests, who bought tickets to watch the performances. Many Capoeiras resented this commercialization of the sport and advocated bringing capoeira back to its African roots and restoring its glory. The *Tribuna da Bahia* stated on September 15, 1981: "Mestre Pastinha became legendary because he taught and disseminated the most authentic capoeira warfare, the one brought from Angola."[61]

The First Regional Seminar on Capoeira and Capoeira Rhythms was organized on a grand scale in 1980. It was held in Salvador for five days and included debates, lectures, and demonstrations that attracted large audiences of tourists, capoeira and physical education teachers, officials, and journalists. It was argued that Capoeira Angola had completely disappeared, and some veteran Capoeiras, incensed at this claim, decided to open a new center of Capoeira Angola where they could meet and create open capoeira circles. In 1982 two academies were opened by Pastinha's devoted student João Pequeno. Today Capoeira Angola is thriving in Salvador, Bahia, in academies run by prestigious teachers. Capoeira Angola has spread throughout the globe, especially in the United States, taught by Mestres João Grande, Acordeon, Cobra Mansa, and others. It is also popular in Europe.[62]

PART 2. SPIRITUAL ASPECTS OF CAPOEIRA

There is, or used to be, a core of witchcraft (*mandinga*) in capoeira.[63] Some think it has to do with the berimbau. The folklorist Edison Carniero pointed out that the *ladainha*, sung before entering the capoeira circle, was an appeal to the gods, adding a touch of mysticism to the ritual.[64] Touching the ground is seen as equivalent to drawing signs in the dust, and kissing the hands of the contestants, crossing oneself, and praying are reminders of long-forgotten traditions, evidence of the Bantus' prayer for divine blessing or aid and for courage in battle.[65] It is clear that despite the institutionalization of capoeira in schools and as a national sport, numerous spiritual elements are still integral to it. Some are overt and familiar; others are covert and obscure or have lost their original significance.

The Bateria

Today the *bateria*, the standard band of the Capoeira Angola circle, consists, in order of importance, of three berimbaus (the *gunga*, the largest, with the deepest sound; the *médio*, of medium size; and the viola, the smallest); two *pandeiros*; an *atabaque*; a large drum used particularly in Candomblé rituals; the *agogô*, a double bell beaten with a wooden stick; and the *reco-reco* (Figure 4.1). The Capoeira Regional band is similar, and capoeira circles can also be organized without the *reco-reco* and the *agogô*.

According to the few written records from the late nineteenth century in Rio de Janeiro, Capoeiras played music when they practiced capoeira, but no details are given as to the instruments.[66] In the early twentieth century in Bahia, the berimbau first appeared as an instrument accompanying capoeira. Manuel Querino wrote in *A Bahia de Outrora*, "In these exercises . . . the Capoeiras danced to the sound of the berimbau—a musical instrument consisting of a flexible wooden bow with edges pressed down by a thin wire. A gourd or a copper coin is tied to the wire."[67] Contemporary Capoeiras, even the oldest, do not re-

FIGURE 4.1. Musical Instruments in Capoeira Circles.

FIGURE 4.2. A Blind Black Playing the Urucungo. From Jean-Baptiste Debret, *Viagem pitoresca e histórica ao Brasil* (São Paulo: Livraria Martins Editôra, 1954), vol. 2, pl. 41. By kind permission of the British Library.

member exactly when and how the berimbau became the leader of the capoeira band. Fu-Kiau thinks that it is an offshoot of the Congo-Angolan *lungungu*, the musical instrument that accompanied the game of *kipura*. José Redinha described this instrument, which he saw in Luanda, Angola, as "the lucungu, an instrument with one string and a sound box made of a gourd."[68] Henrique Augusto de Carvalho's 1890 book about the people of Lunda contains a description of the berimbau, known there as *rucumbo*: "[It] consists of one string stretched on a flexible wooden bow, with a gourd at one end serving as a sound box."[69] There are descriptions and illustrations of this instrument in Brazil from the early nineteenth century. Debret, for example, described the *urucungo* (Figure 4.2): "This instrument consists of half a gourd fixed to a bow made of a bent stick with a copper and zinc wire that the player beats briskly."[70] Henry Chamberlain knew it as *madimba lungungu* (Figure 4.3), "an African musical instrument in the shape of a bow with a wire instead of a string."[71]

Available sources do not link the berimbau with capoeira, at least not until the third quarter of the nineteenth century. Debret's and Chamberlain's illustrations depict men playing it in entirely different social contexts. One depicts a blind beggar, and in the other a man is playing it in a market among women peddlers. This also applies to descriptions by Maria Dundas Graham (1821–1823) and James Wetherell (1856).[72] In 1824 Carl Schlichthorst, a German mercenary, men-

FIGURE 4.3. A Player in the Market (1819). From Henry Chamberlin, *Vistas e costumes da cidade e arredores do Rio de Janeiro*, translated by Rubens Borba de Morās (Rio de Janeiro, 1943). By kind permission of the British Library.

tions the berimbau but describes it as "an instrument often played, consisting of a bow made of pliable wood with one string. Different sounds are produced by applying much or little pressure on the bow, the edge of which is held between the front teeth."[73] Schlichthorst adds that it is a very common instrument, and the footnotes in a book written in the early twentieth century by Emmy Dolt and Gustavo Barroso describe the berimbau as "a small metal instrument shaped like a harp, with a steel tongue between two branches locked into an oval piece, played by pulling the two branches between the teeth while holding a finger on the metal tongue."[74] This is the description of the mouth berimbau whose sound box is the mouth cavity (Figure 4.4).

Angela Comnene's study suggests that this small instrument, known as the "drimba," was popular in many European countries and that in the Middle Ages it was made of metal. In Italy in the sixteenth century its use was forbidden because it was also employed as a weapon. In France until the eighteenth century there was a dance of this name. The Portuguese lexicographer Candido de Figueiredo contends that the Gypsies who roamed through Europe in the thirteenth century brought this instrument with them and that from Europe it reached America. He assumes that "drimba" became "brimba" and eventually "berimbau" or "birimbau," which is more easily pronounced. Sources refer to an instrument called berimbau as early as the sixteenth century but give no description of it. Father Fernão Cardim described Christmas celebrations in 1583: "We gathered with good and appropriate music, and Brother Bernabé gladdened our hearts with his berimbau."[75]

In the nineteenth century, slaves played an instrument that must have originated in Congo Angola known as lungungu, rucumbu, urcungu, or humbo. This consisted of a wooden stick, a metal string, and a gourd sound box that was held in the hands. In the early twentieth century it was already known as berimbau. Another instrument with the mouth serving as the sound box, made of metal and having the same name, was brought from Europe. To distinguish it from the larger berimbau, it was called a mouth berimbau. The African names still known in the mid-nineteenth century of today's berimbau have been forgotten and replaced by the name of another instrument. This does not explain why in the early twentieth century the berimbau reigned supreme over all other instruments in the capoeira circles of Bahia. Fu-Kiau believes that the original "lungungu" was lost and replaced by "berimbau" due to the mispronunciation of the old Bantu war cry, "mbil a mbau," and was made by sounding a gong. In Kongo, under the influence of colonial occupation in the nineteenth century, the r was

FIGURE 4.4. The Mouth Berimbau.

pronounced like *l*, and the battle cry became "mbir a mbau." Slaves brought to Brazil before the colonization of Africa continued to use the old form, but the original meaning of the word was lost and became that of the instrument that accompanies capoeira, the berimbau. This explains its connection with capoeira but does not account for the fact that in the early nineteenth century capoeira was associated with the drum and that there was another instrument with the same name that originated in Europe, the mouth berimbau.

According to Fu-Kiau, another instrument played during a *kipura* was the *ngongi'* (in the Bakongo language), known in Brazil as *agogô* and consisting of a bent metal wire with bells at each end that are struck with a metal rod. It comes in various sizes and is used in different regions of Africa. It is played at Brazilian social events and during African-Brazilian religious ceremonies.[76] It became connected with capoeira only in the twentieth century. Manuel Querino describes another instrument associated with capoeira: "The musician held the berimbau in his left hand, and a small basket containing pebbles, called 'gongo,' in his right hand."[77] This rattle is known today as *caxixi* and was described by Wetherell in 1856: "A sort of rattle is suspended from the other fingers, made of a closed woven basket containing small pebbles that clatter when the hand moves to beat the berimbau string."[78] Kubik says that the word derives from Bantu and means "an instrument that makes a sound like 'xixi.'" He found that in many parts of West and West Central Africa this instrument and similar ones abound but are not necessarily linked to the berimbau.[79]

In the 1930s and 1940s and even in the 1960s and 1970s, musical instruments used for the capoeira circle were not always the same. An announcement of a capoeira performance in which Bimba participated on June 30, 1936, stated that the accompaniment would consist of two berimbais, three tambourines, and a ganza, a metal rattle containing pebbles.[80] In 1965 Carneiro wrote about the instruments used in capoeira games in his time: "Berimbau, ganza (reco-reco) and a tambourine."[81] In fact, until the 1980s there is no specific arrangement, either in the composition of the band or in their place and order in the circle. In photographs of capoeira events held in November 1969 at a tourist center in Salvador, Pastinha plays the drum and stands apart from the other musicians—two berimbais, a tambourine, a *reco-reco*, and an *agogô*. A picture from the 1960s of the Grupo Folclórico da Bahia features two berimbais at each side of the band, two atabaque in the center, one tambourine, and another instrument that is obstructed from view (Figure 4.5).

The berimbau indisputably reigned supreme in the capoeira games, embodying the Bantu worldview and the value attached to a principal instrument. It

FIGURE 4.5. Musical Instruments Used by Grupo Folclórico da Bahia (1969).

had the power to guide the contestants and infuse them with energy, vigor, and magic. Its sounds were its strength. According to Pastinha, "The berimbau is the primitive teacher. It teaches through sound. It charges our body with vibrations (energy) and *ginga*. The percussion band with the berimbau is not a modern-day set-up. No, it is elementary."[82] Pastinha expresses the philosophy of the Africans, for whom the sounds and rhythms of musical instruments are a means of communication infused with supernatural forces, granting strength and energy and conveying messages. In Capoeira Angola, one of the first skills that a beginner learns is the ability to listen carefully and understand the messages of the berimbau. It rules the capoeira circle, and its choice of songs or rhythms determine the pace of the game. It can slow down or accelerate the rhythm and dictate the nature and purpose of the meet as a display of beautifully controlled movements in a show or a competition between two rivals. It authorizes the start and the end of the game. It reproaches and warns if a Capoeirista crosses any red lines. At the start of every event, it is customary for the player of the big berimbau, the *gunga*, to produce sounds that summon the participants to the circle. Many songs refer to the function of the berimbau. For example:

Angolinha, Angola
Angolinha eu vou Jogar
Berimbau ta me chamando
No salão pra vadiar
Se jogar pra mim eu pego
Vou jogar pra te pegar . . .

Angolinha (little Angola), Angola
Angolinha I will play
The berimbau is calling me
To idle in the hall
If you'll play (throw) to me I will catch
I will play to catch you . . .

Once the circle is formed, it is customary that the berimbau held by the teacher should open the event with the introductory song, the ladainha (literally, "prayer"). During the song, the contestants kneel at the feet of the berimbau (pé do berimbau), paying it the respect due to it, and wait for permission to begin playing. The manufacture and preparation of the berimbau are also ceremonial and spiritual in nature. The famous teacher Mestre Acordeon described the long and detailed process involved in the preparation of a good berimbau: "It must be made of good wood. It must be cut from a living tree in the forest, on the right day and under the right moon."[83] In a personal interview with Mestre Valmir (Valmir Santos Damasceno), an expert berimbau builder and owner of a capoeira school in Salvador, it emerges that every step in the manufacture of the berimbau requires the builder's proper physical and spiritual preparation. In addition to waiting for the right day, the right hour, the precise place, the ideal tree, and so on, the builder himself must come prepared, but he refused to divulge what these preparations entailed.[84] The branch also has to go through a set of preparations until it is ready for use, including peeling the bark and drying and shaping it. This process may take months, which makes the berimbau quite expensive. There are huge differences in price between the "simple," cheap instruments sold to tourists or to Capoeiras who do not appreciate the importance of the prolonged process of preparation and first-rate berimbais that were given all the required treatments and possess the desired mystical powers. Berimbais that belonged to deceased old masters are priceless and invaluable and are not for sale. Legends and descriptions adorned with mysticism have arisen around them. Mestre Acordeon has a good story to tell about how he was given Mestre Bimba's berimbau after his death. The description is long and detailed and includes rituals connected to the Candomblé, an exhausting three-day trek, during which he was forbidden to eat and ordered to drink a special blend prepared for him in special bowls and to go through various states of consciousness. Then he met the mestre's widow who gave him the precious berimbau:

> Dona Nair came back with the *mestre*'s berimbau and handed it to me as a talisman of great power. "Take this berimbau Acordeon. When Bimba died two months ago, he told me to give it to you as soon as you arrived." Suddenly everything became clear in my mind and I understood the harmony and hierarchy of the universe. Capoeira assumed its real guise, and this knowledge was like a powerful light that burnt each cell of myself, changing the courses of my life.[85]

The veteran mestre felt it was time to move on and appoint his oldest student as his own heir. He describes how he gave his berimbau with which he walked the capoeira road for twenty years: "Take it to help you along this difficult path, and do not forget that one day I will call you."[86] Acordeon ends this chapter with a pastoral description: "The wind continued blowing through the leaves atop of the trees. Nothing was new, just a repetition of an ancient ritual."[87]

This description is consistent with the mystical significance Capoeiras attribute to the berimbau. Making a berimbau is an art, and a self-respecting Capoeirista will make his own instrument and paint and decorate it. Some tend to tie colored ribbons to it. (The spiritual significance of ribbons was discussed in detail in previous chapters.)

The other instruments played by Capoeiras are also important but lack the spiritual attributes of the berimbau. The mystical power and function of the berimbau is evocative of the status of drums in various African cultures. Fu-Kiau gave me a detailed description of the way the talking drums are manufactured. The process is long and interspersed with religious rituals. Only certain people are allowed to play the drums, and whoever violates this prohibition is liable to the death penalty. The natural materials from which the drum is made must be selected very carefully as regards the day, the hour, and the timing in general. The drum conveys messages between the worlds, indicates the beginning the course and the end of ceremonies, instructs and guides the participants. The drum must be paid respect by bowing down and kneeling in front of it.[88] The authorities put a ban on the capoeira drum in the early and mid-nineteenth century. Under the new circumstances, the Capoeiras had to look for another musical instrument that was free from the unfavorable connotations attached to the drum in the eyes of the authorities. The heir, the berimbau, inherited all the spiritual meanings attached to the drum, as well as its status and spiritual significance in the eyes of even contemporary Capoeiras.

But different Capoeiras show essential differences in the perception of the berimbau's function, significance, and status. Veteran *mestres* express scathing criticism especially against new Regionais who lack the understanding, affinity, and respect for music in general and the berimbau in particular. They say that many Capoeiras regard the music as mere accompaniment and act in the circle as they wish with no regard for the berimbau's instructions. They complain mainly about young white men who lack knowledge and understanding of African-Brazilian cultures and see capoeira as only a sport and martial art accompanied by music that creates the right ambience. This ever-increasing tendency distinguishes even more clearly between the styles, a new phenomenon led by some relatively new white teachers. Since for them capoeira is a martial art and a sport, they focus on its technical-acrobatic aspects (see chapter 5). The wish to present capoeira as a sport and a martial art that surpasses the foreign martial arts has forced out mystical elements and rituals perceived by many Capoeiras as witchcraft or superstitions. These attitudes generated two ways of perceiving capoeira: as a martial art and as a game. This distinction was made not only by the authorities but also by the great founding *mestres*. Pastinha, for example, maintained:

> The musical or rhythm band is not essential in the practice of capoeira, but it is obvious that the Capoeira Angola game, with the rhythm of the typical band accompanying the songs and improvisations of the singers, infuse grace, gentleness, magic and mystery that sparkle with the Capoeiras' spirit.[89]

One may deduce from these words, published in 1964, that Pastinha distinguished between Capoeira Angola as a game and capoeira as a contest. While the latter did not need musical accompaniment, in the former music was an indispensable and vital element imbuing the game with mysticism, elegance, and style. Bimba was also aware of this distinction. A reporter for *A Tarde* (March 16, 1936) asked Bimba in an interview why in the contests between Capoeira Angola and Capoeira Regional they were not able to determine the victor. Bimba answered:

> Very simple: In Capoeira Angola the kicks are prescribed or regulated by the berimbau and the pandeiro. But in real capoeira we defend ourselves and attack the enemy. Do I have to wait for the berimbau to tell me how to react when I am attacked? No berimbau and no pandeiro![90]

This is a very important observation, because it sheds light on the fundamental differences that had evolved in the roles of capoeira. It was now defined as a

martial art that prepares the Capoeirista to defend himself against enemy attacks
and threats and as a wholesome social activity, a game and a pastime, a sport
for the development of physical skills and for practicing the capability to cope
with the vicissitudes of life. This designation of capoeira—as a part of folklore, a
tourist attraction, a field of study, and a national sport—was encouraged by the
authorities and adopted as a policy in the course of the "New State" and during
the military regime. As capoeira spreads throughout the world among young-
sters who are not acquainted with African traditions, ignorance of the status and
function of the berimbau is increasing. In an interview with Capoeiras from different groups of Capoeira Regional, they reacted unanimously to Mestre Acordeon's story about his spiritual journey and the reception of his adored mentor Bimba's berimbau. They saw it as an irrelevant and strange piece of fiction
that depreciates the master's integrity and discredits him. There is, however, an
opposite tendency among many middle-class whites that were not brought up
on these traditions but nevertheless yearn to learn more about them. I discuss
this in chapter 5.

We Will Not Stop Singing

Documents and illustrations from the early nineteenth century bear witness that
musical instruments were played during the capoeira game, but no description
of songs is provided. It is only toward the end of the century that various sources
mention songs connected to capoeira. Abreu wrote that before rival capoeira
groups got into a fight they would challenge their rivals with songs like the one
the Guaiamus sang:

> Jesus' Therezinha
> Open the door and turn off the light
> I want to see a Nagoa dead
> At Good Jesus' door.[91]

The rival team would answer with a challenge of its own:

> The fortress raised a flag
> São Francisco answered with drum beating
> Guaiamu is complaining
> Manuel Preto has shown up.[92]

Manuel Preto was the Santana group leader's nickname and put the fear of God
into his enemies' hearts. The Nagoas used images that belonged to their spiritual
world. The flag, as described above, was used to communicate with the world

of the dead. This is evident in flag waving during funerals (see Figure 1.11). São Francisco, a Catholic saint, used a drumbeat to overcome the Guaiamu. Africans compared their deities to the Catholic saints and worshiped them while hiding their African deities behind the Catholic ones. Saint Francis was syncretized as the *orixá* Orunmila, the great benefactor of humanity and its principal adviser. He reveals the future through the secret of Ifa, the supreme oracle. He is also considered a great healer. The drums warn against imminent danger but also communicate with other worlds and possess supernatural powers that infuse Manuel Preto with such strength that the "Guaiamu is complaining." The Guaiamus were influenced mainly by Christianity, which is evident in their challenging song and their use of the names Therezinha (little Saint Theresa) and Jesus and of the images "open the door and turn off the light," signifying the notion of extinguishing the life of the Nagoa and opening the doors of heaven for his soul. Songs used as challenge were widespread in the Yoruban cultures in the context of war. They had a remarkable psychological influence. Evoking the memory of extolled victories, eminent warriors, spirits, and ancestral fathers that help in the war effort, songs were supposed to cheer up the fighters and frighten their enemy.[93] As the Yoruban culture was very influential among the enslaved population from the mid-nineteenth century onward and as the Capoeiras were increasingly associated with belligerence, we can see why the ritual of challenge was connected to songs in the late nineteenth century.[94] These songs were soon categorized as "war songs." Aluízio Azevedo described a struggle between two capoeira groups in his book *O Cortiço* (1890):

> Chorus songs were heard approaching the Cat's Head gangs. It was the Capoeiras' war song from another neighborhood who came to fight the *carapicus* to avenge with blood the death of their leader Firmo.[95]

In Kongo, the challenge stage was essential before the *kipura* game could begin. It included a ceremony in which one contestant took sand in his hands and held it as if it were glowing embers. The challenged man had to hit the challenger's hand and make him drop the sand. This was the sign for the beginning of the fight—the game of life. This is also the reason it was referred to as "the call to fire." It seems that in connection with capoeira in Brazil, the need for a challenge to start a fight remained, but the ritual of sand dropping was forgotten and replaced by another challenge—songs.

CAPOEIRA SONGS

Today among the Angoleiros as well as among the Regionais three kinds of songs are popular, each of which has unique characteristics, function, manner of performance, and musical instruments. The order of their performance in the capoeira game is as follows:

1. *Ladainha (prayer)*—The prayers are sung solo with no instrumental accompaniment, and their purpose is to convey a message to the audience. They are songs of adoration and praise to capoeira, the city, Brazil, and so on. They also express criticism of events and deeds or gratitude to past teachers and refer to significant facts and stories relating to the history of capoeira. The prayer-song does great honor to its chosen performer, hence only veteran and experienced Capoeiras are bestowed with this sign of respect. In the course of the performance utter silence is maintained, and the game must not begin yet. The contestants about to enter the circle kneel at the feet of the berimbau with heads bent, and the entire crowd respectfully listens to the song. Once the circle is formed, the soloist bursts out into a long cry of "Yê!" The Capoeiras do not know the meaning of this cry, but all of them make it. It has no meaning in Portuguese, but in the Kikongo language it is known as "Ie" and expresses joy or rebuke, which the singer utters at the beginning and end of every song.[96] The following song ends with the word *camará* (fellows), expressing the Capoeiras' sense of brotherhood and preparation for the next stage:

> Yê!
> Brasil nosso Brasil
> Capoeira é a nossa glória
> Eu ja fui juvenil
> Nasci em Salvador
> Capoeira por todo Brasil
> Camara no momento de festa ou de dor.

> Yê!
> Brazil our Brazil
> Capoeira is our pride
> I was once young
> I was born in Salvador
> Capoeira is for the whole of Brazil
> Fellows in festive or painful moments.

2. *Chula / Canto de Entrada (opening song)*—The *chula* is sung as soon as the *ladainha* is finished. Its structure is that of call and response: the chorus repeats the soloist's lines. Its purpose is to prepare the contestants and the spectators for the game about to begin, thus it is more spontaneous, includes improvisations,

and depends on the mood of the participants and on topical events. The opening songs may include a prayer to the gods, greetings to famous teachers, challenges, warnings, or invitations. It is customary that the soloist and other contestants make bodily gestures. In a song glorifying God it is customary to raise the hands up and to the sides; in the references to teachers it is customary to point at the teacher if he is present or to heaven if he is dead (or to his picture). The following is an example of an opening song (the lines in italics are the soloist's lines and are repeated by the chorus):

> *Viva meu Deus!*
> Yê, viva meu Deus, camará
> *Vive meu Mestre!*
> Yê, viva meu mestre, camará
> *Que me ensinou!*
> Yê, que me ensinou, camará
> *A malandragem!*
> Yê, a malandragem, camará,
> *Da capoeira!*
> Yê, da capoeira, camará.

> *Hail my God!*
> Yê, hail my God, fellas
> *Hail my teacher!*
> Yê, hail my teacher, fellas
> *Who taught me!*
> Yê, who taught me, fellas
> *The mischievousness!*
> Yê, the mischievousness, fellas
> *Of capoeira!*
> Yê, of capoeira, fellas.

3. *Corridos (couriers)*—These songs signify the beginning of the game and accompany the Capoeiras who play in the circle. They are also performed as questions and answers, but although the soloist changes his lines, the audience's refrain remains the same. They are accompanied by musical instruments, and their rhythm depends, of course, on the berimbau. Their contents cover a wide variety of subjects, such as stories about previous teachers, challenges, warnings, and precautions, which accompany the events of the game (see chapter 5). The following is an example of a song of this kind:

> *Quando meu filho nascer*
> Maculelê . . . Maracatu
> *Vou perguntar a parteira*
> Maculelê . . . Maracatu
> *O que é que ele vai ser*
> Maculelê . . . Maracatu
> *Ele vai ser um capoeira*
> Maculelê . . . Maracatu
> *Capoeira . . . capu*
> Maculelê . . . Maracatu
> *Mas não tem karatê, não tem kung-fu*
> Maculelê . . . Maracatu.[97]

> *When my son is born*
> Maculelê [stick dance] Maracatu [carnival dance]
> *I will ask the midwife*
> Maculelê . . . Maracatu
> *What will he be*
> Maculelê . . . Maracatu
> *He will be a Capoeirista*
> Maculelê . . . Maracatu
> *Capoeira . . . capu*
> Maculelê . . . Maracatu
> *But there is no karate, no kung-fu*
> Maculelê . . . Maracatu

All three songs and their order are commonly sung in all capoeira schools, but their contents change from one school to the next, depending first on the teacher but also on the students, their goals, socioeconomic status, and so on. While the Regionais sing songs with national messages that highlight the affinity with Brazil, with sport, and with the strengthening of martial art, the Angolairos sing songs about the struggle for freedom, against slavery, against the establishment, for the connection with Africa and the African traditions, and extol black heroes.[98]

The Circle

The first ritual observed in the capoeira game is the formation of a circle. Assisted by the berimbau, the soloist calls all the participants to gather. The spectators converge to the special sounds and create a circle together with the band as part of it. This circle is known as *roda de capoeira* (capoeira circle). Contemporary Capoeiras mostly explain the formation of the *roda* as deriving from slavery, when slaves, in order to hide their activities from their owners, used to form a circle around the trainees. The purpose of the circle was, then, to protect the participants physically, but today Capoeiras admit that the circle grants them strength and power, and together with the singing, music, and hand-clapping they are able to reach high levels of energy and brilliant feats. These explanations convey two ways of perceiving the function of the circle—physical and spiritual.

THE CIRCLE AS A PHYSICAL CONCEPT

The circle of spectators is a boundary and a physical means of defense. A person who is not a member of the group playing the game is not allowed to enter the middle of the circle and start playing. He has to wait for permission from the Capoeiras to join the circle of spectators. Only after some time, with the teacher's permission, will he be allowed to join in as one of the contestants. The circle is, then, a boundary between the participants and the spectators who are not Capoeiras.[99] Today, in many of the capoeira schools, it is customary to draw one or two circles that an individual is allowed to cross only during a capoeira game. The spectators stand beyond the wider circle, a boundary that they must not cross. The smaller circle is the boundary that the contestants must not cross in the course of the game.

I watched a practice of veteran Capoeiras, old students of Mestre Bimba, instructed by his son, Mestre Nenel. They meet once a month in Nenel's house, in a room especially allocated for this purpose. I was surprised to find three circles drawn on the floor with inscriptions clearly denoting the various rhythms that can be practiced within their confines. The first circle denoted the special rhythm called Iuna, which is exercised as homage to famous deceased Capoeiras. It is rather slow, and its purpose is to display beautiful and perfectly performed movements (Figure 4.6). The veteran Capoeiras refused to answer my question as to the meaning of the three circles, which may be a further example of the practical expression of values and beliefs.

Another ritual associated with the circle that apparently has a physical significance is known as *volta ao mundo* (circling the world). It is customary today to stop the game and march around the circumference of the circle, especially after one of the contestants has managed to topple his rival or make fun of him. After a while the Capoeirista walking first usually makes a certain gesture to signal the return to the middle of the circle to resume the game. This practice of

FIGURE 4.6. Three Capoeira Circles and Their Specific Rhythms (1997). By kind permission of Mestre Nenel.

walking around the circle is never done without a reason. It is often done when one of the contestants falls down or shows signs of fatigue or of being at a loss. Capoeiras today tend to explain this ritual as a way to rest, relax, concentrate, and regain their strength so as to continue playing. The relatively slow marching facilitates recovery of breath and pulling oneself together before the game is resumed. This ritual may also be seen as a way to close the symbolic circle that was broken by the failure. This assumption is confirmed by Carneiro's 1965 description of this ritual:

> The first couple appears, kneeling carefully together in front of the band when the soloist sings the *chula*. When the *chula* is concluded the contest begins, but before any kick is released, it is customary that the rivals walk around the fields, their heads bent down. The contestant who walks first will be the first to kick, for the game to be creditable.[100]

In the 1960s it was customary to do the *volta ao mundo* before the contest began. Obviously this ritual was not performed then in order to rest or recover. Carneiro does not explain the meaning of the ritual but states that the order of the kicks guarantees a fair fight. In my opinion, the answer is in the name of the ritual. It is not called circling the field, the lot, or even the capoeira circle but going around the world. Hence the capoeira circle symbolizes the universe, and circling it with the head bent can mean the participants wish to move in the closed and protected circle of the universe that can safeguard their inner circle.

THE SYMBOLIC SIGNIFICANCE OF THE CIRCLE

In Kongo the circle symbolizes the entire universe, the sun's orbit, and the soul. The belief in reincarnation is part of this circle.[101] Man is whole, healthy, and good as long as his circle is protected from breakthroughs and disruptions. To maintain the wholeness of the circle for the safety of newborn babies, it is customary to bind a round wooden disc or a seed around the baby's chest, neck, waist, or ankles.[102] In Kikongo they say, "Lunda lukongolo lwa lunga" (Keep the child's circle intact).[103] By means of the circle, Capoeiras succeed in crossing the physical boundaries and penetrate into higher levels of consciousness or other worlds to consult with or seek help from. Júlio César de Souza Tavares contends that the circle enabled slaves to renew contact with their ancestors and their traditions. The movement, music and song, taking place in the circle enabled them to make a transition into other states of consciousness and preserve their old traditions.[104]

Another ritual that all Capoeiras observe is doing the *au* (turning cartwheels) when they start the game. Many do not know the meaning of this movement but do it as a matter of routine. Turning cartwheels signifies a transition to various states of consciousness in Kongolese culture, hence its profound significance. When the hands touch the ground and the feet are up in the air, the player crosses over to other worlds. The symbolic ritual enables the player to feel and receive the support, encouragement, and strength that he needs in the game by means of the circle. Contemporary studies enable us to reconstruct the lost knowledge and shed light on these rituals, based on what we know about the worldviews of the various cultures.

In Kongolese and Yoruban traditions, spiritual knowledge is often divided into three levels symbolized by three circles. The first and widest signifies the world, the village, or the community, as well as material values. The second, smaller circle stands for the wise men, who are above the material world but still part of it. The third and smallest circle signifies the spiritual world of the initiated.[105] This worldview is expressed in dance by the various circles: the spectators' circle stands for the first circle, the dancers stand for the second circle, and the interaction between the two might place the dancer in the third and inner circle of spiritual knowledge. The dancer needs the larger, supportive circle to be able to bring the good news from the inner circle. This is manifested in religious dances, in which the dancer eventually goes into a trance or is possessed. By "becoming" the god who possessed him, he can convey the message from the transcendental world to the human world.[106]

Capoeira also features three circles, though their existence is "hidden." Interviewing many Capoeiras about the significance of the circle, I learned that the *roda* gives energy to the participants but only when the music and the songs made by Capoeiras who serve as musicians as well as spectators who form the first circle are included. The two participants in the *roda* form the second circle, and the interaction between the two circles may bring the Capoeiras to the inner circle, which is the spiritual world. This was confirmed by Mestre Valmir, who noted that in the *roda* he can go into a trance and turn into another entity. Dr. Decanio, one of the first students of Mestre Bimba, also confirmed that in the *roda* he acts unconsciously. Afterward he cannot remember what he did there. We can see that only a positive interaction between these two circles, the spectators and the dancers, may create a good *roda*, where the participants lose their sense of self and turn into different beings. Mestre Acordeon (Almeida Bira) holds that in order to become a teacher, an applicant must make a three-day journey in which each stage represents a higher level of awareness. The first stage involves learning a physical technique; in the second one, he learns ceremonies, traditions, capoeira philosophy, as well as how to control emotions; the third phase is for spiritual training. Bira describes the difficult goal:

> You might find the way of the masters that is beyond the simple desire of one to reach it. It is not related to strength and technique anymore; it is not the understanding of the philosophy or the control of one's emotions; and it is not found through the guts or the mind either, but only through the heart.[107]

The three stages are represented by the three levels of Capoeirista: student (*discípulo*), teacher's assistant (*contra mestre*), and teacher (*mestre*). The number 3 clearly has special significance. In African-Brazilian religious ceremonies it is customary to dance to the sound of three drums.[108] In contemporary capoeira schools it is customary to play on three berimbais. In the past Capoeiras said three prayers before engaging in battle.[109]

Prayers

Capoeiras customarily kneel at the feet of the berimbau before the beginning of the game. After the end of the opening song and the beginning of the courier song, the berimbau gives the special signal to the participants to enter the circle. At this stage it is also customary to perform a certain ritual—to offer a prayer, each in his way. Some cross themselves and kiss their hands, others touch the ground and kiss their hands, others turn their hands up toward the sky and then kiss them, others kiss the amulet on their neck or draw diverse symbolic signs on the ground, and so on. This is a very personal part of the game; there is no binding rule or format that prescribes the pattern of the activity. Moreover, it is not compulsory, yet all Capoeiras do it tenaciously. The Capoeiras return to this ritual in the course of the game, at times after very successful movements, as signs of gratitude and appreciation, but often also in moments of distress, when they stumble or slip, and sometimes as a warning to their rival (Figure 4.7).

These rituals have assumed the *mestre*'s personal style, and his students simply emulate his movements. A Capoeirista's teacher can sometimes be recognized through his student's prayer movements. In interviews with veteran *mestres*, it emerged that the purpose of these rituals is to receive protection, instruction, and success from God, or to gain a *corpo fechado*. Many teachers of Capoeira Angola are active members in Terreiros de Candomblé. Each has an *orishá* or gods that protect and guide them in their daily life. In exchange for the help and protection they get, the Capoeiras must appease the deities with offerings, special colors, and other rituals that symbolize them. In the past, when the games took place outdoors, Capoeiras would draw symbolic ideographs on the ground or in the sand. This is an ancient tradition brought with slaves from Africa to Brazil. The Bakongo, for example, who had no writing, represented certain essential ideas relating to the earth, the universe, medicine, rules of conduct and law, as well as the spirits of the dead with ideograms they called *bidimbu*. The signs could be drawn in caves, on walls, or on trees. Traditional nations in Angola, especially the Tu-Chokwe and the Lunda, used to draw these symbolic notations, known as *sona* or *lusona*, in the sand.[110] Evidence of such drawings has existed since 1667, in the illustrations of the missionary Cavazzi, who sojourned in Congo and Angola between 1664 and 1667.[111] In addition to endowing the drawer with supernatural powers, these ideograms provided a connection between the physical world and the netherworld when the ground on which they are drawn is touched. According to these traditions, the ancestors are in the ground and can cause the appearance of the other world's power upon the signed ground.[112] In many schools a variety of signs are drawn on the floor. Because in modern capoeira most games take place indoors, in halls and rooms with a tile floor, it is impossible to mark out ideographs on the ground. In Capoeira Angola many of the jumps and leaps involve touching the ground. At two capoeira conventions I attended in summer 1997 and 1999, I saw participants from Germany, France, the United States, and Israel emulating the movements of the famous teachers and trying in their free time to improve their

FIGURE 4.7. Mestre Curió and Mestre Cobra-Mansa Playing Capoeira (1999). By kind permission of Mestre Curió and Mestre Cobra-Mansa.

performance. When I asked why they made certain movements and how they chose which movements to imitate, I received a variety of answers. Many said that they liked certain movements. Others said that the movements they chose added to the fluidity and elasticity of their performance. Some said that their chosen movements characterize Capoeira Angola, their preferred style. Very few admitted that they knew for sure the profound symbolic significance of certain movements but assured me that they would ask their teachers about it when they returned home.[113]

This point reflects the processes dealt with in this book. On the one hand, the imitation of movements and gestures enables the preservation of ancient expressions. On the other hand, the Capoeiras feel free to improvise and embellish according to their skill and faith, leading to changes in the rituals. This is an ongoing process in which the imitation is done without insight or understanding.

The Regionais, for whom capoeira is first of all a sport, tend to make the sign of the cross before engaging in battle. Capoeiras have their own way of crossing themselves, but all of them consider it a prayer for success. In these games, which are very swift, there are hardly any more rituals in the course of the contest. Some groups purposely avoid performing rituals, because they refuse to introduce mystical elements into capoeira. Jewish and Israeli Capoeiras do not cross themselves, but many touch the ground and kiss their hands at the feet of the berimbau.[114] This proves that sometimes rituals one does not understand are easily emulated, while the familiar ones may deter or threaten and are therefore left out.

In present-day capoeira, a clear and consistent order of rituals is observed, starting with the arrival of the musicians, who call on the participants to form a circle. The first two contestants kneel in front of the berimbau and the soloist sings the *ladainha*, which today is a song praising God or commemorating a much-admired *mestre*. This is followed by an entrance song (*canto de entrada*), after which the *mestre* allows the players, using the berimbau, to begin the battle. Having prayed, the participants enter the circle in the customary tumbling stunt, the cartwheel (*au*), and begin practicing.

This is further evidence that in practice the memory of Bantu and Yoruban traditions has been preserved but that the philosophy as a complex of interrelated components has been forgotten.

A major means of communication in Africa is music. Musical instruments are used to assemble the tribesmen to partake in the dance, to go to war, to revolt, to supplicate the gods, and so on. Studies and observations of West and West Central African dance have recorded the established order by which the music invites everybody to join in, followed in most cases by the formation of a circle, so that the event may begin. Capoeira maintains the same pattern of music, inviting the participants to step forward and make a circle.[115] Despite the differences between the diverse West Central African regional cultures and languages, every dance, even for fun in the "secular" dances, is related to the local religious beliefs that the spirits must be appeased and placated and asked for

help and approval. Contact with the gods is established not only through singing but also by means of the music. In Africa musical instruments have a key
role in connecting the world of the living with that of the dead and of the gods.
This is the reason that in West and West Central African dances it is customary
to honor the major instrument by kneeling or bowing in front of it before the
event can begin.[116] This pattern is accurately duplicated in the Capoeiras' kneeling before the berimbau during the *ladainha* and the contestants' prayer.

Catholic-Portuguese influence is more evident in the various groups of Capoeira Regional. Many groups object to any mystical or religious implications
and avoid any ritual expression of the kind mentioned above. This approach
clearly distinguishes between mystical rituals and secular games in the capoeira,
which is possible in the Catholic-Portuguese worldview but foreign to Bantu
and Yoruban consciousness.

FIVE

The Game of Life

Battle of Cultures

By enlarging our studies of bodily "texts" to include dance in all of its forms—among them social dance, theatrical performance, and ritualized movements—we can further our understanding of how social identities are signaled, formed, and negotiated through bodily movement. We can analyze how social identities are codified in performance styles and how the use of the body in dance is related to, duplicates, contests, amplifies, or exceeds norms of nondance bodily expression within specific historical contexts. We can trace historical and geographical changes in complex kinesthetic systems, and can study comparatively symbolic systems based on language, visual representation, display and movement.[1]

THE 1930S AND 1940S were crucial to the history of capoeira. The authorities and intellectuals persisted in trying to present capoeira as a Brazilian product that had evolved from the special circumstances prevailing in Brazil to become Brazil's national sport and folk art. At the same time, capoeira schools founded during those years set themselves apart by their differing styles—Capoeira Angola and Capoeira Regional.

The authorities tried, through legislation, to unite all Capoeiras under one umbrella. The Angoleiros claim that this reflects the whites' ongoing desire to suppress the cultural expressions of the African-Brazilians. Anthropological studies, especially those of the 1990s, support this premise, arguing that the division into styles began only in the 1930s and 1940s and gained impetus in the 1980s, part of the social trend and the re-Africanization processes of the twentieth century.[2]

So what are the differences between Capoeira Angola and Capoeira Regional? What are the reasons for the different attitudes toward capoeira, and what do the differences between them signify?

An examination of the myth, essence, goals, and teaching methods and a review of the kinesthetic aspects of capoeira and the major changes in the perception of aesthetics, time, and space sheds light on the historical and social processes undergone by capoeira. It is evident that despite attempts to impose uniformity and the image of capoeira as a national sport, indigenous to Brazilian folklore, the struggles between different worldviews, rulers and subjects, and Brazilians and African-Brazilians continue.

PART 1. THE FOUNDING MYTH OF CAPOEIRA

Capoeira Regional

ROOTS

Capoeira Regional is presented first as a Brazilian product and second as a legitimate and effective martial art.

This is the upshot of historical, cultural, and social processes in Brazil. The end of World War I ushered in new ideas imported from Europe and the United States. Notions such as modernism began to be disseminated among the intellectual elite, and this was first manifested in art. Concepts such as surrealism penetrated by degrees, and in São Paulo an unprecedented Week of Modern Art was celebrated in 1922. Artists presented plays, shows, readings of poems and stories, concerts, and exhibitions. This was organized by the mulatto artist, musician, and playwright Mário de Andrade—a significant fact given that at this period very few renowned personalities were nonwhite. This was the earliest attempt to present local art that did not emulate European and (North) American ideas and included basically nonwhite elements. This period in Brazil was marked by distrust of the Republican regime, and in 1930 a political coup totally changed Brazil, including its culture. Scholars led by Gilberto Freyre began to highlight the positive effects of African and Indian cultures on Brazilian society. The backwardness of these cultures, until then perceived as race related, was now explained as the result of lack of education and poor hygiene. As of 1937, the year the New State was established, intensive efforts were made to forge a national identity that would include the poor. The endorsement of the carnival, the samba, the Candomblé rituals, and capoeira confirmed the legitimacy of African-Brazilian traditions and blacks. The military regime (1964–1985) underscored this policy, presenting Brazil as nonracist and as a good example of racial integration. This policy gave Brazil entry into the international community and paved the way for diplomatic relations with many European and African states. The authorities supported the African-Brazilian concept in all its aspects and the Centro Folclórico (Folklore Center) was inaugurated in Bahia in the late 1960s for research, performances, and exhibitions on Brazilian folklore, including ca-

FIGURE 5.1. World Capoeira
Association Logo.

poeira, *maculelê* (a battle stick dance), Candomblé, and samba. In addition, the
early 1970s saw the establishment of the African-Brazilian Museum, which dis-
plays the important contributions of the various traditions to the formation of a
Brazilian culture. On March 6, 1974, *A Tarde* declared that Bahia was the only city
that was preserving Brazil's African-Brazilian cultural and mixed-race heritage.[3]
The authorities admitted that there were class differences in Brazil but insisted
they were not race related. Eminent blacks—football players, singers, musicians,
and dancers—exemplified the equality between the races and epitomized their
contribution to the Brazilian nation. In 1972 a special department for capoeira
was opened by the Brazilian Boxing Federation, which taught that capoeira
was a martial art of African-Brazilian origin, a source of pride to all classes of
society, and superior to all other martial arts. The authorities targeted middle-
and upper-class audiences who were increasingly sympathetic to the concept of
Brazil as a nonracist society. Students from these milieus eventually became capoeira teachers and continued to impart the traditions that had been inculcated
in their young minds. The World Capoeira Association (WCA) was established in
February 1979 on the initiative of Mestre Acordeon and his colleagues (Figure
5.1). Their explanations for the elements of the WCA logo were as follows:

> The berimbau symbolizes the importance of music to capoeira. The figures
> in the gourd represent the attitude of balance in unbalanced situations, the
> constant flow of capoeira movements and the action of working together
> with the implied meaning of respect for ourselves and our partners. The
> triangle shows the foundation of the *com-pé* style—the capoeira trilogy:

A. Disciplined training,
B. Respect for the roots, and
C. Applied philosophy.

The inner circle represents the *roda de capoeira* itself, and the outer circle the greater *roda de capoeira* that is life.[4]

CAPOEIRA AS A MARTIAL ART

Where capoeira began is a moot point. Some claim that it was created in the *quilombos*, the refuges for runaway slaves. Others believe the marketplaces were where it all began, and there are also those who locate it in the *senzala*, the slaves' quarters on the plantations.[5] Whatever the origin, the purpose was purely, according to the Capoeiras, to obtain freedom, relief from slavery. Thus, capoeira was legitimate because its cause was just—to fight against what the New State called the oppressive, vile system of slavery. All the components of capoeira were explained as the upshot of slavery. In other words, the prevailing belief about capoeira considers the dance movements, music, and song mere trimmings intended to conceal the slaves' intentions, as was the circle (*roda*). It seems that the *memory* of all the elements of the dance among the African slaves has been preserved, but the *significance* of these elements has been lost.

Capoeira Angola

ROOTS

Pastinha constantly used to declare that capoeira originated in Angola. There is popular song among the Angoleiros: "Sou Angoleiro que vem d'Angola" (I am an Angoleiro who comes from Angola). Pastinha believed that "Capoeira undoubtedly came to Brazil with the African slaves. It was a form of battle with unique characteristics that have been preserved to this day."[6] Cascudo cited the Luanda-born poet, painter, and ethnographer Álbano de Neves e Souza, who contended:

> The Mucope in southern Angola have the zebra dance—the *n'golo*—performed in the course of the Efundula—the girls' rite of passage, when they stop being *muficuemas*—young girls—and become young women, ready to marry and bear children. The boy who wins in the *n'golo* can choose his wife among the new eligible brides without having to pay a dowry. The *n'golo* is capoeira. The slaves who came from the tribes that went there [to Brazil] through the trading port of Benguela, took with them the foot-fighting tradition. With time, what was first a tribal tradition became a defensive and

FIGURE 5.2. Fundação Internacional de Capoeira Angola Logo, Bahia affiliate.

offensive weapon for survival in a hostile environment.... Another reason that convinces me that capoeira originated in Angola is that hoodlums in Brazil play an instrument called the berimbau which we call *m'bolumbumba* or *hungu*, depending on the place, which is played [in Africa] by the herdsmen."[7]

This explanation is accepted as the founding myth of Capoeira Angola. It is quoted to establish the Brazilians' affinity with Angola, the country of origin of their Capoeiras. The logo of the Fundação Internacional de Capoeira Angola (FICA) features a zebra coming out of the African continent and meeting a South American Capoerista (Figure 5.2).

The Angoleiros have two major goals: first, to designate capoeira as the activity of free Africans, perpetuated by their proud descendants; and second, to link capoeira to the ongoing struggle of blacks for equality in Brazil's inequitable society. What began as a demand for freedom is based today on the yearning to reestablish black heritage.

AFRICAN PRIDE

Emphasis on the affinity between capoeira and African rituals, traditions, and customs was evident mainly in the last years of the military regime—from the 1980s onward, characterized mainly by a gradual *distensão* (relaxing) of oppression and a slow process of political liberalization, the *abertura* (opening), occurring in Brazil at the time. The popularity of soul music in the United States inspired many black Brazilians from the suburbs to indulge in punk dance and to form carnival groups like the Ile Aiye, formed in 1975. In the processions, other black groups performed skits about the history of Brazil and its blacks in which such themes as slave revolts and opposition to slavery also included capoeira.[8] Slogans such as "Black Is Beautiful" and "Black Power," imported from the United States, were welcomed. New styles of clothing, hairdos, music, and dance were followed by renewed interest in Africa and its traditions. The carnivals, capoeira shows, samba dances, and Candomblé meets became tourist attractions that, besides being remunerative, resulted in greater self-esteem and awareness of these cultural expressions.[9]

EQUALITY AND SOCIAL JUSTICE

Middle-class blacks now began to speak out against the latent racism in Brazil that barred their way to all key positions. They contended that national identity was merely another form of discrimination. In 1978 black social and political organizations such as the Movimento Negro Unificado (United Black Movement) were established. These movements supported and helped the black community, finding jobs, building shelters for homeless children, instituting education for children and adults, and so on.[10] The Angoleiros were also struggling for justice and social equality. The popular Angoleiro songs deal with slavery, extolling the heroes of the struggle for independence and stressing the contribution of capoeira to Brazil. A song about Pastinha runs:[11]

> A capoeira rasga o véu dos algoles
> Na convicção da fé contra escravidão
> Doce voz dos teus filhos e heróis
> A capoeira ama abolição.

> Capoeira tore the veil of the hangman
> With conviction of faith against slavery
> Sweet voice of your sons and heroes
> Capoeira loves the abolition [of slavery].

Zumbi, the last king of Palmares, the biggest and best-known *quilombo* for runaway slaves, is another case in point. The blacks still revere him and see him as their model in the ongoing struggle. Capoeira songs extol his valor, and Palmares, established in the early seventeenth century, became the symbol of the

African slaves' struggle for freedom and self-rule, standing firm against the un-relenting attacks of the army. In 1694 a large force headed by Domingo Jorge Velho lay siege to Palmares. After twenty-one days of blockade and fierce battles, during which two hundred of the besieged jumped from a cliff to their deaths, two hundred more were killed, and five hundred were captured and sold, the city was conquered and demolished. King Zumbi escaped, after appointing succes-sors who would continue the fight, but he was finally captured and executed.[12] Many Capoeiras maintain that capoeira was a form of active resistance in the *quilombos*, though there is no concrete evidence for this.

A song by one of the most famous contemporary teachers, Mestre Moraes, sums up the essence and function of capoeira today:

> Capoeira é uma arte
> Que o negro inventou
> Foi na briga de duas Zebras
> Que o N'golo se criou
> Chegando aqui no Brazil
> Capoeira se chamou
> Ginga e dança que era arte
> Em arma se transformou .
> Para libertar o negro da senzala do senhor
> Hoje aprendo essa cultura para me conscientizar
> Agradeço ao pai Ogum
> A força dos Orixás
> Camaradinha.

> Capoeira is an art
> Invented by the black man
> In the fight between two zebras
> The N'golo was created
> Arriving in Brazil
> It was called capoeira
> Ginga and dance that became art
> Became arms
> To liberate the black from the masters' slave quarters
> Today I study this culture for my conscience
> I am grateful to father Ogum [god of war]
> To the power of Orixás [the deities]
> Comrade.

PART 2. CAPOEIRA TODAY: ANGOLA AND REGIONAL

There is ongoing discussion as to whether Capoeira Angola is the original African "Capoeira mãe" (Capoeira Mother). To distinguish between Capoeira Angola and Capoeira Regional, largely since the 1980s, Angoleiros emphasize elements they believe to be "traditionally African." Luíz Vieira claims that "the Capoeira Angola practiced in some academies in Bahia is actually a product of an effort to reconstitute the capoeira of times past in present conditions."[13] Mestre Camisa, founder of Capoeira Abadá, one of today's most influential Capoeira Regional groups, explains, "Capoeira Angola was invented to fight capoeira Regional" for legitimation.[14] What is clear is that both capoeira styles have changed. Capoeira Regional has been "whitened" and Brazilianized, and Capoeira Angola has become more "African." These differences are more a matter of ideologies—"Brazilianists" versus "Africanists"—than skin color. Since the 1980s, and especially today, there are white Angoleiros as well as black Regionais.

Learning and Teaching Capoeira

Many Capoeiras claim that the most significant change in the status of capoeira is attributable to Mestre Bimba, who emphasized the martial aspects of the art and left out other features. He created "a method of systematic study, to facilitate the learning for those in whose veins the African cultural heritage of the movements and rhythms of the Candomblé did not flow."[15] This "revolutionary solution" had, however, been attempted earlier—in the *Handbook of Capoeira and Brazilian Gymnastics* published in 1907 in Rio de Janeiro. The handbook was divided into chapters containing detailed explanations of the correct stance, basic postures, and modes of defense and attack.[16] Another handbook, *National Gymnastics (Capoeiragem)*, published in 1928, also gave accurate descriptions of the rules of capoeira and its history.[17] Bimba, who was illiterate (like many Capoeiras in his time), understood the need to adapt capoeira for the elite. Methodical teaching, certification, medals, and other such features brought him closer to the hearts and pockets of the whites. The Angoleiros, on the other hand, initially tried to resist the changes. Capoeira had been learned in the streets and squares and on the beaches by emulating the movements of more experienced Capoeiras. The degrees of importance and respect were positively related to the Capoeirista's personality, skill, and style, reflecting the African concept of teaching through experience, but the renaissance of Capoeira Angola in the 1980s compelled the Angoleiros to accept the inevitable. To gain recognition and help from the authorities, they tried to create a unified setup that would be acceptable to all *mestres* of Capoeira Angola, to no avail. The conflict between the need to attract more students and the desire to maintain the "purity" of capoeira and its traditional values stood in their way. Angoleiro José Luis Oliveira, better known as Bola Sete, wrote in his book *Capoeira Angola na Bahia*:

> In order to build a better organization for Capoeira Angola and to encourage those who train in the "national battle," we were obliged under the circumstances to set up a system of grades. For the time being, this system is modified according to the wishes of the *mestres* in their own schools.[18]

In Bola Sete's school there were five grades, each with a different belt in the colors of the flags of Bahia and Brazil.[19] Other groups chose colors associated with the Candomblé and/or the gods. A capoeira group in São Paulo, for example, graded the students on a scale of one to seven. The first grade was green, symbolizing Oxossi, defender of hunting and wild animals, protector of lost souls by setting them on the right path. The second degree was brown, for Omulo, god of medicine, who can change the body. By this stage, the student has gained some control over his body. The third degree, yellow, represents Oxum, goddess of rivers and waterfalls. She is soft as a lake and deep as the seas. At this stage the Capoeirista knows how to use capoeira to his advantage. The fourth degree is violet, the color of Xangô, god of courage and justice. The fifth stage symbolizes Yemanjá, goddess of creativity and the sea. At this stage, when the Capoeirista virtually wrestles with the ocean, he can give expression to all his creativity. The sixth stage symbolizes Ogum, the mighty god of war, whose color is red. At this important stage, the Capoeirista is qualified to impart his skills to other students. The last and seventh stage is symbolized by white, the color of Oxalá, supreme god of the sky, of light and serenity, the highest rank for a Capoeirista.[20] Among the Angoleiros, it is the teacher who decides the color of the belts, the number of grades, the ceremonies, and the badges. He can interpret their significance according to his beliefs.

Role-Playing — Musicians as Both Players and Spectators

In the capoeira circle, the observers may become participants at any stage; the contestants become observers when their own contest is over, and the musicians are constantly changing. The soloist sings his call and the observers respond in chorus and these roles may also change during the game. This interesting pattern is also one of the traditional practices of the Bantu and Yoruban ethnic groups and in capoeira, in which a player may influence the rhythm, structure, and form of a contest and a soloist can introduce a song with a unique rhythm and style.[21] The responses of the audience may also alter the course of events in the circle, and the two contestants are obviously affected by and affect the interaction between themselves and their audience.

The berimbau controls the circle, determining when the game begins and ends and its pace. But sometimes it yields to other factors, such as the *chamada* (the call), a game within a capoeira game. Even when the *mestre* instructs the players to stop the game, if one of them makes a "call" the berimbau must yield and allow the game to continue. Thus the *chamada* is an act of defiance against the berimbau. Because the musicians are replaced by the spectators, a berimbau sometimes refuses to cede his position to a member of the crowd. In this case the soloist may sing:

> Esse Gunga é meu
> Esse Gunga é meu
> Foi meu pai que me deu.

> This Gunga is mine
> This Gunga is mine
> My father gave it to me.

This is his way of saying, "I do not intend to give up my place so easily or so fast. Go back to your place."

The berimbau sometimes responds to a challenge, for example, by a spectator singing a new song that reflects a specific situation. Such songs are intended to cheer, criticize, warn, threaten, and even ridicule the players, and the spectators can thus affect and be affected by what happens in the *roda*. When the contestants are of unequal skills, the spectators may sing the following song:[22]

> Essa cobra te morde
> Olhe a cobra mordeu
> Oi o bote da cobra
> O veneno da cobra
> Oi a casca da cobra
> O que cobra danada
> O que cobra malvada
> Olhe o buraco, velho
> Ele tem cobra dentro
> Olhe o pulo da cobra.

> This snake will bite you
> Look, the snake has bitten

Oh, watch out the snake's attack
Oh, the snake's venom
Oh, look the snake's skin
Oh, it's an evil snake
Oh, it's a cruel snake
See that hole, old man
There's a snake inside
See the snake leap.

The song is a warning to a young player tackling a more experienced one. Another song, in the form of a prayer, may also be sung, requesting God's aid, for example, if the contestants are unmatched—"Valha me deus, sinho São Bento" (Watch over me, God and blessed Saint Benedict)—but the tone of the song may vary. If a new student decides to challenge a more experienced Capoeirista, the chorus may poke fun at the overconfident youngster, ridiculing his presumption. But if a player stumbles into such a situation unwittingly, the audience may well encourage him with the same song.

A game may sometimes become violent. Then the soloist, as well as the spectators, can try to soothe tempers with songs such as the following:

Vou quebrar tudo hoje
E amanhã nada quebra.

I will break everything today
And tomorrow nothing will break.

This song levels criticism at contestants who have apparently broken the rules; so that by tomorrow there will be nothing left to break. Another song is an entirely different approach to the same situation. Instead of ridicule and defiance, the spectators moralize about the contestants' conduct, demanding that they start playing properly and not be so cocky:

Por favor meu mano
Eu não quero barulho aqui, não.

Please, my brother
I don't want any noise here, no.

The contestants themselves can also convey messages to the spectators and try to intimidate their opponents. In a fight in 1944 between Mestre Bimba and a less celebrated guest who decided to flex his muscles against the famous *mestre*, Bimba sang the following song:[23]

> The day I shone
> In Itabaiana
> No man rode a horse
> No woman took out a chicken
> The nuns who prayed
> Forgot the prayer.

The rival answered with a challenge of his own:

> The bird was bewitched
> When she stood on the fountain
> She was shrewd and agile
> But capoeira killed her.

Bimba responded again:

> A prayer for a strong arm
> A prayer to Saint Matthew
> The bones will go to the cemetery
> Your bones, not mine.

At this stage the chorus intervened, hoping to make the game begin:

> Zum zum zum
> Capoeira killed one
> Zum zum zum
> Only one remained in the field.

But the mysterious rival did not give in. Insisting on having the last word, he sang:

> And I was born on Saturday
> Walked on Sunday
> And on Monday
> I played capoeira.

After this the chorus responded and the game began. This example of the dynamics of the game shows that within the prescribed rules there is room to maneuver, extemporize, and react.

All this is changing, especially in Capoeira Regional. The musicians, the observers, and the music have become mere accompaniments to the contestants. Pastinha said, "The secret of capoeira dies with me and the other *mestres*. Today there is much acrobatics and little capoeira."[24] Many Regional games are short and very fast. After two minutes at the most, the participants are exhausted and replaced by the next contestants in line. Angoleiros, however, can last for ten minutes or more, so that the dialogue between all the participants can continue.

Time and Space

In the course of the nineteenth century, despite their hard labor, the slaves would meet on Sundays and holidays to dance their traditional dances. At first the Europeans viewed these dances as barbaric, not only because of movements they considered shameless and provocative movements but also because these events took place outdoors at night, in big circles, often around bonfires, and were disorderly and noisy.[25]

West and West Central African dances tend to be unrestricted and are not separated from the audience. The dancers mingle with the spectators and make physical contact with them. A dance could spread to the squares, streets, beaches, or any other public space and continue for as long as the audience, dancers, and musicians cared to stay. The Bantu and Yoruban concept of dance allows, or rather expects, refinement, improvisation, innovation, and change so that each dancer can display his skill.[26] This is also true of capoeira.

Nineteenth-century European dances such as the polka, minuet, and waltz also took place out of doors as a rule but were very structured and stylized. One had to learn the rhythm and the steps, and there was no deviation from the pattern. The choreography was not a matter of improvisation or spontaneity, and each dance was performed separately, in order, one at a time. The aristocrats who adopted these dances stylized the movements and limited their space and time even more.[27]

In the early eighteenth century, the Brazilian elite tried to imitate the European fashion, and dancing took place indoors, either in a hall or on a stage. Hazard-Gordon found that many slave owners who knew that banning the dances could lead to a revolt tried to impose limits on their space and duration.[28] Nonetheless, some black dances—the fofa, fado, batuque maxixe, and samba—were adopted by whites even among the aristocracy who took to dancing outside.[29]

The same is true of capoeira. At first the circles were formed spontaneously outdoors, unrestricted by time or space. Whenever a few Capoeiras met and the atmosphere and the mood were right, they would start a game. The institutionalization of capoeira resulted in limitations of space, time, and training that later became even more restricted when capoeira was played inside a circle drawn on the academy floor. Even outdoor circles were circumscribed. Presentations were held at certain times and locations, and advance notices were issued.

Today members of capoeira schools and academies perform in streets, squares, and beaches, both for fun and to attract new students. These meets are also pre-arranged in regard to time, place, and number of participants. The organizing group wears the uniform of its school and is set apart from the rest of the audience. Capoeiras who are not invited to participate may not join the game.

Capoeira has also to represent Brazilian culture and folklore. The Ministry of Tourism in Bahia sponsors and initiates capoeira shows. They are of two kinds, distinguishable as influenced by either "African" or "white" concepts of time, space, and choreography: The "African" version—outdoor performances—is presented in the city squares on Saturdays and Sundays in popular tourist areas. Their object is profit. The participants are mainly from the lower classes, most of them unskilled or unemployed, trying to supplement their income. The circles are not prearranged, and the participants change from week to week. They are not bound by opening or closing times, and it all depends on the spectators, the participants, and the atmosphere.

The other kind, which I call Showcase Capoeira, is created especially for tourists. These performances, which are advertised as representing Brazilian culture and folklore, are usually performed in halls, sometimes in town squares, for profit and/or publicity. The performers are professional dancers, and the show is a regular staged performance with stylized and choreographed movements that remains the same each time. There is no interaction between the audience and the artists.

The highlight of conventions organized throughout the year, to which many capoeira schools are invited, is the *roda aberta* (open circle) where everybody is invited to participate. These circles are usually held outdoors and can continue for hours on end, not necessarily at the original site.

Aesthetics

When the Capoeiras themselves distinguish between Capoeira Angola and Capoeira Regional, they describe them respectively as *jogo baixo* (low game), and *jogo alto* (high game). These definitions are based on style. In Capoeira Angola the players bend over and frequently touch the ground, and their movements are relatively slow. In Capoeira Regional the movements are fast, vertical, and upward, involving acrobatics and kicks. This is why very few Capoeiras are considered good Regionais or possess the necessary speed, agility, fitness, flexibility, and acrobatic skills—which also naturally decline with age. In Capoeira Angola there is no such problem. The slower tempo and the rounded, bending movements allow almost anybody at any age to participate. In Capoeira Re-

gional schools there are hardly any older participants, whereas among the Angoleiros some are quite elderly. Some Capoeira Regional adherents believe that
the founder of Capoeira Angola, Mestre Pastinha, adapted capoeira to his own
physical limitations. He was fifty-two when he opened his capoeira school in
1941, and he died at the age of ninety-two. This is another example of the lack of
comprehension of the essence of West and West Central African dance.

The dancer Deborah Bertonoff has defined the essence of classical ballet as
follows:

> In that ancient Greek world which is the source and origin of all European
> art the dominant ideal was the vertical line, the upward aspiration of spirit
> and soul; and they were the supreme behest of the dancer. This principle
> still exists today in the classical ballet. . . . From our very first lesson we
> dancers train ourselves ceaselessly in this elevation above and withdrawal
> from the soil. Dancing has always borne the stamp of the virtuoso, the one
> capable of leaping and hovering in the air.[30]

Dancing, which demands high standards and unnatural movements, is an art
form only few can master; the same applies to Capoeira Regional.

In West and West Central African dances one part moves against another,
and movements can issue simultaneously from different centers. The dance is
also polyrhythmic, with different parts of the body moving in different rhythms.
The knees are bent to strengthen the connection with the ground.[31] As observed
by Esther Dagan:

> The natural bends provide the dancer with freedom in his choice of move-
> ment, drawn from a large repertoire of natural movement vocabulary with
> unlimited options for variation, combination, and improvisation. More-
> over, the natural bends allow each individual in the community to perform
> the dance up to his or her ability. Therefore dance in Africa is accessible to
> everyone.[32]

This approach is similar to the underlying concept of Capoeira Angola.

Yoruban and Kongolese religions are geocentric, based on the benevolent
forces of nature or on polytheistic characteristics representing aspects of the
nature of man. The gods are connected with man when they are personified
in ceremonial dances. This also explains the constant need to reach down and
feel the ground with legs bent. Christianity is a paternalistic, monotheistic belief
that God is not in man but far above him. For Christians, especially Protestants,
the soul and the spirit are separate from the body, which is the locus of original
sin and must be kept under control.[33] These beliefs are expressed in the dance,

embodied in the aspiration to elevate the dancer to exalted spiritual heights. The Christian Capoeiras tried to straighten the body, turning somersaults and cartwheels with legs outstretched and with less downward bending and touching the ground. However, in the 1980s Capoeira Angola returned, and the Angoleiros emphasized, even more vigorously, the bent knees and direct contact with the ground.

The Philosophy of Capoeira

Many Capoeiras of both schools see capoeira as a way of life that provides them with all they need for coping successfully with their difficulties and problems. The basic trait underlying capoeira ideology, according to Capoeiras and scholars alike, is *malícia*, a term meaning cunning, suspicion, alertness, readiness, flexibility, and adaptation. The implication is that one needs to know how to use capoeira skills to one's advantage when the need arises.

MALÍCIA

Mestre Pastinha explicated *malícia* as follows:

> The Capoeirista resorts to an endless number of tricks to confuse and distract his opponent. He pretends to step back but he returns quickly; jumps from side to side; lies down and gets up; advances and retreats; pretends not to see the opponent to deceive him; turns in all directions; and shrinks in a cunning and bewildering *ginga*.[34]

Gregory Downey explains:

> Malícia, not coincidentally, is the quality, or constellation of qualities, that the ideal Capoeirista should most evidence in his or her everyday life: a combination of wariness, quick wit, savvy, unpredictability, opportunism, playfulness, viciousness, and a talent for deception.[35]

Today every capoeira teacher, regardless of style, emphasizes that *malícia* is vital to capoeira. Even in the first lesson, the teacher inculcates the principle that Capoeiras should never trust anybody. They must always be on the alert and never take their eyes off their rival. The ability to fool, distract, and deceive the opponent is the key to success. In capoeira, *malícia* is present from the very first movement—the *ginga*—and in the songs and all the other rituals of the game.

The basic movement in capoeira, the *ginga*, is a constant fluid movement backward and forward, and a good Capoeirista will use *malícia* in the *ginga* to deceive his opponent.

According to Cesar Barbieri:

Capoeiras unanimously affirm that the *ginga* is the first principle of capoeira. The constant, ceaseless movement of the body—*gingar*—is the principle that creates snares of deception, of trickery, by which the adversary
can be taken unawares.[36]

Ginga has thus became one of the most distinctive features of capoeira. Moura
explains:

The trickery or negation of the fight, and the flexibility that constant exercise gave to those who practiced Capoeiragem, gave them a distinctive
walk[,] [t]he swaying stride—*andar gingando* [rowing the body].[37]

Malícia appears in many other tricky movements to mislead an adversary, for
example, keeping a poker face during complex or difficult moves or laugh-
ing, smiling, or shaking the legs in response to an opponent's successful attack.
Today's capoeira teachers praise past Capoeiras' cunning and thus reinforce its
significance. There is a story about the famous Capoeirista Besouro who once
fell to the ground during a game, crying like a woman and begging for mercy.[38]

Another form of *malícia* is epitomized in a kick called the *benço* (blessing);
the name hints at the contradiction between the movement and its intention.
Capoeiras say that when a slave owner met his slaves in the morning, mainly on
Sundays, he would give them his blessing. They had to bend their heads, bow
down, and thank him, and this after he had not only blessed them but also made
them work to exhaustion, punished them atrociously, and humiliated them in-
discriminately. The kick reflects the attitude of the slave who bends to receive his
master's blessing but at the same time swings his foot forward to kick his opponent in the belly.

Malícia also features in songs:

> Vamos quebrar coquinha
> Enquanto a polícia não vem
> Se a polícia chega
> Nós quebra com ela também.

> Let's bang our heads
> While the police are not coming
> If the police arrive
> We will bang with them too.

The chorus responds to the soloist with the same words, but when the song is
repeated, the last two lines are sung differently:

FIGURE 5.3. The *Chamada* (Call) during a Capoeira Game (1997).

> Quando a polícia chega
> Bota água no café e chama a polícia também
>
> When the police arrive
> Put on the water for coffee and call in the police too

The new ending is unexpected. Instead of "banging" with the police, they make fun of them and invite them in for a cup of coffee.

One of the common capoeira rituals in which *malícia* is emphasized is the *chamada*. Here, a participant stands in the center of the circle and stretches his arms out to the sides or behind his back, calling his opponent to come closer. This call cannot be refused: once the *chamada* has started the game must go on. The second player approaches the caller with special movements and touches him. As soon as physical contact has been made the ritual continues with a *passo a dois* (pas de deux) in which the two contestants walk backward and forward (Figure 5.3).

Malícia is expressed when the contestants separate and one of them makes a sudden movement. Mestre Curió says, "The chamada is the philosophy of the Angoleiro and his cunning."[39] The ritual is less popular among Regionais. Many believe it is a way to gain time and do not use it often. Others, especially older Capoeiras, contend that it adds a bit of tension to the game. Some think it is an echo of slavery, when slaves mocked their owners' dances—which, to them, were lacking in interest, originality, and rhythm—and that their amusing imitations and songs were parodies of these dances.

HOW MALÍCIA EMERGED

Contemporary investigators endeavoring to explain *malícia* refer back to slavery. Lewis Lowell suggests:

> Through the give and take of plantation life, a culture of slavery was created, a complex system with the constant threat of violence. . . . It is the value of deception, of apparent accommodation, which I hope to show is at the heart of the play in capoeira. . . . The complex drama of adaptation to domination through Malícia keeps vitality in the game of capoeira one hundred years after the abolition of that terrible institution from which it was born.[40]

The anthropologist Iria D'aquino writes:

> From the very beginning Capoeiras used *malícia*. They were *malicioso* in deceiving their masters into believing that their practice of a dangerous fight form was harmless pastime. They were *maliciosos* in their confrontations that emphasized the sudden and unexpected attack.[41]

Later, with the abolition of slavery, the tradition was preserved, because life for a freedman was also a ceaseless struggle. Maria Angela Borges Salvadori maintains that in the early twentieth century the characteristic Capoeira, as described by the authorities, in dictionaries, and in the press, is quite similar to the emerging type of urban citizen who was a constant source of trouble—the *malandro* (punk). She contends that the *malandro* superseded the black Capoeirista in his quest for freedom and merged with him. In this period, both Capoeiras and punks were considered louts and thieves.[42] A samba song written in 1933 by Wilson Batista is titled "Lenço no pescoço" (A Kerchief around the Neck):

> Meu Chapéu de lado
> Tamanco arrastando
> Lenço no pescoço
> Navalha no bolso
> Eu passo gingando
> Provoco e desafio
> Eu tenho orgulho
> De ser tão vadio

Sei que eles falam
Desse meu proceder
Eu vejo quem trabalha
Andar na miséria
Eu sou vadio
Por que tive inclinação
Eu me lembro era criança
Tirava samba-canção

My hat turned down
Clogs dragging
A kerchief around the neck
A razor in my pocket
I sway *gingando*
I provoke and defy
I am proud
Of being such an idler
I know they talk
About my conduct
I see that whoever works
Remains poor
I am an idler
Because that's my inclination
I remember when I was a child
I composed samba-canção [type of samba song]

The anthropologist Gregory Downey finds a connection between *malícia* and the *malandro*. The punk is seen today as a national figure, characteristic of the Brazilian's stamina and pluck. He copes successfully with the social inequities of present-day Brazil, not with a view to reforming the system, but for his own advantage and welfare. This is the only way for the weak to overcome the strong, for the few to overcome the many. Shrewdness, resourcefulness, and craft can help you to beat the system. These qualities are evident in football, another sport that characterizes Brazil, in samba songs, in the *sambistas'* (samba dancers) movements, and obviously in capoeira.[43] *Malícia* was accepted as the Capoeiras' philosophy deriving from the Brazilian reality as an upshot of the slaves' struggle.

However, I think that the origin of *malícia* is found in the African traditions that the slaves brought with them and that is associated with the Bantu and Yoruban game of life. For the Bantu, play is a way to understand life, to prepare for it—integral to it.[44] For the Yoruba, the game is an engaging transformational process that is often competitive. Margaret Drewal noted: "Playing involves spending time with people for its own sake, engaging them in a competition of wits verbally and/or physically, and playing it out tactically to disorient and be disoriented, to surprise, and be surprised, to shock and be shocked."[45]

In Christianity there are clear diametrical oppositions—good/evil, sacred/profane, black/white, work/play. But in the Bantu and Yoruban philosophies this is the way of the world: every good contains some bad, in every spiritual ritual there are secular aspects, and vice versa. Balance is achieved only where contradictory elements meet. Exu (Eshu), the Yoruban orishá, is a case in point. The Christian slave owners regarded him as the devil, while in Yorubaland and in the African-Brazilian Candomblé he is the trickster, a messenger, a mediator between men and gods, thus combining good and bad.[46]

This concept of complementary opposites is also reflected in *malícia*. The Capoeirista Nestor Capoeira explains:

> The philosophy underlying capoeira—the Capoeirista's perspective, how he copes with life, with the world and with other people—is cynical, realistic, crude, ironic and humorous, vital, poetic and intuitive. Paradoxical? No. In the capoeira game—dance and fight, laughter and wisdom—contradictions meet and blend. This foundation, this specific way of seeing things, this particular belief—those who use it spontaneously and naturally in the circle and in everyday life fondly call it *malícia*.[47]

Malícia reflects, then, a philosophy of life from which the Capoeirista learns how to come to grips with the challenges of the capoeira circle and hence with the demands of everyday life. Mestre Acordeon describes the stages every student must go through until he can assimilate capoeira philosophy and master the invaluable malícia:

> On the first level, students begin to learn clear and defined movements of attack and defense, developing discipline and self-control. . . . They are lost in space; they see nothing. . . . I call this stage "playing in the dark." Capoeiras progressively gain a clear perception of their own movements. I call this stage "playing in the water." . . . In the next stage, "playing in the light," students work to perfect their movements, the timing and rhythm of their fighting. . . . At this point, the emphasis in training must change from physical achievement to controlling emotions and comprehending the philosophy.[48]

This, according to Acordeon, is the stage of the *contra mestre* (assistant teacher), of acquiring the real craft after many years of strenuous exercises and training in basic physical skills. Acordeon believes that only a real *mestre*, can reach the fourth and last stage that he calls "playing in the mind"—the ability to anticipate an opponent's intentions and, more significant, influence his mind. He goes on to expound his views about stories dealing with ancient Capoeiras who were said to possess supernatural powers and could extricate themselves from impossible situations, like Besouro. These extraordinary men succeeded, in other words, in "closing the body."[49] Acordeon is not alone. Some Angoleiros claim that *malícia* is in fact *mandinga*, a term that signifies both witchcraft and the desirable kinesthetic quality of play. Movements with *mandinga* are deceptive, humorous, treacherous, and oblique. André Lacé Lopes suggests that while the classic movements of *mandinga* were probably intended as magical summons to supernatural forces, today they signify the "secret" experiential knowledge that distinguishes between those who simply play capoeira and those who truly embody it.[50] Mestre João Pequeno claims that he teaches his students how to play capoeira, but they should learn *malícia* for themselves since it cannot be taught. Many Capoeiras believe that the technical and systematic teaching methods based on Bimba's *sequências* (limited sequence movements), which are used today in Capoeira Regional, contribute to the loss of *malícia*, creativity, and spontaneity. Downey calls this "mechanical" capoeira, which "exhibits little joy, malice, or playfulness, evidencing a kinesthetic concern with efficiency that seems to override all other considerations."[51] Regionais and Angoleiros alike see *malícia* as the philosophy of capoeira, but they use it differently and thus alter its meanings and significance.

The ongoing efforts to unify capoeira and unite the Capoeiras began in the 1970s, both in the government and among capoeira *mestres*. These efforts continue today, especially among *mestres* of Capoeira Regional, many of whom believe that they teach both *jogo baixo* and *jogo alto*. Some maintain that "capoeira é uma só" (there is only one capoeira). This attempt to bridge the gap between the Regional and the Angola capoeiras only deepens the misinterpretation of the processes that capoeira has undergone.

Capoeira was initially the provenance of the slaves, the indigents, and the rioters whom the authorities persecuted with laws, arrests, punishment, and even exile. To get rid of the stigma attached to it, capoeira had to be institutionalized, nationalized, a healthy sport embodying both the policy of the government and the wants of the people. The authorities wanted to gain more control and reduce the resentment of the masses, while the masses wanted legitimacy and recognition for their values and traditions.

As more Christian students and teachers from the upper classes became capoeira participants, so the ideologies and philosophies began to be overlooked or forgotten. At first this was confined to oral memories, but gradually the original West and West Central African rituals were also forgotten. It appears that the "white" influence is steadily growing, and this is causing the estrangement between Capoeira Angola and Capoeira Regional. The Catholic-Portuguese concept of dance has made capoeira an artistic and competitive sport practiced by few, in bounded spaces (capoeira schools, private studios, and halls), and at fixed times (duration of performance, training, and practice periods). Capoeira seems to be losing its spontaneity. Today one must go to a capoeira school and take regular lessons at regular times from a certified teacher. In contemporary Capoeira Regional the technical and professional aspects take precedence over the Bantu and Yoruban philosophies and traditions. The West Central African rituals performed before the battle are gradually being pushed aside, and the role of the musical instruments that once determined the rhythm and style of the game has been reduced to mere accompaniment. Capoeira Angola highlights the "African" elements such as the natural "inclination," community and entertainment, and *malícia*. Some scholars and Capoeiras agree that today's Capoeira Atual (actual capoeira), also known as capoeira *contemporânea* (contemporary capoeira) has been created by Capoeiras who are trying to replace the lost African tradition of Capoeira Angola and merge it with Capoeira Regional.

Social and political processes and expediency have affected and will continue to affect the practical and oral memory of capoeira. I believe this is the result of the dichotomy between the Catholic-Portuguese and the African beliefs that confront each other daily in Brazilian life and have led to the mixed nature of capoeira. There are tensions that draw some Capoeiristas toward "Africa" and the others toward "Brazil," though both trends are explained in Catholic-Christian terms.

It's time, it's time
It's time, it's time, comrade
Let's go,
Let's go, comrade
Out into the world,
Out into the world, comrade
What the world provides,
What the world provides, comrade
Take a turn around the world,
Take a turn around the world, comrade

IN BRAZIL, THE written sources of the nineteenth century were mainly produced by whites and obviously reflect their outlook on life. For them Africa was a backward continent, deprived of European culture. Their views were supported by theories about the inferiority of the black race, supposedly stuck in the primitive stage of human development, so that they were comparable to animals or had the intelligence and mental ability of singing and dancing children. These attitudes, together with the needs of the slave owners, were translated into a policy that constantly attempted to prevent or annihilate any of the blacks' cultural expressions, including capoeira.

The terms the white authorities and tourists used to describe capoeira in the early 1800s were "slave games," "dances," "battles," and the like, the result of their attempts to define an activity that was beyond their comprehension. Capoeira consisted of music, dancing, and singing, a social event conducted in a circle, and hence defined as a dance. However, it also included maneuvers such as jumping and kicking, which were consistent more or less with the definition of a martial art. From the white person's point of view, dancing does not go hand in hand with boxing. Moreover, the movements of capoeira presented a specific kind of martial art—with no physical contact—thereby lending the entire activity the semblance of a game.

For the African slaves in Brazil at that time, capoeira was a social expression that incorporated all the basic African elements: the circle, the dance, the music, the spectators, as well as the rituals, symbols, and other components. It also contained all the ingredients of a game from the Kongolese perspective: a means to train and prepare for life, providing the experience needed to strengthen the body and the soul. Moreover, like any other activity, it contained elements that combined the sacred and the secular. The gods and/or the dead were active participants. It was necessary to appease them; there were ways to obtain their help; and there were customs, garments, accessories, gestures, songs, and sounds that guaranteed the desired results. Capoeira was not merely a dance or a diversion to while away the time; neither was it a martial art for vanquishing the masters or other enemies, or a game for the sake of fun, in Western terms. Rather, it was a complex interaction among people, encompassing their physical and spiritual essence and involving the gods and spirits of their ancestors. It was a synthesis of symbols, rituals, and traditional customs. These aspects, partially and sketchily described in the early 1800s, gradually diminished and had almost disappeared at the turn of the nineteenth century, when capoeira was legally defined as a practice of movement and a physical skill. When other social groups began practicing capoeira—native Brazilians, persons of mixed race, white immigrants, and even local aristocrats—many of them saw capoeira only as a martial art for acquiring fitness and agility to enable them to cope with the dangers of daily life. But this concept of capoeira, as a martial art and a violent solution for problems presented by the authorities, was both partial and biased. Its objective was to abolish capoeira because, it was claimed, it was a danger to public order. The lower classes, however, were not only trying to preserve their traditions but also to find other ways to express their criticism of the authorities. For many Capoeiras, mainly those from the lower strata of society, capoeira retained its values. There are reports about Capoeiras dancing, leaping, and hopping in front of military parades and religious processions, reportedly disturbing the peace and behaving improperly. They used amulets and participated in rituals to protect themselves against injury. They wore special accessories and made music to connect with arcane worlds and with their gods and forefathers, to secure protection against evil spirits. While the authorities labeled them as dangerous and violent hoodlums, the people admired them and their deeds. However, they did not remain isolated and segregated. Other influences infiltrated the patterns of their customs and rituals. Their links with their countries of origin broke when the transatlantic slave trade was stopped in 1850, so that the traditions transmitted from generation to generation depended on memory and on oral teaching, which were inevitably influenced by external factors.

In the late nineteenth and early twentieth centuries, the concept of whitening prevailed in Brazil, based on quasi-scientific racial theories that were taking root in Europe and the United States, utilizing biological "evidence" to affirm the superiority of the white race. The experts claimed that for the sake of eugenics, it was imperative to take certain measures as a means to minimize the influence of blacks and to improve the whites' genes. These measures included encouraging massive immigration from Europe, prohibiting immigration of blacks and Asians, and forbidding intermarriage. By that time capoeira was no longer a purely black activity; it also included mulattos and whites, most of whom had regular occupations and incomes, though they were stigmatized as drifters and idlers whose sources of livelihood were theft, extortion, and murder.

In the 1930s scholars led by Gilberto Freyre began stressing the beneficial influence of African and Indian cultures on Brazilian society. Their "backwardness," perceived up to that time as the result of their origin, was now regarded differently and was explained in terms of cultural differences, lack of education, and poor hygiene. There began an intensive preoccupation with the creation of a national identity, with emphasis on homogeneity as embodied in the new mixed type—the Mestiço. Getúlio Vargas's Estado Novo, or New State, policy of 1937–1945 advocated the image of a unified Brazil in which whites, blacks, mulattos, Mestiços and others could live in harmony, without racial strife.

Capoeira was adopted as Brazil's national sport. In order to get rid of its negative connotations, it became necessary to transform it and show it in a new light. The "negative" Rio de Janeiro brand of capoeira was rejected, and all eyes turned to Bahia—the capoeira center that now became the symbol of African-Brazilian authenticity. Capoeira, like other cultural manifestations such as samba, Candomblé, and carnival had metamorphosed from an activity associated exclusively with blacks into a respectable and significantly Brazilian entity. Its remodeled "history" linked capoeira with the activities of Brazil's African slaves. Capoeira had undergone a "face lift," had been adapted to conform to patterns compatible with national values. It was now closely supervised. From a spontaneous activity, it mutated into a sport, a martial art learned in official schools, at regular times, under systematic instruction. Many Capoeiras, led by Mestre Pastinha, who wished to preserve the spirit of the "pure" capoeira, demonstratively refused to accept this regime. Their style, the "real" capoeira brought from Angola, would keep alive the values, movements, rituals, and aesthetics of African cultures.

In the 1980s, until the collapse of the military regime in 1985, and while similar processes were taking place in the United States, Brazil underwent a massive return to its "sources," an attempt to connect once more with the traditions of the "homeland." There were antigovernment protests against seeing Brazilian identity as embodied in a single national type, which in the protesters' view was intended to conceal the dichotomies between whites and blacks, between rich and poor, thereby perpetuating discrimination and racism. New Capoeira Angola groups stressed, even more strongly, capoeira's "African" aspects and rekindled interest in this almost defunct style. New students enrolled in these schools, first in Brazil and later in the United States and Europe. African Americans and African Brazilians, men and women alike, wished to study their ancestral culture in depth. The whites saw all this as a novel and exotic activity, a pathway to the spirituality so lacking in their own culture. The Angoleiros' efforts to separate Capoeira Angola defeated the attempts of the authorities and the social elite in the 1970s to unify capoeira as the Brazilians' national sport.

Today, more than ever before, there are still Capoeiras who are trying to bridge the gap between Angola and Regional, adopting what they like from the two styles, and creating countless hybrids, depending mostly on the mestres' predilections. This very intricate process is in constant flux, because of all the different cultures, traditions, attitudes, values, and customs that find their expression in contemporary capoeira.

I suggest that the encounter between the diverse cultures has not culminated in the emergence of one universal capoeira. Neither does the assertion that the twentieth century (in particular, the 1980s) witnessed the division into Capoeira Angola and Capoeira Regional comply with our findings; though according to new studies and the statements of contemporary Angoleiros, this trend is gaining impetus. Indeed, the opposite seems to be true: the encounter has generated an ongoing process that began when African slaves transported to Brazil encountered other cultures and experienced (with them) a reality in constant flux economically, socially, and politically. This reality included Capoeiras of various ethnic origins, backgrounds, and socioeconomic status. Thus the goals, essence, characteristics, and language of capoeira have become diversified. Variations incorporate traditions that are influenced, among other things, by different perceptions of aesthetics, space, time, and teaching methods, as well as by African, African-Brazilian, and Christian convictions, rituals, symbols, and religious beliefs. The controversies concerning every aspect of contemporary capoeira confirm the great variety of views and interests that divide the authorities, capoeira instructors, students, and the media, pulling capoeira in different directions and molding it in accordance with their views. Cultural manifestations have always reflected people's outlook on life—be it in dance, music, movement, faith, ritual, or symbol. An in-depth investigation of the cultural and historical modifications of these elements in capoeira reveals the ebb and flow of the struggles in Brazilian society, from the early 1800s, when the Brazilian Empire was established, throughout the rise and fall of the Republic and the dictatorships to today. The sociopolitical strife between blacks and whites—subjects and rulers—which did not erupt in civil wars, uprisings, revolutions, or bloodshed—is manifest in the ongoing covert and overt cultural conflicts, in the different perceptions of time, space, aesthetic norms, rituals, and symbols.

So what is capoeira? It is the game of life; the depth, wealth, and variation of the capoeira language; the Capoeiras' social and cultural legacy; their encounters, conflicts, and fusion.

"Take a turn around the world, comrade."

Introduction

1 Mello Filho Barreto and Hermeto Lima, *História da polícia do Rio de Janeiro: Aspectos da cidade e da vida carioca* (Rio de Janeiro: Editôra A Noite, 1939), pp. 144–147; Plácido de Abreu, *Os Capoeiras* (Rio de Janeiro: Tip. Seraphim Alves de Britto, 1886); Aluízio Azevedo, *O Cortiço* (Rio de Janeiro: Technoprint, 1890).

2 *Guia do capoeira ou ginástica brasileira* (Rio de Janeiro, 1907); Annibal Burlamaqui, *Ginástica nacional (Capoeiragem)* (Rio de Janeiro: Obra Inédita, 1928).

3 Gilberto Freyre, *The Masters and the Slaves*, translated by Samuel Putman (New York: Knopf, 1970); Gilberto Freyre, *Order and Progress*, translated by Rod W. Horton (New York: Knopf, 1970); Viriato Correia, *Casa de Belchior* (Rio de Janeiro: Ed. Civilização Brasileira, 1936); Edison Carneiro, *Religiões negras: Negros bantos* (Rio de Janeiro: Civilização Brasileira, 1991), Edison Carneiro, *Capoeira* (Rio de Janeiro: Ministério da Educação e Cultura, Instituto Nacional de Livro, 1977); Edison Carneiro, *Dinâmica do folclore* (Rio de Janeiro: Of. Gráfica do Jornal do Brasil, 1965); Edison Carneiro, *A sabedoria popular* (Rio de Janeiro: Ministério da Educação e Cultura, Instituto Nacional de Livro, 1957); Arthur Ramos, *The Negro in Brazil*, translated by Richard Pattee (Washington, D.C.: Associated Pub., 1951).

4 Iria D'aquino, "Capoeira: Strategies for Status, Power and Identity" (Ph.D. dissertation, University of Illinois at Urbana-Champaign, 1983); Lewis Lowell, *Ring of Liberation: Deceptive Discourse in Brazilian Capoeira* (Chicago: University of Chicago Press, 1992); Leticia Reis, V.S., "Negros e brancos no jogo da capoeira: A reinvenção da tradição" (M.A. thesis, Universidade de São Paulo, 1993); Gregory John Downey, "Incorporating Capoeira: Phenomenology of a Movement Discipline" (Ph.D. dissertation, University of Chicago, 1998).

5 Marcos Luíz Bretas, "A queda do Império da Navalha e da Rasteira: A república e os Capoeiras," *Estudos Afro-Asiáticos* 20 (1991): 239–256; "Navalhas e Capoeiras—Uma outra queda," *Ciência Hoje* 19.59 (1989): 56–64; Thomas Holloway, "A Healthy Terror: Police Repression of Capoeiras in Nineteenth-Century Rio de Janeiro," *Hispanic American Historical Review* 69.4 (1989): 637–676; Maria A. Borges Salvadori, "Capoeiras e malandros: Pedaços de uma senora tradição popular, 1890–1950" (M.A. thesis, Universidade Estadual de Campinas, 1990); Antônio Liberac Pires, "A capoeira no jogo das cores: Criminalidade, cultura e racismo na cidade do Rio de Janeiro, 1890–1937" (M.A. thesis, Campinas, 1996); Antônio Liberac Pires, *Bimba, Pastinha e Besouro de Manganga* (Goiana: Editôra Grafset, 2002); Carlos Eugênio Líbano Soares, *A capoeira escrava e outras tradições rebeldes no Rio de Janeiro, 1808–1850* (Campinas: Editora da UNICAMP, 2001); Carlos Eugênio Líbano Soares, *A negregada instituição: Os Capoeiras no Rio de Janeiro*

(Rio de Janeiro: Prefeitura da Cidade do Rio de Janeiro, 1994); Luíz Renato Vieira and Mathias Röhring Assunção, "Mitos controvérsias e fatos: Construindo a história da capoeira," *Estudos Afro-Asiáticos* 34 (1998): 81–120; Luíz Renato Vieira, *O jogo da capoeira: Cultura popular no Brasil* (Rio de Janeiro: Editora Sprint, 1998); Luíz Renato Vieira, "Da vadiação a Capoeira Regional: Uma interpretação da modernização cultural no Brasil" (M.A. thesis, Universidade de Brasília, 1990); Mathias Röhring Assunção, *Capoeira: The History of an Afro-Brazilian Martial Art* (London: Routledge, Taylor and Francis Group, 2005).

6 Bira Almeida (Mestre Acordeon), *Capoeira: A Brazilian Art Form* (Berkeley: North Atlantic Books, 1986); Nestor Capoeira, *Capoeira: Os fundamentos da malícia* (Rio de Janeiro: Editora Record, 1997); Angelo Augusto Decanio, *A herança de Pastinha: A metafísica da capoeira* (Salvador: author's edition, 1996); Angelo Augusto Decanio, *A herança do Mestre Bimba: Lógica e filosofia africanas da capoeira* (Salvador: author's edition, 1996); Angelo Augusto Decanio, *Falando em capoeira* (Salvador: author's edition, 1996); José Luíz Oliveira (Mestre Bola Sete), *Capoeira Angola na Bahia* (Salvador: Empresa Gráfica da Bahia, 1989).

7 "Kongolese" refers to the historical area today known as Congo and Angola.

8 Júlio Cesar de Souza Tavarez, "Dança da guerra" (M.A. thesis, Universidade de Brasília, 1984).

9 Kenneth Michael Dossar, "Dancing between Two Worlds: An Aesthetic Analysis of Capoeira Angola" (Ph.D. dissertation, Temple University, 1994); T. J. Desch-Obi, "Engolo: Combat Traditions in African and African Diaspora History" (Ph.D. dissertation, University of California, Los Angeles, 2000), pp. 30, 52–60.

10 For further discussion on the origin of capoeira, see Desch-Obi, "Engolo"; Cascudo L. da Câmara, *Folclore do Brasil* (São Paulo: Fundo de Cultura, 1967), pp. 182–187.

Chapter 1

1 John Luccock, *Notas sobre o Rio de Janeiro e partes meridionais do Brasil tomadas durante uma estada de dez anos nesse país, de 1808 a 1818* (São Paulo: Livraria Martins, 1942), pp. 28–29; Mary Karasch, *Slave Life in Rio de Janeiro 1808–1850* (Princeton: Princeton University Press, 1987), p. 242.

2 John Robertson, *Letters on Paraguay* (New York: AMS Press 1970), pp. 164–169.

3 João Maurício Rugendas, *Viagem pitoresca através do Brasil* (São Paulo: Livraria Martins, 1954), p. 196–197.

4 Rugendas, *Viagem*, p. 198.

5 Resolution 413 of October 31, 1821, calls for "administering corporeal punishments in the public squares to all the Blacks referred to as capoeiras." *Coleção Cronológica das Leis, Decretos, Resoluções de Consulta, Provisões etc. do Império do Brasil*, tomo 3, p. 235. Six days later "it was decided about the steps that should

be taken against the Black capoeiras in the Province of Rio de Janeiro" (Decisão (414) de 5 novembro de 1821, *Coleção Cronológica das Leis*, 1837, tomo 3, p. 235). A month later it says: "Sending the capoeira slaves caught committing a crime to be flogged" (Decisão de 6 de janeiro de 1822, *Coleção das Decisões do Governo Império do Brasil*, 1887, pp. 3–4). Resolution 122 of 28 May 1824 says: "We have been apprised . . . that Blacks entitled Capoeiras carry on their insolence and raise havoc in the streets. To make sure that these disturbances stop once and for all, you are ordered to punish outright every slave caught disturbing the peace, whoever his owner, with the customary punishment or even twice as hard, when the severity of the crime requires it" (Decisão (02) de 22 de Maio, 1824, *Coleção das Decisões do Governo Império do Brasil*, 1886, p. 87). *Documentação Jurídica sobre o negro no Brasil* (0438), 1808–1888; *Índice analítico*, Arquivo Público do Estado da Bahia (hereafter APEB).

6 In July 1825 there is a further request to beef up the vigilance, patrols, and protection of the citizens from undesired capoeira gatherings (Códice 327, vol. 1, 06.07.1825, fol. 159, AN; Soares, *A capoeira escrava*, p. 172.

7 Códice 403, vol. I, 30 Sept. 1812, Arquivo Nacional (hereafter AN).

8 Ibid., 2 Jan. 1813, p. 111, AN.

9 Ibid., vol. II, 5 Jan. 1819, AN.

10 Ibid., 3 Jan. 1821, AN.

11 Leila Mezan Algrante, *O feitor ausente: Estudos sobre a escravidão urbana no Rio de Janeiro, 1808–1822* (Petrópolis: Vozes, 1988), pp. 209–210.

12 Soares, *A capoeira escrava*, p. 249.

13 *Coleção das Decisões*, 1886, p. 128; *Documentação Jurídica sobre o negro no Brasil* (0446), 1808–1888; *Índice analítico*, (APEB).

14 Códice 327, Registro de Ofícios de Polícia ao Comandante da Real depois Imperial Guarda de Polícia, 1815–1831, vol. I, fol. 37, 06.04.1816, AN; in Soares, *A capoeira escrava*, pp. 178–179.

15 Paulo Coelho de Araújo, "A capoeira: A transformação de uma atividade guerreira numa atividade lúdica" (Ph.D. dissertation, Universidade de Porto, 1995), p. 97.

16 Decisão (02) de 22 de maio, 1824, *Coleção das Decisões*, 1886, p. 87 (APEB).

17 Códice 327, vol. I, 04.12.1823, fol. 115, AN; in Soares, *A capoeira escrava*, p. 184.

18 Série Justiça, IJ 6 166, 26 June 1833, AN.

19 Ibid., IJ 6 166, 18 Nov. 1833, AN.

20 *Coleção das Decisões*, 1866, Decisão (205) de 27 de julho 1831 (APEB).

21 Charles Ribeyrolles, *Brasil pitoresco: História, descrições, viagens, colonização, instituições*, translated by Gastão Penalva (São Paulo: Editôra da Universidade de São Paulo, 1941), p. 38.

22 See John F. Szwed and D. Roger Abrahams, *After Africa* (New Haven: Yale University Press, 1983), pp. 229, 233, 244, 293.

23 Códice 327, vol. I, 04.10.1816, fol. 69; in Soares, *A capoeira escrava*, p. 236 n. 39.

24 In Karasch, *Slave Life*, p. 243.

25 Códice 327, vol. I, 03.04.1821, fol. 96, AN; in Soares, *A capoeira escrava*, p. 236 n. 39.

26 *O Universo*, Regulamento de Providências Policiais a Respeito de escravos e taverneiros—M.G—B.H. APM; in Araújo, *A capoeira*, p. 122.

27 Probably a game played with the peels of fruits. Códice 327, vol. I, 09.10.1816, fol. 69, AN; in Soares, *A capoeira escrava*, pp. 179–180.

28 Karasch, *Slave Life*, pp. 226, 243, 366–367. V. Ferreira, "Legislação Portuguesa Relativa ao Brasil," *Revista do Instituto Histórico Geográfico Brasileiro* 159 (1929): 199–240; Carl Schlichthorst, *O Rio de Janeiro como é 1824–1826*, translated by Emmy Dodt and Gustavo Barrosso (Rio de Janeiro: Editôra Getúlio Costa, 1943), p. 132.

29 Códice 327, vol. II, 05.07.1830, fol. 13, AN; in Soares, *A capoeira escrava*, p. 188.

30 Karasch, *Slave Life*, p. 16.

31 Ibid., pp. 14–21.

32 Soares, *A capoeira escrava*, pp. 124–128.

33 See Araújo, "A capoeira"; Abreu, *Os Capoeiras*, p. 1; D'aquino, "Capoeira," p. 24.

34 Many Capoeiras believe that capoeira was developed by runaway slaves in Palmares, a state founded by slaves that flourished in northeastern Brazil throughout most of the seventeenth century. Zumbi, the last leader of the Quilombo of Palmares, embodies for many Brazilians, especially those of African descent, the strongest resistance to the slave-based colonial regime and consequently the struggle for economic and political justice. See *Quilombo*, Videorecording, CDK Produções Ltda., 1984.

35 Soares, *A capoeira escrava*; Gerhard Kubik, *Angolan Traits in Black Music, Games, and Dances of Brazil: A Study of African Cultural Extensions Overseas* (Lisbon: Centro de Estudos de Antropologia Cultural, 1979), p. 27.

36 In John Thornton, "Art of War in Angola, 1575–1680," *Comparative Studies in Society and History* 30:3 (1988): 364–365. See also John Thornton, "African Dimensions of the Stono Rebellion," *American Historical Review* (1991): 1101–1113.

37 See Luís da Câmara Cascudo, *Folclore do Brasil* (São Paulo: Fondo de Cultura, 1967), p. 18; Assunção, *Capoeira*, pp. 24, 49–55.

38 Desch-Obi, "Engolo," pp. 30, 52–60.

39 Assunção, *Capoeira*, pp. 52–56.

40 Soares, *A capoeira escrava*, p. 89.

41 Códice 403, vol. II, 4 Feb. 1818, AN.

42 Códice 403, 3 Mar. 1820, AN; in Holloway, "A Healthy Terror," p. 647 n. 17.

43 IJ 6 166, 27 July 1831, AN; in Holloway, "A Healthy Terror," p. 651.

44 Códice 403, vol. II, 25 Nov. 1819, AN.

45 Ibid., vol. I, 14 Apr. 1812, AN.

46 Ibid., vol. II, 25 July 1817, AN.

47 Ibid., 25 July 1817, AN.

48 Ibid., 4 Feb. 1818, AN.

49 Ibid., 3 Jan. 1820, AN.

50 Correspondência recebida, 10 Aug. 1836, AG/PMERJ; in Holloway, "A Healthy Terror," p. 651.

51 For more information, see João José Reis, *Slave Rebellion in Brazil* (Baltimore: Johns Hopkins University Press, 1993).

52 Elísio de Araújo, *Estudos históricos sobre a polícia da Capital Federal, 1808–1831* (Rio de Janeiro: Tip. Leuzinger, 1898), p. 120.

53 Jair Moura, "Evolução, apogeu e declínio de Capoeiragem no Rio de Janeiro," *Cadernos RioArte* 1.3 (1985): 86–93.

54 Reis, "Negros e brancos," pp. 24–25.

55 Lewis Lowell, *Ring of Liberation: Deceptive Discourse in Brazilian Capoeira* (Chicago: University of Chicago Press, 1992), p. 46.

56 Araújo, *A capoeira*, pp. 106–107, 127; Pires, *Capoeira no jogo das Cores*; Assunção, *Capoeira*, p. 79.

57 Soares, *A capoeira escrava*, p. 336.

58 Ibid., p. 412.

59 *Diário do Rio de Janeiro*, 17 June 1828, fol. 1, Biblioteca Nacional do Rio de Janeiro (hereafter BN).

60 Robert Walsh, *Notices of Brazil in 1828–1829* (London, 1830), p. 130; in Soares, *A capoeira escrava*, p. 329.

61 Ibid., p. 330.

62 Códice 319, Registro de portarias e avisos expedidos pelas diversas Secretarias de Estado sobre assuntos referentes a polícia, 12.06.1828, ofício do ministro da justiça ao intendente de polícia, fol. 56, AN; in Soares, *A capoeira escrava*, p. 333; my emphasis.

63 Soares, *A capoeira escrava*, p. 335.

64 Karasch, *Slave Life*, p. 63.

65 Reis, *Slave Rebellion*, pp. 129–138.

66 Códice 334, Correspondencia reservada da polícia, 1833–1846, 17.03.1835 AN; in Soares, *A capoeira escrava*, p. 361.

67 CLIB, 1835, Justiça, 18.03.1835, p. 57; in Soares, *A capoeira escrava*, p. 370.

68 See Maria Ines Cortes de Oliveira, "Quem eram os 'negros da Guiné'? Sobre a origem dos africanos na Bahia," paper presented at the conference "Identifying Enslaved Africans: The Nigerian Hinterland and the African Diaspora," Toronto, 1997.

69 IJ 6 17, 8 Apr. 1835, AN.

70 Códice 334, 13.05.1835, AN; in Soares, *A capoeira escrava*, p. 363.

71 GIFI 5B 425, 3 Jan. 1837, AN; in Holloway, "A Healthy Terror," p. 637.

72 For further details, see Downey, "Incorporating Capoeira," pp. 79–80.

73 Rugendas, *Viagem pitoresca*, p. 197.

74 The interviews were conducted in summer 1997, spring and fall 1998, and summer 1999 with groups of Capoeira Regional and Capoeira Angola.

75 A. Tierou, *Doople: The Eternal Law of African Dance* (Paris: Hawood Academic Publishers, 1992), p. 2.

76 A. L. Kaeppler, "Memory and Knowledge in the Production of Dance," in *Images of Memory*, edited by Sussane Kuchler and Walter Melion (Washington, D.C.: Smithsonian Institution Press, 1991).

77 William Bosman, *New and Accurate Description of the Coast of Guinea* (London, 1705), pp. 386–387.

78 Rugendas, *Viagem pitoresca*, p. 196.

79 Michel Huet, *The Dances of Africa* (New York: Harry N. Abrams, 1996), p. 8; Katrina Hazard-Gordon, *Jookin': The Rise of Social Dance Formations in African-American Culture* (Philadelphia: Temple University Press, 1990), p. 4.

80 Esther Dagan, "Origin and Meaning of Dance's Essential Body Position and Movements," in *The Spirits' Dance in Africa*, edited by Esther Dagan (Westmount: Galerie Amrad African Arts, 1997), p. 117; Thornton, "African Dimensions of the Stono Rebellion," p. 1112; Desch-Obi, "Engolo," p. 55.

81 Jan Vansina, *The Tio Kingdom of Middle Congo 1880–1892* (London: Oxford University Press, 1973), pp. 45, 163, 215.

82 Interview with Dr. Fu-Kiau, 20–21 Aug. 1999, Salvador, Bahia.

83 Desch-Obi, "Engolo," p. 57.

84 Conversations with Dr. Fu-Kiau, Aug. 1999, Salvador, Bahia.

85 Vicente Ferreira Pastinha, *Capoeira Angola* (Salvador: Escola Gráfica N.S. de Loreto, 1964), p. 31; Reis, "Negros e brancos," p. 82.

86 D'aquino, "Capoeira," p. 24.

87 Rego, *Capoeira Angola*, p. 58.

88 Ashenafi Kebede, *Roots of Black Music: The Vocal, Instrumental, and Dance Heritage of Africa and Black America* (Trenton: Africa World Press, 1995), p. 94; Sterling Stuckey, *Slave Culture* (New York: Oxford University Press, 1987), p. 20; Ivan Livingstone, "Dances for Gods in Benin," in *The Spirits' Dance in Africa*, edited by Esther Dagan (Westmount: Galerie Amrad African Arts, 1997), p. 197; interview with Fu-Kiau, Salvador, 1997; Wyatt MacGaffey, *Religion and Society in Central Africa* (Chicago: University of Chicago Press, 1986), pp. 239–240.

89 Códice 403, vol. II, 16 Dec. 1818, AN.

90 Maria Dundas Graham, *Journal of a Voyage to Brazil and Residence There during Part of the Years 1821, 1822, 1823* (New York: Praeger, 1969), p. 199.

91 Ribeyrolles, *Brasil pitoresco*, p. 38.

92 Kia Bunseki Fu-Kiau, "African Diasporadical Languages: Unspoken but Alive and Powerful," paper presented at the 31st Annual Conference on African Linguistics, Boston University, 2000.

93 Kubik, *Angolan Traits*, pp. 27–28.

94 Thornton, "Art of War," p. 366.

95 Filippo Pigafetta, *Report of the Kingdom of Congo* (London: Frank Cass, 1970).

96 Robert Farris Thompson, *Four Moments of the Sun: Kongo Art in Two Worlds* (Washington, D.C.: National Gallery of Art, 1981), pp. 106–107.

97 Interview with Fu-Kiau, 20–21 Aug. 1999, Salvador, Bahia.

98 O. Olutoye and J. A. Olapade, "Implements and Tactics of War among the Yoruba," in *War and Peace in Yorubaland, 1793–1893*, edited by Adeagbo Akinjogbin (Ibadan: Heinemann Educational Books, 1998), p. 211.

99 In Peter Fryer, *Rhythms of Resistance: African Musical Heritage in Brazil* (London: Pluto, 2000), p. 57.

100 Códice 403, vol. II, 5 Dec. 1820, AN.

101 Karasch, *Slave Life*, p. 233.

102 MacGaffey, *Religion and Society*, pp. 90, 107; Vansina, *The Tio Kingdom*, pp. 208; Georges Balandier, *Ambiguous Africa: Cultures in Collision* (London: Chatto and Windus, 1966), p. 43; Michel Huet, *The Dance, Art and Ritual of Africa* (New York: Pantheon, 1978), p. 13.

103 Códice 403, vol. I, 13 Dec. 1814, AN.

104 Códice 403, vol. I; in Soares, *A negregada instituição*, p. 28.

105 Códice 403, vol. I, 17 May 1815, p. 248, AN.

106 Ibid., vol. II, 18 Nov. 1818, AN.

107 Ibid., vol. II, 28 Feb. 1820; in Soares, *A negregada instituição*, p. 28. My emphasis.

108 Códice 403, vol. II, 19 Nov. 1818, AN.

109 Ibid., vol. II, 9 Aug. 1821, AN.

110 Ibid., 22 Dec. 1820; in Soares, *A capoeira*, p. 59.

111 See also MacGaffey, *Religion and Society*, pp. 42–51.

112 Olfert Dapper, *Description de l'Afrique* (Paris: Fondation Dapper, 1990).

113 Robert Farris Thompson, *Face of the Gods: Art and Altars of Africa and the African Americas* (New York: Museum for African Art, 1993), p. 131.

114 Jean-Baptiste Debret, *Viagem pitoresca e histórica ao Brasil* (São Paulo: Livraria Martins, 1954), vol. II, p. 180.

115 Ibid., vol. I, p. 237.

116 Thompson, *Face of the Gods*, p. 128.

117 Pigafetta, *Report of the Kingdom of Congo*, p. 108.

118 Ann Hilton, *The Kingdom of Kongo* (New York: Oxford University Press, 1985), p. 96.

119 Thompson, *The Four Moments*, p. 35.

120 Ibid., pp. 35–37; see also MacGaffey, *Religion and Society*, pp. 148–160.

121 MacGaffey, *Religion and Society*, p. 153.

122 Thompson, *Face of the Gods*, p. 76.

123 Ibid., p. 153.

124 Debret, *Viagem pitoresca*, vol. I, p. 269.

125 Luíz de Edmundo, *O Rio de Janeiro no tempo dos vice-reis* (Rio de Janeiro: Imprensa Nacional, 1938), p. 32.

126 Schlichthorst, *O Rio de Janeiro*, pp. 130–131.
127 Ibid., p. 132.
128 In Karasch, *Slave Life*, p. 130.
129 Schlichthorst, *O Rio de Janeiro*, p. 132.
130 Ibid.

Chapter 2

1 An advertisement was published in *Diário do Rio de Janeiro* on January 29, 1849, about a runaway slave named Izias. He was described as "a light-skinned Pardo [of mixed black and white descent] with black curly hair, tall, strong, good looking, a tailor by profession" (fol. 4, BN). A few months later the same paper published another advertisement asking the public to help capture a slave who had escaped on October 21 from José Maria da Conceição, citizen of Engenho Novo. The fugitive was described as "a Creole, of fula color, with a beard; . . . a vegetable vendor, well known to the pedestres (a special unit of police founded in 1841 to patrol the streets and maintain public order); a Capoeirista." A reward was promised for returning him to his owner. Holloway, "A Healthy Terror," p. 667.

2 Holloway, "A Healthy Terror," p. 654.

3 Ibid.

4 S. Chalhoub, "Slaves, Freedman and Politics of Freedom in Brazil: The Experience of Blacks in the City of Rio," *Slavery and Abolition* 10.3 (1989): 64; Karasch, *Slave Life*, p. 65.

5 Chalhoub, "Slaves, Freedman and Politics," pp. 64–84.

6 SDM-AM OPJ (1829–1836) 1 9.593, 28/03/1836, Ofício no. 2167; in Soares, *A capoeira escrava*, p. 290.

7 *Diário do Rio de Janeiro*, 29 Jan. 1849, fol. 4, BN.

8 Ofícios Recebidos, 1.9.602, 24.03.1840. Juiz de Paz do 1 Distrito do Sacramento, SDM-AM; in Soares, *A capoeira escrava*, p. 299.

9 Códice 398, Relação de Prisões no Rio de Janeiro, 1849–1850, 22.12.1849, fol. 27v., AN; in Soares, *A capoeira escrava*, p. 115.

10 For more details, see J. P. Marques, "Manutenção do tráfico de escravos num contexto abolicionista: A diplomática portuguesa 1807–1819," *Revista Internacional de Estudos Africanos* 10–11 (1989): 65–99; E. Santos, "Escravatura e antropologia dos portugueses," *Ultramar* 5–6 (1973): 51–98.

11 Holloway, "A Healthy Terror," p. 670.

12 Soares, *A negregada instituição*, p. 117.

13 Ibid., p. 103.

14 Manuel Antônio de Almeida, *Memórias de um sargento de milícias* (São Paulo: Technoprint, 1945), p. 48.

15 Karasch, *Slave Life*, pp. 223–224.

16 IJ 6 216, 15 Oct. 1853, AN.

17 IJ 6 484, 24 Feb. 1859, AN; in Holloway, "A Healthy Terror," p. 665.

18 *Correio Mercantil* (Rio de Janeiro), 14 Dec. 1855, p. 1, BN.

19 Ordens do Dia no. 11., 16 Dec. 1869, AG/PMERJ; in Holloway, "A Healthy Terror," p. 667.

20 OPJ. 1848, 1.9.606 04.01.1848. Da Secretaria de Polícia da Côrte ao Inspetor do Arsenal, SDM-AM; in Soares, *A capoeira escrava*, p. 301.

21 Ibid., 05.04.1848; Inspetor do Arsenal; in In Soares, *A capoeira escrava*, p. 301.

22 Série Justiça, IJ 6 212, 13 Nov. 1849, AN.

23 Ibid., IJ 6 484, 19 Jan. 1859, AN.

24 Ibid., IJ 6 19 (Polícia Avisos), 4 Sept. 1869, AN.

25 IJ 6 212, 25 Apr., 16 June 1489, AN; in Holloway, "A Healthy Terror," p. 653.

26 Série Justiça, IJ 6 212, AN; Série Justiça, IJ 6, AN.

27 OP. 1848, 1.9.606 04.01.1848, Da Secretaria de Polícia da Côrte ao Inspetor do Arsenal SDM-AM; in Soares, *A capoeira escrava*, p. 301.

28 OP. 1848, 05.04.1848, Da Secretaria de Polícia da Côrte ao Inspetor do Arsenal. In Soares, *A capoeira escrava*, p. 301.

29 Códice 323, vol. 15, 29.03.1841, fol. 148, AN; in Soares, *A capoeira escrava*, p. 217.

30 Série Justiça, IJ 6 212, AN.

31 Ibid., p. 10, AN.

32 *Diário do Rio de Janeiro*, 7 July 1849, fol. 2, BN.

33 Holloway, "A Healthy Terror," pp. 641–642.

34 Soares, *A capoeira escrava*, p. 119.

35 *Correio da Tarde*, Rio de Janeiro, 3 Nov. 1849, BN.

36 Série Justiça, IJ 6 217, 20 Jan. 1854, AN.

37 Daniel Parrish Kidder and James Cooley Fletcher, *O Brasil e os brasileiros* (São Paulo: Companhia Editôra Nacional, 1941), p. 138.

38 Ibid., p. 152.

39 Karasch, *Slave Life*, p. 299.

40 Mello Moraes Filho, *Festas e tradições populares do Brasil* (São Paulo: Livraria Itatiaia Editôra, 1979), p. 259.

41 For more details, see Soares, *A capoeira escrava*, pp. 150–151.

42 Ofício expedido pelo chefe de Polícia ao Comandante dos Permanentes, Códice 323, vol. 14, 2 May 1838, fol. 95v., AN; in Soares, *A capoeira escrava*, p. 218.

43 Códice 323, vol. 16, 3 Aug. 1842, Ofício do chefe do polícia ao inspetor do Arsenal de Marinha, AN; in Soares, *A capoeira escrava*, p. 379.

44 Kidder and Fletcher, *O Brasil*, p. 151.

45 Relatório do Chefe de Polícia da Côrte, 1872, pp. 22–23, Annex to Relatório do Ministério de Justiça, 1872, AN.

46 Soares, *A negregada instituição*, pp. 72–79; Holloway, "A Healthy Terror," 662–676; Karasch, *Slave Life*, pp. 299–300; Lowell, *Ring of Liberation*, pp. 47–48.

47 James C. Scott, *Weapons of the Weak* (New Haven, Yale University Press, 1985), p. 26.

48 Manuel Querino, *A Bahia de outrora* (Salvador: Progresso, 1946), p. 79; *Jornal do Commercio*, 22 Jan. 1872; *Diário do Rio de Janeiro*, 22 July 1872, in Soares, *A negregada instituição*, p. 260.

49 Moraes Filho, *Festas*, pp. 258–259.

50 Relatório do Chefe de Polícia da Côrte, 1872, pp. 22–23. Annex to Relatório do Ministério de Justiça, 1872, AN.

51 Relatório do Chefe de Polícia da Côrte, 1875, p. 184. Annex to Relatório do Ministério de Justiça, 1875, AN.

52 Freyre, *The Mansions and the Shanties*, p. 325.

53 *Diário do Rio de Janeiro*, 17 Jan. 1872.

54 Ibid., 5 Mar. 1872; in Soares, *A negregada instituição*, p. 74.

55 Ibid.

56 Moraes Filho, *Festas*, p. 258.

57 Abreu, *Os Capoeiras*, p. 4.

58 *Diário do Rio de Janeiro*, 11 Mar. 1872.

59 *Jornal do Commercio Rio de Janeiro*, 28 Jan. 1878.

60 *Diário do Rio de Janeiro*, 11 Mar. 1872.

61 19 Jan. 1859, Série Justiça, IJ 6 484, AN.

62 Kidder and Fletcher, *O Brasil*, p. 152.

63 *Jornal do Commercio*, 10 Mar. 1874.

64 Moraes Filho, *Festas*, p. 258.

65 Soares, *A negregada institução*, p. 74.

66 Moraes Filho, *Festas*, p. 259.

67 For more details about women in capoeira, see Maya Chvaicer, "The Complexity of Capoeira: Encounter, Collision, and Fusion of Cultures. Rio de Janeiro and Bahia, Nineteenth and Twentieth Centuries" (Ph.D. dissertation, University of Haifa, 2000), pp. 316–324; *Jornal do Commercio*, 29 Jan. 1878;

68 Abreu, *Os Capoeiras*, p. 5.

69 *Jornal do Commercio*, 29 Jan. 1878, p. 1, BN.

70 AJ, Fernando Isidoro da Conceição, réu, mss. Caixa 49, processo 9, APERJ; in Soares, *A negregada instituição*, p. 276.

71 Carl von Koseritz, *Imagens do Brasil* (São Paulo: Livraria Martins, 1943), p. 52.

72 *Jornal do Commercio*, 28 Jan. 1878, BN.

73 Reis, "Negros e brancos," pp. 24, 46.

74 Ibid.

75 *O Mosquito*, Rio de Janeiro, 26 Aug. 1871; in Soares, *A negregada instituição*, p. 78.

76 *Gazeta de Notícias*, Rio de Janeiro, 26 Feb. 1878, p. 1, BN.

77 Roberto da Matta, *Carnivals, Rogues and Heroes: An Interpretation of the Brazilian Dilemma* (Notre Dame: University of Notre Dame Press, 1991), pp. 76–77.

78 Debret, *Viagem pitoresca*, vol. II, pp. 21–22.

79 Ibid., p.26.

80 Luíz Agassis and Elizabeth Cary Aggasis, *Viagem ao Brasil 1865–1866* (Belo Horizonte: Editôra Itatiaia Limitada, 1975), p. 76.

81 Kidder and Fletcher, *O Brasil*, pp. 165–167.

82 Debret, *Viagem pitoresca*, pp. 23–24.

83 Ibid., p. 24.

84 Ibid., p. 180.

85 Ibid.

86 Rugendas, *Viagem*, p. 199.

87 Kidder and Fletcher, *O Brasil*, p. 172.

88 Ibid., p. 167.

89 *Anais da Câmara dos Deputados*, 5 sept. 1887, p. 21; in Soares, *A negregada instituição*, p. 75.

Chapter 3

1 Richard Graham, *Britain and the Onset of Modernization in Brazil 1850–1914* (New York: Cambridge University Press, 1968), pp. 27–29.

2 *Jornal do Commercio*, 22 Apr. 1870, BN.

3 Ministério dos Negócios da Justiça, 1871; in Soares, *A negregada instituição*, p. 194.

4 Relatório do Chefe de Polícia da Côrte, 1872, pp. 22–23. Annex to Relatório do Ministério de Justiça, 1872.

5 Relatório do Chefe de Polícia da Côrte, 1875, p. 184. Annex to Relatório do Ministério de Justiça, 1875.

6 *Diário do Rio de Janeiro*, 9 Mar. 1874, BN.

7 *Jornal do Commercio*, 1 Mar. 1874, BN.

8 Ibid., 28 Nov. 1878, BN.

9 Ibid., 29 Nov. 1878, BN.

10 Koseritz, *Imagens do Brasil*, pp. 238–239.

11 Soares, *A negregada instituição*, pp. 142–143.

12 Hasting Charles Dent, *A Year in Brazil with notes on the abolition of slavery, the finances of the empire, religion, meteorology, natural history* (London: K. Paul, Trench and Company, 1886), p. 239.

13 Bretas, "A queda do Império," p. 241.

14 Ibid.

15 Soares, *A negregada instituição*, p. 151.

16 Holloway, "A Healthy Terror," p. 658.

17 Soares, *A negregada instituição*, p. 176.

18 José Murilho de Carvalho, *Os bestializados: O Rio de Janeiro e a República que não foi* (São Paulo: Companhia das Letras, 1991), p. 17.

19 Soares, *A negregada instituição*, p. 175.

20 *Vida Policial*, 23 Jan. 1926, pp. 15–16, BN.

21 Rego, *Capoeira Angola*, pp. 305–307.

22 *Diário do Rio de Janeiro*, 17 Feb. 1872, BN.

23 Abreu, *Os Capoeiras*, p. 4.

24 Ibid.

25 Moraes Filho, *Festas*, p. 258.

26 Edmundo, *O Rio de Janeiro no tempo dos vice-reis*, pp. 37–40.

27 Silvio Romero, "Poesia popular brasileira," *Revista Brasileira* 1 (1879): 273.

28 Azevedo, *O Cortiço*, p. 103.

29 Moraes Filho, *Festas*, p. 258.

30 Abreu, *Os Capoeiras*, p. 7.

31 Ibid., p. 3.

32 Soares, *A negregada instituição*, pp. 40–49.

33 Agenor Lopes de Oliveira, *Toponímia carioca* (Rio de Janeiro: Prefeitura do Distrito Federal, 1935), vol. II, 13, 6, 1, BN.

34 Oliveira, "Quem eram," p. 22.

35 Abreu, *Os Capoeiras*, p. 5.

36 Soares, *A negregada instituição*, pp. 54, 95.

37 Assunção, *Capoeira*, pp. 89–90.

38 Moraes Filho, *Festas*, p. 258.

39 Abreu, *Os Capoeiras*, p. 6.

40 Ibid.

41 Relatório do Chefe de Polícia da Corte, 1875, p. 184. Annex to Relatório do Ministério de Justiça, 1875.

42 *Vida Policial*, 23 Jan. 1926, p. 15, BN.

43 Emilia Viotti Costa, *The Brazilian Empire: Myth and Histories* (Chicago: University of Chicago Press, 1985), pp. 22–23, 60.

44 José Murilho de Carvalho, *Teatro de sombras* (São Paulo: Hucitec, 1988), pp. 141–142.

45 *Anais da Câmara dos Deputados*, 6 Feb. 1873; in Soares, *A negregada instituição*, p. 196.

46 *Kosmos*, Ano III no. 3, Mar. 1906, BN.

47 *A Reforma*, 25 Aug. 1872, BN.

48 Costa, *The Brazilian Empire*, p. 71.

49 The law provided for the registration of all slaves and their children and that all children of slaves born after the law were to be free. When the child was eight, the slave owner could receive a government payment or enjoy the labor of the child until age twenty-one.

50 *A Reforma*, 22 Aug. 1872; in Soares, *A negregada instituição*, p. 202.

51 *A República*, 19 Sept. 1872, BN.

52 *Cidade do Rio*, 10 Dec. 1889, BN.

53 *Gazeta de Notícias*, 12 Dec. 1889, BN.

54 Edmundo, *O Rio de Janeiro do meu tempo*, p. 387.

55 Moraes Filho, *Festas*, p. 262.

56 *A República*, 2 Mar. 1873, BN.

57 *A Comédia Popular*, 28 Jan. 1878; in Soares, *A negregada instituição*, p. 330.

58 *Gazeta de Notícias*, 25 Jan. 1878, BN.

59 Ibid., 6 Feb. 1878, BN.

60 Nelson Werneck Sodre, *Panorama do Segundo Império* (São Paulo: Companhia Editôra Nacional, 1939), pp. 181–183.

61 Rego, *Capoeira Angola*, p. 314.

62 *Novidades*, 15 Jul. 1889, BN.

63 Carvalho, *Os bestializados*, pp. 19–24.

64 Bretas, "A queda do Império," p. 249.

65 *Gazeta de Notícias*, 12 Dec. 1889, BN.

66 Carvalho, *Os bestializados*, p. 19.

67 Ibid., p. 24; Bretas, "A queda do Império," p. 240.

68 Eduardo Prado, *Fastos da ditatura militar no Brasil*, pp. 323; in Bretas, "A queda do Império," p. 251.

69 Processo Crime de Otávio Carlos (reu) 7c.115, 1893, AN.

70 Processo Crime de Tomas do Rego, T8. 122, 1902, AN.

71 Processo Crime Federico J. de Freitas (reu) T8. 1904, AN.

72 *Kosmos*, 10 Mar. 1906, BN.

73 Moraes Filho, *Festas*, p. 258.

74 Ibid.

75 Abreu, *Os Capoeiras*, p. 19.

76 Moraes Filho, *Festas*, p. 261.

77 Abreu, *Os Capoeiras*, p. 2.

78 Luís da Câmara Cascudo, *Dicionário do Folclore* (Belo Horizonte: Itatiaia, 1984), p. 369.

79 Anita Jacobson-Widding, *Red-White-Black as a Mode of Thought* (Uppsala: Stokholn, Almquist and Wikseu, 1979), p. 188; Vansina, *The Tio Kingdom*, p. 235; MacGaffey, *Religion and Society*, p. 53; Hilton, *The Kingdom of Kongo*, p. 51.

80 Freyre, *The Masters and the Slaves*, p. 102.

81 Neto Coelho, *O Bazar* (Porto: Livraria Chardon de Lello e Irmãos, 1928), p. 137.

82 Abreu, *Os Capoeiras*, pp. 3–4.

83 Giovani Antonio Cavazzi, *Descriçao histórica dos três reinos do Congo, Matamba e Angola*; in James Sweet, *Recreating Africa: Culture, Kinship, and Religion in the African Portuguese World, 1441–1770* (Chapel Hill: University of North Carolina Press, 2003), p. 141.

84 Hilton, *The Kingdom of Kongo*, p. 18.

85 MacGaffey, *Religion and Society*, p. 37.

86 A young Kongolese woman claimed to be possessed by Saint Anthony; see John Thornton, *The Kongolese Saint Anthony: Dona Beatriz Kimpa Vita and the An-*

tonian Movement, 1684–1706 (Cambridge: Cambridge University Press, 1998), p. 133.

87 Cavazzi, *Descrição histórica dos três reinos*; in Ezio Bassani, ed., *Un Cappuccino nell'Africa nera del seicento: I disegni dei Manoscritti Araldi del Padre Giovanni Antonio Cavazzi da Montecuccolo* (Quaderni Poro, no. 4, 1987), pl. 33.

88 MacGaffey, *Religion and Society*, p. 85.

89 Robert Farris Thompson, *Flash of the Spirit: African and Afro-American Art and Philosophy* (New York: Random House, 1983), p. 117.

90 Among the Tio of the middle Kongo amulets were also in wide use and were called *kaa*. For further details, see Vansina, *The Tio Kingdom*, p. 188.

91 Hilton, *The Kingdom of Kongo*, pp. 18–19; MacGaffey, *Religion and Society*, p. 139.

92 In MacGaffey, *Religion and Society*, p. 205.

93 Ibid., p. 206.

94 Karasch, *Slave Life*, pp. 224–225.

95 Debret, *Viagem pitoresca*, vol. I, p. 268.

96 Ibid., p. 269.

97 Ibid., vol. II, p. 163.

98 Sweet, *Recreating Africa*, p. 180.

99 Interview with Fu-Kiau, Salvador, Bahia, Sept. 1999.

100 Paraná arm of a large river separated by an island from the main course.

101 Olutoye and Olapade, "Implements and Tactics," in *War and Peace in Yorubaland*, p. 210.

102 Thompson, *Face of the Gods*, p. 160.

103 Freyre, *The Masters and the Slaves*, p. 317.

104 Elizabeth W. Kiddy, "Who Is the King of Congo?" in *Central Africans and Cultural Transformations in the American Diaspora*, edited by Linda Heywood (New York: Cambridge University Press, 2002), p. 178.

105 Karasch, *Slave Life*, p. 232.

106 Fryer, *Rhythms of Resistance*, p. 19; Thompson, *Flash of the Spirit*, pp. 160, 162.

107 Moraes Filho, *Festas*, p. 258.

108 Azevedo, *O Cortiço*, p. 49; in Salvadori, *Capoeiras e malandros*, p. 123.

109 Ibid., p. 125.

110 Edmundo, *O Rio de Janeiro*, p.383.

111 Reis, "Negros e brancos," p. 92.

112 Rego, *Capoeira Angola*, p. 44.

113 Edmundo, *Rio de Janeiro do meu tempo*, pp. 385–386: "Fui saindo de barriga e, quando o grillo estrilou, abri o arco e cahi no mundo. Na minha meia hora vou longe, que eu sou do povo da lyra e tenho o corpo fechado."

114 Interview with Fu-Kiau, August 1999.

115 MacGaffey, *Religion and Society*, p. 85.

116 Thompson, "Capoeira," *Spoleto Festival U.S.A.* (1987), p. 25.

NOTES TO PAGES 102–113

117 Cavazzi, *Descrição histórica*; in Sweet, *Recreating Africa*, p. 142.

118 Inquisição de Lisboa, Cadernos do Promotor, Processo no. 3641, Arquivo Nacional de Torre de Tombo; in Sweet, *Recreating Africa*, p. 142.

119 Oliveira, *Capoeira Angola na Bahia*, p. 84.

120 Interview with the researcher and Capoeirista, Aug. 1997.

121 The Bible: 2 Sam. 16:16.

122 Edmundo, *Rio de Janeiro no tempo dos vice-reis*, p. 34.

123 Pires, *Bimba, Pastinha e Besouro de Manganga*, pp. 17–34.

124 Rego, *Capoeira Angola*, p. 265.

125 Edmundo, *Rio de Janeiro no tempo dos vice-reis*, p. 36.

126 João do Rio, *História da gente alegre*; in Salvadori, *Capoeiras e malandros*, p. 138.

127 Kidder and Fletcher, *Brasil e os brasileiros*, pp. 111–112.

128 Ibid., p. 108.

129 Jair Moura, "Capoeirista de Antigamente não 'brincava em serviço,'" *A Tarde*, 10 July 1971, BN.

130 Interview with Fu-Kiau, Salvador, Bahia, Aug. 1999.

131 Moura, "Capoeirista de Antigamente."

132 Ibid.

133 Daniel Coutinho, *O ABC da Capoeira Angola: Os manuscritos do Mestre Noronha*, p. 28; in Downey, "Incorporating Capoeira," p. 327.

134 Josephus Flavius, *The Antiquities of the Jews* (Jerusalem: Mass, 1940), chap. 8, 2:5, or 42–49.

135 Jean Chevalier and Alain Gheerbrant, "Star," in *A Dictionary of Symbols*, translated by John Buchanan-Brown (Oxford: Blackwell, 1994), p. 924.

136 Rachel Milstein, *Solomon's Seal*, pp. 36, 50–54.

137 William Vantuono, *Sir Gawain and the Green Knight* (New York: Garland Publishing, 1991), pp. 37–38.

138 Preinterview with Mestre Curió, Salvador, Bahia, Sept. 1998.

Chapter 4

1 Carvalho, *Os bestializados*, pp. 39–40.

2 L. C., "A capoeira," *Kosmos* RJ. Ano III, no. 3, 1906, BN.

3 *Guia do Capoeira*, introd.

4 Ibid., p. 3.

5 L. C., "A capoeira."

6 Burlamaqui, *Ginástica nacional (Capoeiragem)*, pp. 3–5.

7 Coelho, *O Bazar*, p. 134.

8 Ibid., p. 139.

9 *Revista Vida Policial*, Jan.–Feb., 23 Jan. 1926, p. 16.

10 Penna, *Subsídios para o estudo do treinamento*; in Reis, "Negros e brancos," p. 63.

11 Ibid., p. 69.
12 Dunshee, *Atas e atos do Governo Provisório*, RJ, 1930; in Salvadori, *Capoeiras*, p. 148.
13 Corrêia, *Casa de Belchior*, pp. 144, 147–155.
14 Ibid., p. 138.
15 Pires, *Capoeira*, chap. 3.
16 Ibid.
17 Reis, "Negros e brancos," pp. 73–74.
18 In Vieira, *O jogo da capoeira*, p. 64.
19 Ibid., p. 65.
20 Ibid., p. 70.
21 Interviews with Mestre Acordeon (Almeida Bira), Decanio (Angelo Augusto Decanio Filho), Itapoan (Raimundo Cesar Alves de Almeida), and Jair Moura, summer 1997, 1998, 1999, Salvador, Bahia.
22 Reis, "Negros e brancos," p. 77.
23 D. Kim Butler, *Freedoms Given, Freedoms Won* (New Brunswick: Rutgers University Press, 1998), p. 168.
24 Interviews with Mestre Cobra Mansa (Cinésio Feliciano Peçanha) and Mestre Angolinha, Salvador, Bahia, August 1999.
25 Rachel Elizabeth Harding, "Candomblé and the Alternative Space of Black Being in Nineteenth-Century Bahia" (Ph.D. dissertation, Brown University, 1997), pp. 88–90.
26 Nina Rodrigues, *Os Africanos no Brasil* (Brasília: Editora UNB, 1988), pp. 215–216.
27 In Lourdes Martinez-Echazabal, "O culturalismo dos anos 30 no Brasil e na América Latina: Deslocamento retórico ou mudança conceitual?" in *Raça ciência e Sociedade*, edited by Marcos Chor Maio and Ricardo Ventura Santos Raça (Rio de Janeiro: Editôra Fiocruz, 1998), p. 116.
28 James Wetherell, *Stray Notes from Bahia* (Liverpool: Webb and Hunt, 1860) pp. 119–120.
29 *Alabama* 12.04.1870; in Assunção, *Capoeira*, p. 102.
30 Querino, *A Bahia de outrora*, p. 74.
31 Holloway, "A Healthy Terror," p. 674; Tavarez, "Dança de guerra," pp. 8–9; Soares, *A negregada instituição*; D'aquino, *Capoeira*, pp. 9, 25.
32 Araújo, *A capoeira*, p. 115.
33 In Rio until 1811, 96.2 percent of imported slaves were from West Central Africa. Only 2 percent were brought directly from West African ports, and an additional 6 percent were transported from Bahia to Rio. Karasch, *Slave Life*, p.14.
34 Reis, *Slave Rebellion*, pp. 43–44.
35 Ibid., pp. 147–148.
36 Silvia Bezerra. *Repertório de Fontes sobre a Escravidão Existentes no Arquivo Municipal de Salvador* (Salvador: Fundação Gregorio de Matos, n.d.).
37 Assunção, *Capoeira*, pp. 106–108.

38 Frederico José Abreu, *"Bimba é Bamba"*: *A Capoeira no Ringue* (Bahia: P&A Gráfica e Editôra, 1999), p. 25.

39 Ibid.

40 Alceu Maynard Araújo, "Batuque," in *Folclore Nacional*, vol. II (São Paulo: Edições Melhoramentos, 1964), pp. 231–237; Cascudo, *Dicionário do folclore brasileiro*, pp. 114–115.

41 Interviews with Mestre Acordeon and Cobra Mansa, Aug. 1999, Salvador, Bahia.

42 This contention is probably incorrect because it is known that other schools were opened previously but did not receive the recognition Bimba's did, which is why they faded from the collective memory. Moreover, different records cite various dates for the opening of his school. For example, Moura's article in the newspaper *Tribuna da Bahia* dated 5 Mar. 1975 states that Bimba first opened his school in 1928 (p. 13).

43 Rego, *Capoeira Angola*, pp. 282–283.

44 *Tribuna da Bahia*, 2 Dec. 1924; in Abreu, *Bimba é Bamba*, p. 30.

45 *A Tarde*, 23 Mar. 1968; in Abreu, *Bimba é Bamba*, p. 30.

46 *Estado da Bahia*, 30 June 1936.

47 *A Tarde*, 10 Aug. 1936; in Jair Moura, *Capoeira: A luta regional bahiana* (Salvador: Cadernos de Cultura, 1979), p. 31.

48 Letter from Juracy Magalhães to Waldeloir Rego, 10 May 1966; in Rego, *Capoeira Angola*, p. 316.

49 Jorge Amado, *Bahia de Todos os Santos: Guia das ruas e dos mistérios da cidade do Salvador* (São Paulo: Livraria Martins, 1958), p. 183.

50 Reis, "Negros e brancos," p. 92.

51 Moura, *Capoeira: A luta regional bahiana*, p. 25.

52 Jair Moura, "Bimba, mestre dos mestres no jogo da Capoeira," *A Tarde*, 15 Apr. 1967.

53 Reis, "Negros e brancos," pp. 117–121.

54 Evaldo Bogado Almeida and Marcos Jose Gomes Souza, *Associação de Capoeira Barravento* (Niterói: Marcos Andre F. de Almeida, 1995), p. 14.

55 In Reis, "Negros e brancos," p. 126.

56 His followers therefore claim that Pastinha has the exclusive right to the first capoeira school. For example, the Capoeirista José Luís Oliveira, known as Bola Sete, writes about it in his book *A Capoeira Angola na Bahia*, p. 28.

57 Vicente Ferreira Pastinha, *Esportivo de Capoeira Angola* (Salvador, 1963), pp. 5–6.

58 Jair Moura, "Mestre Bimba: A crônica da capoeiragem" (1991), manuscript, p. 23.

59 Amado, *Bahia de Todos os Santos*, p. 209.

60 Angelo Augusto Decanio, *A herança de Pastinha: A metafísica da capoeira* (Salvador: author's edition, 1996), pp. 15–16.

61 Fatima Goes, "Mestre Pastinha pede ajuda," *Tribuna da Bahia*, Salvador, 15 Sept. 1981.

62 Assunção, *Capoeira*, pp. 170–208.

63 Thompson, "Capoeira," p. 25; Moura, "Capoeirista de Antigamente não 'brincava em serviço'"; Tavarez, "Dança de guerra," p. 92; Carneiro, *Religiões negras*, p. 213.

64 Carneiro, *Religiões negras*, p. 213.

65 The Bakongo believe that the combined force of drawing symbolic signs on the ground and singing Ki-kongo words invoke God and the ancestors and will result in the appearance of the other world's power on that signed ground. Thompson, *Flash of the Spirit*, p. 110.

66 Abreu, *Os Capoeiras*, p. 5.

67 Querino, *A Bahia de outrora*, p. 75.

68 Redinha, *Album etnográfico*, p. 85; in Kay Shaffer, "O Berimbau de Barriga e seus toques," in *Monografias Folclóricas* (Rio de Janeiro: Ministério da Educação e Cultura, Secretaria de Assuntos Culturais, Fundação Nacional de Arte, Instituto Nacional de Folclore, 1977), p. 10.

69 Henrique Augusto Dias de Carvalho, *Etnografia e história tradicional dos povos da Lunda* (Lisbon, 1890); in Shaffer, "O berimbau de Barriga," p. 10.

70 Debret, *Viagem pitoresca*, vol. I, p. 253.

71 Chamberlain, *Vistas e costumes*; in Karasch, *Slave Life*, p. 236.

72 Graham, *Journal of a Voyage to Brazil*, p. 199; Wetherell, *Stray Notes from Bahia*, pp. 106–107.

73 Schlichthorst, *O Rio de Janeiro*, p. 141.

74 Ibid.

75 Tinhorão, *Os sons dos negros no Brasil: Cantos, danças, folguedos, origem*, São Paulo: Art Editôra, 1988, p. 26.

76 Kazadi Va Mukuna, "O Contato musical transatlântico: Contribuição banto a música popular brasileira" (Ph.D. dissertation, University of California, Los Angeles, 1978), p. 96.

77 Querino, *Bahia de outrora*, p. 75.

78 Wetherell, *Stray Notes from Bahia*, pp. 106–107.

79 Kubik, *Angolan Traits*, p. 35.

80 *Estado da Bahia*, 30 June 1936, BN.

81 Carneiro, *Dinâmica do folclore*, p. 52.

82 In Downey, "Incorporating Capoeira," p. 141.

83 Almeida, *Capoeira*, p. 72.

84 Interview, Salvador, Bahia, Oct. 1998.

85 Almeida, *Capoeira*, p. 139.

86 Ibid., p. 140.

87 Ibid.

88 Interview, Salvador, Bahia, Oct. 1998.

89 Pastinha, *Capoeira Angola*, p. 39.

90 In Abreu, *Bimba é Bamba*, p. 68.

91 Abreu, *Os Capoeiras*, p. 5.

92 Ibid., p. 5.

93 Folabo Ajayi, "Kinesics of Fight or Flight: An Analysis of Ijaye War Songs and Dance," in *War and Peace*, pp. 245–260; Philip D. Curtin, "Osifekunde of Ijebu," in *Africa Remembered: Narratives by West Africans from the Era of the Slave Trade*, edited by Philip D. Curtin (Madison: University of Wisconsin Press, 1968), p. 280; Robert Farris Thompson, "Dance and Culture," *African Forum* 2 (1966): 96.

94 It is interesting that even today the Yoruba conduct boxing matches/games when a contestant challenges the rival he wishes to fight. The challenge consists of raising the hand, and the answer is a similar gesture. Alyce Taylor Cheska, *Traditional Games and Dances in West African Nations* (Bloomington: Indiana University Press, 1987), p. 56.

95 Azevedo, *O Cortiço*, p. 127.

96 Interview with Fu-Kiau, Salvador, Bahia, Aug. 1999.

97 From a booklet titled *A música da Capoeira Angola* sold at the Capoeira Angola convention in Salvador, Bahia, Aug. 1999. The booklet is not paginated, and no other identifying features are provided.

98 For more details, see Downey, "Incorporating Capoeira," pp. 122–126; D'aquino, *Capoeira*, p. 125.

99 D'aquino, *Capoeira*, pp. 112–113.

100 Carneiro, *Dinâmica*, p. 52.

101 MacGaffey, *Religion and Society*, p. 44; Thompson, *Flash of the Spirit*, p. 109; Stuckey, *Slave Culture*, pp. 12, 36.

102 MacGaffey, *Religion and Society*, pp. 84–85, 123, 204.

103 Thompson, *Face of the Gods*, p. 57.

104 Tavarez, "Dança da guerra," p. 75.

105 Tierou, *Doople*, pp. 33–34.

106 For more details, see Erica Bourguignon, "Ritual Dissociation and Possession Belief in Caribbean Negro Religion," in *Afro-American Anthropology*, edited by Norman E. Witten and John F. Szwed (New York: Free Press, 1970), pp. 87–102.

107 Almeida, *Capoeira*, pp. 33–34.

108 Fryer, *Rhythms of Resistance*, p. 18.

109 Lowell, *Ring of Liberation*, p. 117.

110 Thompson, *Four Moments*, p. 43.

111 Ibid., p. 47; Thompson, *Flash of the Spirit*, p. 113.

112 Reis, "Negros e brancos," p. 210.

113 Interviews with Capoeiras at the Capoeira Angola conventions, Salvador, Bahia, Aug. and Sept., 1998, 1999.

114 Interviews with Israeli Capoeiras, members of the groups ABADA and Capoeira-ginga, Haifa and Tel Aviv, 1997.

115 Deborah Bertonoff, *Dance Towards the Earth* (Tel Aviv: Alityros Books, 1963), p. 125; Ivan Livingstone, "Dances for Gods in Benin," p. 203; Fryer, *Rhythms of Resistance*, p. 18,

116 Livingstone, "Dances for Gods in Benin," p. 197; interviews with professional Afri-

can dancers at the 7th International Benefit Dance Concert and Conference, New York, Apr. 1999.

Chapter 5

1 Jane Desmond, "Embodying Difference: Issues in Dance and Cultural Studies," in *Everynight Life: Culture and Dance in Latino/a America*, edited by Celeste Fraser and José Esteban Muñoz (Durham: Duke University Press, 1997), 33–34.
2 Downey, "Incorporating Capoeira"; Vieira and Assunção, "Mitos controvérsias e fatos"; Vieira, *O jogo da capoeira*.
3 Jocelito Teles dos Santos, "A Mixed-Race Nation: Afro-Brazilians and Cultural Policy in Bahia, 1970–1990," in *Afro-Brazilian Culture and Politics*, edited by Hendrik Kraay (New York: M. E. Sharpe, 1998), pp. 122–123.
4 Almeida, *Capoeira*, p. 64.
5 Carneiro, *Dinâmica do folclore*, p. 51; Rego, *Capoeira Angola*, p. 24; Almeida, *Capoeira*, pp. 15–6; Araújo, *A capoeira*, p. 11; Oliveira, *Capoeira Angola*, p. 22.
6 Pastinha, *Capoeira Angola*, p. 29.
7 Cascudo, *Folclore do Brasil*, p. 18.
8 Butler, *Freedoms Given*, p. 180.
9 Robert M. Levine, "The Social Impact of Afro-Brazilian Cult Religion," *Estudos Interdisciplinários de América Latina y el Caribe* 5:1 (1995): 45–47.
10 Downey, "Incorporating Capoeira," p. 15; Butler, *Freedoms Given*, pp. 88–128.
11 Pastinha, *Esportivo de Capoeira Angola*, p. 15.
12 R. K. Kent, "Palmares, an African State in Brazil," *Journal of African History* 7 (1965): 173.
13 Vieira, "Da vadiação a Capoeira Regional," p. 107.
14 In Downey, "Incorporating Capoeira," p. 267.
15 Decanio, *Falando*, p. 11.
16 *Guia do Capoeira*, pp. 4–15.
17 Burlamaqui, *Ginástica nacional (Capoeiragem)*, pp. 11–54.
18 Oliveira, *Capoeira*, p. 153.
19 Ibid.
20 Reis, "Negros e brancos," pp. 183–184.
21 Jacqui Malone, *Steppin' on the Blues: The Visible Rhythms of African American Dance* (Urbana: University of Illinois Press, 1996), pp. 12–13.
22 *A música da Capoeira Angola*.
23 Moura, "Mestre Bimba," pp. 72–74.
24 In Reis, "Negros e brancos," p. 103.
25 Thomas Lindley, *Narrativa de uma viagem ao Brasil* (São Paulo: Companhia Editôra Nacional, 1969), p. 179; G. W. Freyreiss, *Viagem ao interior do Brasil* (Belo Horizonte: Editôra Itatiaia, 1982), p. 65; Schlichthorst, *O Rio de Janeiro*, p. 142; Agassiz and Agassiz, *Viagem ao Brasil 1865–1866*, p. 45.

26 Ajayi, "Kinesics," p. 35; Henry Drewal and Margaret Thompson Drewal, *Gelede: Art and Female Power among the Yoruba* (Bloomington: Indiana University Press, 1983); Margaret Drewal Thompson, *Yoruba Ritual: Performance, Play, Agency* (Bloomington: Indiana University Press, 1992), pp. 15–19. Esther Dagan, "The Absurdity of Staging Dances in Gabon in 1966," in Dagan, ed., *The Spirits' Dance in Africa*, pp. 220–224.

27 Desmond, "Embodying Difference," p. 38.

28 In the mid-nineteenth century many councils banned black dances. The municipal council of Canavieiras (Bahia) prohibited all dances after 9:00 P.M. The council of Nazaré determined in March 1845 that all drumming and dances were forbidden except for those approved by the authorities. See Repertório de Fontes sobre a Escravidão, pp. 51, 62, 63, 65, 66, 71, 75.

29 J. R. Tinhorão, *História social da música popular brasileira* (São Paulo: Editôra 34, 1998), p. 73–74; Hermano Vianna, *The Mystery of Samba: Popular Music and National Identity in Brazil*, edited and translated by John Charles Chasteen (Chapel Hill: University of North Carolina Press, 1999).

30 Bertonoff, *Dance Towards the Earth*, p. 120.

31 Brenda Dixon Gottschild, *Digging the Africanist Presence in American Performance, Dance and Other Contexts* (London: Greenwood, 1996), p. 8.

32 Dagan, *The Spirits' Dance in Africa*, p. 103.

33 Gottschild, *Digging the Africanist Presence*, p. 10.

34 Pastinha, *Capoeira Angola*, p. 37.

35 Downey, "Incorporating Capoeira," pp. 184–185.

36 C. Barbieri, *Um jeito brasileiro de aprender a ser* (Brasília: DEFER, Centro de Informação sobre a Capoeira, 1993), p. 59.

37 Moura, "Mestre Bimba," pp. 13–14.

38 Downey, "Incorporating Capoeira," p. 196.

39 Ibid., p. 153.

40 Lowell, *Ring of Liberation*, p. 40.

41 D'aquino, *Capoeira*, p. 99.

42 Salvadori, *Capoeiras e malandros*, pp. 170–171.

43 Downey, "Incorporating Capoeira," p. 183.

44 Interview with Fu-Kiau, Salvador, 1997.

45 Drewal, *Yoruba Ritual*, p. 17.

46 Magalhães, *Orixás da Bahia*, p. 169.

47 Capoeira, *Capoeira*, p. 121.

48 Almeida, *Capoeira*, pp. 144–145.

49 Ibid., p. 150.

50 In Downey, "Incorporating Capoeira," p. 335.

51 Ibid., p. 487.

Agogô: Percussion instrument of African origin made of two metal or wood bells.

Angoleiros: Practitioners of the Capoeira Angola style.

Atabaque: A kind of drum used in Africa and African-Brazilian religious and entertainment events.

Au: Cartwheel, capoeira movement.

Axé: Divine energy in African-Brazilian religions.

Bamba: "Tough guy," a term to describe a professional capoeirista.

Bateria: Set of percussion instruments in a samba and capoeira orchestra.

Batuque: 1. Generic denomination for drumming. 2. Generic designation of Afro-Brazilian dances. 3. Early combat game in Bahia.

Batuqueiro: Practitioner of batuque.

Berimbau: Musical bow that originated in Central Africa; since the early twentieth century, a key instrument in capoeira.

Brincadeira: A children's game; used to describe the capoeira game.

Cabra: 1. A goat. 2. A dark-skinned mulatto.

Candomblé: African-Bahian religions.

Canto de Entrada: Capoeira song following the *ladainha*; consists of praises and exhortations sung by the lead singer and repeated by the chorus. Also known as *chula*.

Capoeira Angola: Twentieth-century term to denominate the traditional style of capoeira.

Capoeira Regional: A new capoeira style invented by Mestre Bimba that includes movements from other martial arts.

Capoeiragem: Synonym for the martial art of capoeira used in nineteenth-century Brazil.

Capoeirista: The contemporary term for a capoeira practitioner.

Caxixi: A kind of rattle made of straw filled with beans.

Chamada: "Call." A game within the capoeira game mainly practiced in Capoeira Angola.

Chula: *See* Canto de Entrada.

Contra Mestre: Intermediary stage between advanced student and mestre.

Corrido: Call and response song used during a capoeira game.

Efundula: Female puberty ceremonies in southern Angola that included combat between young men. Some maintain it resembles capoeira movements.

Ginga: Basic step of capoeira.

Gunga: The biggest and deepest berimbau used in the capoeira orchestra and the one that usually controls the rhythm.

Jogo: Play, game.

Kalunga: Kikongo word that had many meanings, including "great ocean" and the cosmological line between the world of the dead and the world of the living.

Ladainha: Literally, "litany." Introductory song in Capoeira Angola that usually contains a story or wisdom of life.

Maculelé: Stick fight dance. Adopted by capoeira groups as a form of exercise; part of capoeira performances.

Macumba: Generic term referring to African-Brazilian religions in Rio de Janeiro.

Malandragem: Trickery, cunning.

Malandro: Rogue, vagrant.

Malícia: Cunning, trickery. A key feature of capoeira philosophy.

Malta: A gang. A common term for capoeira gangs in nineteenth-century Rio de Janeiro.

Mandinga: 1. Name of tribes in West Africa. 2. Witchcraft, sorcery. 3. Spiritual power and cunning in capoeira.

Mandingueiro: 1. Sorcerer. 2. Someone who knows how to use mandinga in capoeira.

Médio: Berimbau with medium-size gourd.

Mestiço: A term traditionally applied to people of mixed European and indigenous Amerindian ancestries.

Mestre: The highest rank in capoeira; teacher who knows the capoeira world.

Moleque: Young boy. A derogatory term for unreliable young person, usually black.

Navalha: Razor. A popular weapon used by capoeiras in nineteenth- and early-twentieth-century Rio de Janeiro and Bahia.

N'golo: Zebra dance. The mythical Angolan origin of the Brazilian capoeira.

Orixá: Yoruba/Nagô deity in African-Brazilian religions.

Pandeiro: Tambourine used in the capoeira orchestra.

Pardo: Mulatto and by extension any person of mixed origin.

Patuá: Amulet.

Quilombo: Hiding place of fugitive slaves.

Rabo de Arraia: Literally, "sting ray's tail"; a well-known capoeira kick.

Rasteira: Sweeping, counterattack.

Reco-reco: Scraper made of wood mainly used in the Capoeira Angola orchestra.

Roda de capoeira: Circle of participants where the capoeira game takes place.

Samba: Dance and music of Central African origin. Became the national dance of Brazil during carnival.

Senzala: Slave quarters.

Terreiro: Public place where African-Brazilian religions are practiced.

Toque: Rhythmic pattern in capoeira.

Umbanda: Syncretic religion derived from African-Brazilian, Catholic, and other traditions and beliefs.

Vadiação: Vagrancy. In Bahia a synonym for capoeira game.

Vadiar: Literally, "to be idle." Synonym for playing capoeira.

Valentão: Tough guy.

Viola: 1. A guitar. 2. A violin. 3. The berimbau with the smallest gourd, thus making the highest sound.

Volta do mundo: Literally, "turn around the world." Today it is the period during which Capoeiras rest while walking around in the circle.

Primary Sources

Manuscripts

Arquivo Municipal de Salvador (AMS)

    Repertório de Fontes sobre a Escravidão: Câmara Municipal Carinhanha FCM liv.
    119.6 fl. 11v. 06, 22 Apr. 1837. *Câmara Municipal Salvador* FCM liv. 119.5 fl. 38, 70
    25 Feb. 1831. *Câmara Municipal Sento Sé* FCM liv. 119.6 fl. 17, 17, 22 Apr. 1837.

Arquivo Nacional, Rio de Janeiro (AN)

    Códice 403, Relações de presos feitos pela polícia, 1812–1826. 3 vols.

    Decretos do Governo Provisório, Imprensa Nacional, Rio de Janeiro, 1890, pp.
    2734–2735.

    Ofícios do Chefe de Polícia, Série Justiça: IJ 6 165 19, July 1831; IJ 6 166, 19 July 1831,
    7 June 1833, 26 June 1833, 18 Nov. 1833; IJ 6 17, 8 Apr. 1835; IJ 6 172, 26 Jan. 1836;
    IJ 6 173, 3 Dec. 1836; IJ 6 174, 5 Jan. 1837; IJ 6 212, 14 June 1849; IJ 6 212, 16 June
    1849; IJ 6 212, 13 Nov. 1849; IJ 6 215, 9 Oct. 1852; IJ 6 216, 15 Oct. 1853; IJ 6 217,
    20 Jan. 1854; IJ 6 484, 19 Jan. 1859; IJ 6 19, 4 Sept. 1869.

    Processo Crime: 7C. 115 1893,7C. 358 1901, T8 809 1901, T7 0242 1902, T8 1022 1902,
    T8 1551 1904, T8. 1904, 7C 932 1905, MW. 586 1906, 7G 734 1907, T7 671 1907,
    MW. 1123 1907, MW 2059 1908, T8 3223 1908, T8 3878 1911, 72.382 1912, *Pretória*
    Criminal 71–217 1915.

    Relatório do Chefe de Polícia da Corte, 1872, pp. 22–23. Annex to Relatório do
    Ministério de Justiça, 1870, 1872, 1875.

Arquivo Público do Estado da Bahia (APEB)

    Coleção Cronológica dos Leis, Decretos, Resoluções de Consulta Provisões etc. do
    Império do Brasil 1837, 413—Decisão 31 Oct. 1821, 414—Decisão 5 Oct. 1821.

    Coleção das Decisões do Governo do Império do Brasil, 1886, Decisão 22 May 1824,
    No. 122 Justiça 28 May 1824, No. 182, Justiça 30 Aug. 1824, No. 193 Justiça 13
    Sept. 1824, No. 215 Justiça 9 Oct. 1824, No. 205 Justiça 27 July 1831, No. 148
    Decisão 17 Apr. 1834.

    Coleção das Decisões do Governo do Império do Brasil. 1887. Decisão 4 Jan. 1822,
    Decisão 6 Jan. 1822.

    Documentação Jurídica sobre o negro no Brasil (0438). 1808–1888. *Índice analítico.*

Biblioteca Nacional, Rio de Janeiro (BN)

    Anais da Biblioteca Nacional do Rio de Janeiro 37, 1918.

    Coleção de Leis do Império do Brasil 6 Jan. 1822.

    Brasil Policial, Oct. 1951.

    A Cidade do Rio, 14 July 1888, 24 July 1888, 10 Dec. 1889.

    Correio da Tarde (Rio de Janeiro), 3 Nov. 1849.

Correio Mercantil (Rio de Janeiro), 14 Dec. 1855.

Diário de Notícias, 13 July 1888, 13 Dec. 1889, 19 Jan. 1890, 9 Apr. 1890.

Diário do Rio de Janeiro, 24 Dec. 1826, 17 June 1828, 29 Jan. 1849, 7 July 1949, 3
    Nov. 1849, 17 Jan. 1872, 17 Feb. 1872, 5 Mar. 1872, 11 Mar. 1872, 27 July 1872, 9
    Mar. 1874,

Estado da Bahia, 9 June 1936, 30 June 1936.

Folha Nova, 5 Jan. 1885.

Gazeta de Notícias, 4 Jan. 1878, 26 Feb. 1878, 12 Dec. 1889.

Jornal do Commercio, 22 Apr. 1870, 09 Jan. 1872, 1 Mar. 1874, 10 Mar. 1874, 28 Jan.
    1878, 29 Jan. 1878, 28 Nov. 1878, 29 Nov. 1878.

Kosmos, Mar., no. 3, 1906.

Novidades, 15 July 1889.

O Mosquito, 26 Aug. 1871.

A Reforma 25 Aug. 1872, 10 Sept. 1872.

A República, 6 Aug. 1872, 3 Sept. 1872, 2 Mar. 1873.

Revista Ilustrada, 3 Mar. 1888.

Vida Policial, 25, Mar. 1925, 31 Mar. 1925, 23 Jan. 1926.

Published Books

Abreu, Frederico José. *"Bimba é Bamba": A capoeira no Ringue.* Bahia: P&A Gráfica e
    Editôra, 1999.

Agassis, Luíz, and Elizabeth Cary Agassis. *Viagem ao Brasil 1865–1866.* Belo
    Horizonte: Editôra Itaiaia, 1975.

Allain, Emile. *Rio de Janeiro, quelques donnes sur la capital et sur l'administration du
    Bresil.* Paris: L. Frinzine; Rio de Janeiro: Lachaud, 1886.

Almeida, Manuel Antônio de. *Memórias de um sargento de milícias.* São Paulo:
    Technoprint, 1945.

Ave-Lallemant, Robert. *Viagem pelo norte do Brasil no ano de 1859.* Rio de Janeiro:
    Instituto Nacional do Livro, Ministério da Educação e Cultura, 1961.

Azevedo, Aluízio. *O Cortiço.* Rio de Janeiro: Technoprint, 1890.

Bosman, William. *New and Accurate Description of the Coast of Guinea.* London:
    J. Knapton, 1705.

Burlamaqui, Annibal. *Ginástica Nacional (Capoeiragem).* Rio de Janeiro: Obra
    Inédita, 1928.

Coelho, Neto. *O Bazar.* Porto: Livraria Chardon de Lello e Irmãos, 1928.

Dapper, Olfert. *Description of Benin (1668).* Madison: University of Wisconsin, 1998.

Debret, Jean-Baptiste. *Viajem pitoresca e histórica ao Brasil.* São Paulo: Livraria
    Martins Editôra, 1954.

Dent, Hasting Charles. *A Year in Brazil with Notes on the Abolition of Slavery, the
    Finances of the Empire, Religion, Meteorology, Natural History.* London: K. Paul,
    Trench and Company, 1886.

D'Evreux, Yves. *Viagem ao norte do Brasil*. Rio de Janeiro: Freitas Bastos, Livraria Leite Ribeiro, 1929.

Documentos acerca do tráfico da escravatura. Lisbon, 1840.

Freireyss, G. W. *Viagem ao interior do Brasil*. Belo Horizonte: Editôra Itatiaia, 1982.

Graham, Maria Dundam. *Journal of a Voyage to Brazil and Residence there during part of the years 1821, 1822, 1823*. New York: Praeger, 1969.

Guia do Capoeira ou ginástica brasileira. Rio de Janeiro, 1907.

Josephus, Flavius. *The Jewish War*. Jerusalem: Mass, 1940.

Kidder, Daniel Parrish. *Reminiscências de viagem e permanência no Brasil*. São Paulo: Livraria Martins, 1951.

Koseritz, Carl von. *Imagens do Brasil*. São Paulo: Livraria Martins, 1943.

Koster, Henry. *Viagens ao Nordeste do Brasil*. São Paulo: Companhia Editôra Nacional, 1942.

Lindley, Thomas. *Narrativa de uma viagem ao Brasil*. São Paulo: Companhia Editôra Nacional, 1969.

Luccock, John. *Notas sobre o Rio de Janeiro e partes meridionais do Brasil tomadas durante uma estada de dez anos nesse país, de 1808 a 1818*. São Paulo: Livraria Martins, 1942.

Morley, Helena. *The Diary of Helena Morley*. Translated by Elisabeth Bishop. New York: Ecco Press, 1977.

Pigafetta, Filippo. *Report of the Kingdom of Congo*. London: Frank Cass, 1970.

Ribeyrolles, Charles. *Brasil pitoresco: História, descrições, viagens, colonização, instituições*. Translated by Gastão Penalva. São Paulo: Editôra da Universidade de São Paulo, 1941.

Robertson, John. *Letters on Paraguay*. New York: AMS Press, 1970.

Rugendas, João Maurício. *Viagem pitoresca através do Brasil*. São Paulo: Livraria Martins Editôra, 1954.

Schlichthorst, Carl. *O Rio de Janeiro como é 1824–1826*. Translated by Emmy Dodt and Gustavo Barrosso. Rio de Janeiro: Editôra Getúlio Costa, 1943.

Spix, Johann B. von, and Carl Friedrich P. von Martius. *Viagem pelo Brasil*. Translated by Lucia Furquim Lahmeyer. Rio de Janeiro: Imprensa Nacional, 1938.

Wetherell, James. *Stray Notes from Bahia*. Liverpool: Webb and Hunt, 1860.

Secondary Sources

Abreu, Plácido de. *Os Capoeiras*. Rio de Janeiro: Tip. Seraphim Alves de Britto, 1886.

Adefila, J. A., and S. M. Opeola. "Supernatural and Herbal Weapons in 19th-Century Yoruba Warfare." In *War and Peace in Yorubaland, 1793–1893*, edited by Adeagbo Akinjogbin. Ibadan: Johnmof Printers, 1998.

Agier, Michel. *Racism, Culture, and Black Identity in Brazil*. Oxford: Elsevier Science, 1995.

Ajayi, Folabo. "Kinesics of Fight or Flight: An Analysis of Ijaye War Songs and Dance." In *War and Peace in Yorubaland 1793–1893*, edited by Adeagbo Akinjogbin. Ibadan: Johnmof Printers, 1998.

Algranti, Leila Mezan. "Os ofícios urbanos e os escravos ao ganho no Rio de Janeiro colonial (1808–1822)." In *História econômica do período colonial*, edited by Tama Szmrecsanyi. São Paulo: Editôra Hucitec, 1996.

———. *O feitor ausente: Estudos sobre a escravidão urbana no Rio de Janeiro 1808–1822*. Petrópolis: Vozes, 1988.

———. "Slave Crimes: The Use of Police Power to Control the Slave Population of Rio de Janeiro." *Luso-Brazilian Review* 25:1 (1988): 26–48.

Almeida, Bira (Mestre Acordeon). *Capoeira: A Brazilian Art Form*. Berkeley: North Atlantic Books, 1986.

Almeida, Evaldo Bogado, and Marcos Jose Gomes Souza Silva. *Associação de Capoeira Barravento*. Niterói: Marcos Andre F. de Almeida, 1995.

Almeida, Raimundo Cesar Alves de (Mestre Itapoan). *Bibliografia crítica da Capoeira*. Brasilia: DEFER Centro de Informação e Documentação sobre a Capoeira, 1993.

Almeida, Renato. "O brinquedo da capoeira." *Revista do Arquivo Municipal* 88 (1942): 155–161.

———. "O folclore no Brasil." *Revista Brasileira de Folclore* 8.21 (1968): 105–118.

Amado, Jorge. *Bahia de Todos os Santos: Guia das ruas e dos mistérios da cidade do Salvador*. São Paulo: Livraria Martins Editôra, 1958.

———. *Jubiaba*. São Paulo: Livraria Martins Editôra, 1965.

Araújo, Alceu Maynard. *Folclore nacional*. São Paulo: Edições Melhoramentos, 1964.

Araújo, Elísio de. *Estudos históricos sobre a polícia da capital federal, 1808–1831*. Rio de Janeiro: Tip. Leuzinger, 1898.

Araújo, Paulo Coelho de. "A Capoeira: A transformação de uma atividade guerreira numa atividade lúdica." Ph.D. dissertation, Universidade de Porto, Porto, 1995.

Areias, Almir das. *O que é capoeira*. São Paulo: Brasiliense, 1983.

Assunção, Mathias Röhring. *Capoeira: The History of an Afro-Brazilian Martial Art*. London: Routledge, Taylor & Francis Group, 2005.

Barbieri, C. *Um jeito brasileiro de aprender a ser*. Brasília: DEFER, Centro de Informação e Documentação sobre a Capoeira, 1993.

Barreto, Mello Filho, and Hermeto Lima. Pref. by Filinto Muller. *História da Polícia do Rio de Janeiro: Aspectos da cidade e da vida carioca*. Rio de Janeiro: Editôra A Noite, 1944.

Bastide, Roger. *The African Religions of Brazil: Toward a Sociology of the Interpenetration of Civilizations*. Baltimore: Johns Hopkins University Press, 1978.

Beaurepaire-Rohan, Visconde de. "Capoeira." In *Dicionário de vocábulos brasileiros*. Salvador: Editôra Progresso, 1956.

Beckles, Hilary McD. "War Dances: Slave Leisure and Anti-Slavery in the West Indies." Paper presented at the conference "More than Cool Reason: Black

Responses to Enslavement, Exile and Resettlement," University of Haifa, Haifa, 1998.

Beattie, M. Peter. *The Tribute of Blood: Army, Honor, Race and Nation in Brazil, 1864–1945*. London: Duke University Press, 2001.

Bertonoff, Deborah. *Dance Towards the Earth*. Tel Aviv: Alityros Books, 1963.

Bezerra, Silvia Martha Castello Branco. *Repertório de Fontes sobre a escravidão existente no Arquivo Municipal de Salvador*. Salvador: Instituto de Estudos Brasileiros, 1988.

Bhabha, Homi K. *The Location of Culture*. London: Routledge, 1994.

Borges, Dain Edward. *The Family in Bahia, Brazil, 1870–1945*. Stanford: Stanford University Press, 1992.

Bourguignon, Erica. "Ritual Dissociation and Possession Belief in Caribbean Negro Religion." In *Afro-American Anthropology*, edited by Norman E. Witten and John F. Szwed. New York: Free Press, 1970.

Boxer, Charles Ralph. *The Golden Age of Brazil, 1695–1750*. Berkeley: University of California Press, 1969.

———. *The Portuguese Seaborne Empire 1415–1825*. London: Hutchinson, 1969.

———. *Race Relations in the Portuguese Colonial Empire, 1415–1825*. Westport: Greenwood Press, 1985.

Brasil, Hebe Machado. *A música na cidade do Salvador 1549–1900*. Salvador: Publicação da Prefeitura Municipal do Salvador, 1969.

Bretas, Marcos Luiz. "Navalhas e Capoeiras—Uma outra queda." *Ciência Hoje* 19.59 (1989): 56–64.

———. "A queda do império da Navalha e da Rasteira: A república e os Capoeiras." *Estudos Afro-Asiáticos* 20 (1991): 239–256.

Brown, Diana. *Umbanda: Religion and Politics in Urban Brazil*. Michigan: UMI Research Press, 1985.

Browning, Barbara. "Headspin: Capoeira's Ironic Inversion." In *Everynight Life: Culture and Dance in Latin/o America*, edited by Celeste Fraser and Jose Esteban Munoz. Durham: Duke University Press, 1997.

Butler, D. Kim. *Freedoms Given, Freedoms Won*. New Brunswick: Rutgers University Press, 1998.

Camara, M. E. "Afro-American Religions Syncretism in Brazil and the United States: A Weberian Perspective." *Sociological Analysis* 48 (1987): 299–318.

Canevacci, Massimo. *Sincretismos: Uma exploração das hibridações culturais*. São Paulo: Livros Studio Nobel, 1996.

"Capoeira da Bahia, 4 séculos de história." *Gazeta Mercantil* (São Paulo), 12 May 1972.

Capoeira, Nestor. *Capoeira: Os fundamentos da malícia*. Rio de Janeiro: Editôra Record, 1997.

Carneiro, Edison. *Capoeira*. Rio de Janeiro: Ministério da Educação e Cultura, Instituto Nacional de Livro, 1977.

———. *Dinâmica do folclore*. Rio de Janeiro: Of. Gráfica do Jornal do Brasil, 1965.

————. *Religiões negras: Negros bantos*. Rio de Janeiro: Civilização Brasileira, 1991.

————. *A sabedoria popular*. Rio de Janeiro: Ministério da Educação e Cultura, Instituto Nacional de Livro, 1957.

Carvalho, Henrique Augusto Dias de. *Etnografia e história tradicional dos povos da Lunda*. Lisbon, 1890.

Carvalho, José Murilho de. *Os bestializados: O Rio de Janeiro e a república que não foi*. São Paulo: Companhia das Letras, 1991.

————. *A formação das almas: O imaginário da república no Brasil*. São Paulo: Companhia das Letra, 1990.

————. *Teatro de sombras*. São Paulo: Hucitec, 1988.

Carybé, Hector Bernabó. *Iconografia dos Deuses africanos no Candomblé da Bahia*. São Paulo: Raízes, 1980.

————. *As sete portas da Bahia*. Rio de Janeiro: Editôra Record, 1976.

Cascudo, Luís da Câmara. *Dicionário do folclore*. Belo Horizonte: Itatiaia, 1984.

————. *Folclore do Brasil*. São Paulo: Fundo de Cultura, 1967.

Castro, Jeanne Berrance de. *A milícia cidadã: A Guarda Nacional de 1831 a 1850*. São Paulo: Companhia Editôra Nacional, 1977.

Chalhoub, Sidney. "Slaves, Freedman and Politics of Freedom in Brazil: The Experience of Blacks in the City of Rio." *Slavery and Abolition* 10.3 (1991): 64–84.

————. *Visões de liberdade: Uma história das duas últimas decadas da escravidão na corte*. São Paulo: Companhia das Letras, 1990.

Chediak, Adriano. "Capoeira: Da senzala para o campus." *Revista Capoeira* 1.1 (1998): 4–12.

Cheska, Alyce Taylor. *Traditional Games and Dances in West African Nations*. Bloomington: Indiana University Press, 1987.

Chevalier, Jean, and Alain Gheerbrant. *A Dictionary of Symbols*. Translated by John Buchanan-Brown. Oxford: Blackwell, 1994.

Correia, Viriato. *Casa de Belchior*. Rio de Janeiro: Ed. Civilização Brasileira, 1936.

Costa, Emilia Viotti. *The Brazilian Empire: Myth and Histories*. Chicago: University of Chicago Press, 1985.

Costa, Lamaratine Pereira de. *Capoeira sem mestre*. Rio de Janeiro: Edições de Ouro, 1962.

Costa, Michael. *The Pentagram, Solomon's Seal, and the Star of David*. Tel Aviv: Hakibutz Hameuchad, Sifriat Poalim, 1990.

Costa e Silva, Alberto da. "Buying and Selling Korans in Nineteenth-Century Rio de Janeiro." Paper presented at the conference "Rethinking the African Diaspora: The Making of a Black Atlantic World," Emory University, Atlanta, 1998.

Cruls, Gastão. *A aparência do Rio de Janeiro*. Rio de Janeiro: Livraria José Olympio Editôra, 1965.

Curtin, Philip D. *Africa Remembered: Narratives by West Africans from the Era of the Slave Trade*. Madison: University of Wisconsin Press, 1968.

————. *The Atlantic Slave Trade*. Madison: University of Wisconsin Press, 1969.

Dagan, Esther. "The Absurdity of Staging Dances in Gabon in 1966." In *The Spirits' Dance in Africa*, edited by Esther Dagan. Westmount: Galerie Amrad African Arts Publications, 1997.

———. "Origin and Meaning of Dance's Essential Body Position and Movements." In *The Spirits' Dance in Africa*, edited by Esther Dagan. Westmount: Galerie Amrad African Arts Publications, 1997.

D'aquino, Iria. "Capoeira: Strategies for Status, Power and Identity." Ph.D. dissertation, University of Illinois at Urbana-Champaign, 1983.

———. *Description de l'Afrique*. Paris: Fondation Dapper, 1990.

D'Avila, C. "Com proteção de Xango eles fazem maculelê e capoeira." *A Tarde*, 10 July 1969.

Davis, David Brion. *Slavery and Human Progress*. New York: Oxford University Press, 1984.

Decanio, Angelo Augusto. *Falando em capoeira*. Salvador: author's edition, 1996.

———. *A herança do Mestre Bimba: Lógica e filosofia africanas da capoeira*. Salvador: author's edition, 1996.

———. *A herança de Pastinha: A metafísica da capoeira*. Salvador: author's edition, 1996.

Desch-Obi, T. J. "Engolo: Combat Traditions in African and African Diaspora History." Ph.D. dissertation, University of California, Los Angeles, 2000.

Desmond, Jane. "Embodying Difference: Issues in Dance and Cultural Studies." In *Everynight Life: Culture and Dance in Latin/o America*, edited by Celeste Fraser and José Esteban Muñoz. Durham: Duke University Press, 1997.

Dias, Luis Sergio. "Quem tem medo da capoeira? 1890–1904." Master's thesis, Universidade Federal do Rio de Janeiro, 1993.

———. "A turma da lira: A sobrevivência negra no Rio de Janeiro pos-abolicionista." Manuscript, Rio de Janeiro, 1995.

Dias, Luis Sergio, and Paulo Knauss Mendonça. *Capoeira: Vida e morte no Rio de Janeiro*. Rio de Janeiro: Museu Histórico da Cidade do Rio de Janeiro, Projeto Gonzaga de Sá, 1986.

Dirks, R. "Slaves' Holiday." *Natural History* 84.10 (1975): 82–90.

Donaldson, G. A. "A Window in Slave Culture: Dances at Congo Square in New Orleans, 1800–1862." *Journal of Negro History* 69.2 (1984): 63–72.

Dossar, Kenneth Michael. "Dancing between Two Worlds: An Aesthetic Analysis of Capoeira Angola." Ph.D. dissertation, Temple University, 1994.

Downey, Gregory John. "Incorporating Capoeira: Phenomenology of a Movement Discipline." Ph.D dissertation, University of Chicago, 1998.

Drewal, Henry J., and Margaret Thompson Drewal. *Gelede: Art and Female Power among the Yoruba*. Bloomington: Indiana University Press, 1983.

Drewal, Margaret Thompson. *Yoruba Ritual: Performance, Play, Agency*. Bloomington: Indiana University Press, 1992.

Edmundo, Luíz. *O Rio de Janeiro do meu tempo*. Rio de Janeiro: Imprensa Nacional, 1938.

———. *O Rio de Janeiro no tempo dos vice-reis*. Rio de Janeiro: Imprensa Nacional, 1932.

Elmir, C. P. "O escravo urbano na visão de um viajante." *Estudos Ibero-Americanos* 16 (1990): 117–136.

Eltis, David. "The Ninteenth-Century Transatlantic Slave Trade." *Hispanic American Historical Review* 67.1 (1987): 109–138.

Federação de Capoeira Desportiva do Estado do Rio de Janeiro. *Exame para obtenção do título de contra-mestre e mestre de capoeira*. Rio de Janeiro, 1996.

Ferreira, V. "Legislação portuguesa relativa ao Brasil." *Revista do Instituto Histórico Geográfico Brasileiro* 159 (1929): 199–240.

Fonseca, Eduardo. *Dicionário antológico da cultura Afro-Brasileira: Portuguese-Yoruba-Nago-Angola-Gege*. Florianópolis: Yorubana do Brasil Sociedade Editôra Didática Cultura, 1995.

Fraga, Filho Walter. *Mendigos, moleques e vadios na Bahia do século XIX*. São Paulo: Editôra Hucitec, 1996.

Freyre, Gilberto. *The Mansions and the Shanties*. Translated by Harriet Deonis. New York: Knopf, 1968.

———. *The Masters and the Slaves*. Translated by Samuel Putman. New York: Knopf, 1970.

———. *Order and Progress*. Edited and translated by Rod W. Horton. New York: Knopf, 1970.

Fryer, Peter. *Rhythms of Resistance: African Musical Heritage in Brazil*. London: Pluto, 2000.

Fu-Kiau, Kia Bunseki. "African Diasporadical Languages: Unspoken, but Alive and Powerful." Paper presented at the 31st Annual Conference on African Linguistics, Boston University, 4 Mar. 2000.

Galvão, Flavio A. P. "Reabilitação da Capoeira." *O Estado de São Paulo*, 2 Nov. 1956, p. 8.

Geertz, Clifford. *The Interpretation of Cultures*. [In Hebrew] Translated by Joash Meisler. Jerusalem: Keter, 1990.

Ghiberti, A. "Ésporte ou cultura?" *Capoeira: A Arte Marcial do Brasil* 1 (1983): 65.

Goes, Fatima. "Mestre Pastinha pede ajuda." *Tribuna da Bahia* (Salvador), 15 Sept. 1981.

Gottschild, Brenda Dixon. *Digging the Africanist Presence in American Performance, Dance and Other Contexts*. London: Greenwood, 1996.

Graham, Richard. *Britain and the Onset of Modernization in Brazil 1850–1914*. New York: Cambridge University Press, 1968.

———. "Causes for the Abolition of Negro Slavery in Brazil: An Interpretive Essay." *Hispanic American Historical Review* 46.2 (1966): 123–137.

Graham, S. L. "Documenting Slavery." *Luso-Brazilian Review* 21.2 (1984): 95–99.

Hahner, June E. *Poverty and Politics: The Urban Poor in Brazil, 1870–1920.* Albuquerque: University of New Mexico Press, 1986.

Hamilton, R. G. "The Present State of African Cults in Bahia." *Journal of Social History* 3 (1970): 357–373.

Harding, Rachel Elizabeth. "Candomblé and the Alternative Space of Black Being in Nineteenth-Century Bahia." Ph.D. dissertation, Brown University, 1997.

Hasenbalg, Carlos. "Entre o mito e os fatos: Racismo e relações raciais no Brasil." Edited by Marcos Chor Maio and Ricardo Ventura Santos. *Raça, Ciência e Sociedade.* Rio de Janeiro: Editôra Fiocruz, 1998.

Hazard-Gordon, Katrina. *Jookin': The Rise of Social Dance Formations in African-American Culture.* Philadelphia: Temple University Press, 1990.

Hess, David J. *The Brazilian Puzzle.* New York: Columbia University Press, 1995.

Hilton, Anne. *The Kingdom of Kongo.* New York: Oxford University Press, 1985.

Holloway, Thomas. "A Healthy Terror: Police Repression of Capoeiras in Nineteenth Century, Rio de Janeiro." *Hispanic American Historical Review* 69.4 (1989): 637–676.

Huet, Michel. *The Dance, Art and Ritual of Africa.* New York: Pantheon Books, 1978.

———. *The Dances of Africa.* New York: Harry N. Abrams, 1996.

Huggins, N. I. "The Deforming Mirror of Truth: Slavery and the Master Narrative of American History." *Radical History Review* 49 (1991): 25–48.

Jacobson-Widding, Anita. *Red-White-Black as a Mode of Thought.* Uppsala: Stokholn, Almquist and Wikseu, 1979.

Kaeppler, A. L. "Memory and Knowledge in the Production of Dance." In *Images of Memory*, edited by Sussane Kuchler and Walter Melion. Washington, D.C.: Smithsonian Institution Press, 1991.

Karasch, Mary C. *Slave Life in Rio de Janeiro, 1808–1850*, Princeton: Princeton University Press, 1987.

Kebede, Ashenafi. *Roots of Black Music: The Vocal, Instrumental, and Dance Heritage of Africa and Black America.* Trenton: Africa World Press, 1995.

Kent, R. K. "Palmares: An African State in Brazil." *Journal of African History* 7 (1965): 161–175.

Kidder, Daniel Parrish, and James Cooley Fletcher. *O Brasil e os brasileiros.* São Paulo: Companhia Editôra Nacional, 1941.

Kiddy, Elizabeth W. "Who Is the King of Congo?" In *Central Africans and Cultural Transformations in the American Diaspora*, edited by Linda Heywood, pp. 153–182. New York: Cambridge University Press, 2002.

Klein, Herbert. *African Slavery in Latin America and the Caribbean.* New York: Oxford University Press, 1986.

———. *The Atlantic Slave Trade.* Cambridge: Cambridge University Press, 1999.

———. "The Trade in African Slaves to Rio de Janeiro, 1795–1811: Estimates of Mortality and Patterns of Voyages." *Journal of African History* 10:4 (1969): 540.

Krich, John. *Why Is This People Dancing? A One-Man Samba to the Beat of Brazil.* New York: Simon and Schuster, 1993.

Kubik, Gerhard. *Angolan Traits in Black Music, Games, and Dances of Brazil: A Study of African Cultural Extensions Overseas.* Lisbon: Centro de Estudos de Antropologia Cultural, 1979.

————. "Oral Notation of some West and Central African Time-Line Patterns." *Review of Ethnology* 3 (22): 169–176.

Law, Robin. "European Sources: Regional Focus versus Archival Dispersal." Paper presented at the conference "Identifying Enslaved Africans: The 'Nigerian' Hinterland and the African Diaspora," York University, Toronto, 1997.

Levine, Robert M. *Brazil, 1822–1930.* New York: Garland, 1983.

————. "The Social Impact of Afro-Brazilian Cult Religion." *Estudos Interdisciplinários de América Latina y el Caribe* 5.1 (1995): 37–57.

Levine, Robert M., and José Carlos Sebe bom Meihy. *The Life and Death of Carolina Maria de Jesus.* Albuquerque: University of New Mexico Press, 1995.

Lima, Oliveira. *D. João VI no Brasil.* Rio de Janeiro: Topbooks, 1996.

Lima, Tânia. *Sincretizmo religioso: O ritual afro.* Recife: Editôra Massangana, 1996.

Livingstone, Ivan. "Dances for Gods in Benin." In *The Spirits' Dance in Africa*, edited by Esther Dagan. Westmount: Galerie Amrad African Arts, 1997.

Lopes, Andre Luiz Llace. "A Mulher na Capoeira." *Jornal dos Sports*, 4 Feb. 1996.

Lovejoy, Paul E. "Identifying Enslaved Africans: Methodological and Conceptual Considerations in Studying the African Diaspora." Paper presented at the conference "Identifying Enslaved Africans: The 'Nigerian' Hinterland and the African Diaspora," York University, Toronto, 1997.

————. "The Volume of the Atlantic Slave Trade." *Journal of African History* 23 (1982): 473–501.

Lowell, Lewis. *Ring of Liberation: Deceptive Discourse in Brazilian Capoeira.* Chicago: University of Chicago Press, 1992.

MacGaffey, Wyatt. *Religion and Society in Central Africa.* Chicago: University of Chicago Press, 1986.

Magalhães, Elyette Guimares de. *Orixás da Bahia.* Salvador: Secretaria da Cultural e Turismo, 2003.

Malone, Jacqui. *Steppin' on the Blues: The Visible Rhythms of African American Dance.* Urbana: University of Illinois Press, 1996.

Martínez-Echazabal, Lourdes. "O culturalismo dos anos 30 no Brasil e na América Latina: Deslocamento retórico ou mudança conceitual?" In *Raça, ciência e sociedade*, edited by Marcos Chor Maio and Ricardo Ventura Santos. Rio de Janeiro: Editôra Fiocruz, 1998.

Matta, Roberto da. *Carnival, Rogues and Heroes: An Interpretation of the Brazilian Dilemma.* Notre Dame: University of Notre Dame Press, 1991.

McGowan, Chris. *The Brazilian Sound: Samba, Bossa Nova and the Popular Music of Brazil.* New York: Billboard Books, 1991.

McLaren, Peter. "White Terror and Oppositional Agency: Towards a Critical Multiculturalism." In *Multicultural Education, Critical Pedagogy and the Politics of Difference*, edited by Christine E. Sleeter and Peter L. McLaren. New York: State University of New York Press, 1995.

Meireles, Cecília. *Batuque, samba e macumba: Estudos de gesto e de ritmo*. Lisbon: Mundo Portuguese, 1935.

Miller, Joseph C. *Way of Death*. Madison: University of Wisconsin Press, 1988.

Milstein, Rachel. *Solomon's Seal*. Jerusalem: David Tower Museum, 1996.

Moraes Filho, Mello. *Festas e tradições populares do Brasil*. São Paulo: Livraria Itatiaia Editôra, 1979.

Morais, Evaristo de. *Da monarquia para a república (1870–1889)*. Brasília: Editôra Universidade de Brasília, 1985.

Moura, Jair. "Bimba, a lendária figura do mestre na luta/dança capoeira." *Tribuna da Bahia*, 5 Mar. 1975.

——. "Bimba, mestre dos mestres no jogo da capoeira." *A Tarde*, 15 Apr. 1967.

——. *Capoeira: A luta regional baiana*. Salvador: Cadernos de Cultura, 1979.

——. *Capoeiragem, arte e malandragem*. Salvador: Cadernos de Cultura, 1980.

——. "Capoeirista de Antigamente não 'brincava em serviço.'" *A Tarde*, 10 July 1971.

——. "Evolução, apogeu e declínio da capoeiragem no Rio de Janeiro." *Caderno RioArte* 1.3 (1985): 86–93.

——. "O Mestiço e a capoeiragem carioca." *Revista Capoeira*, June–Aug. 1998, pp. 4–5.

——. "Mestre Bimba: A crônica da capoeiragem." Manuscript.

Mullin, Michael. *Africa in America: Slave Acculturation and Resistance in the American South and the British Caribbean, 1736–1831*. Urbana: University of Illinois Press, 1992.

Mukuna, Kazadi Va. "O contato musical transatlântico: Contribuição banto a música popular brasileira." Ph.D. dissertation, University of California, Los Angeles, 1978.

Mutti, Maria, *Maculelê*. Salvador: Prefeirtura Municipal, 1978.

Ojo, Jerome O. *Yoruba Customs from Ondo*. Wein: Elisabeth Stiglmayr, 1976.

Oliveira, Agenor Lopes de. *Toponímia carioca*. Rio de Janeiro: Prefeitura do Distrito Federal, 1935.

Oliveira, José Luíz (Mestre Bola Sete). *Capoeira Angola na Bahia*. Salvador: Empresa Gráfica da Bahia, 1989.

Oliveira, Maria Inês Cortes de. "Quem eram os 'negros da Guiné'? Sobre a origem dos africanos na Bahia." Paper presented at the conference "Identifying Enslaved Africans: The 'Nigerian' Hinterland and the African Diaspora," York University, Toronto, 1997.

Olutoye, O. and J. A. Olapade. "Implements and Tactics of War among the Yoruba." In *War and Peace in Yorubaland, 1793–1893*, edited by Adeagbo Akinjogbin. Ibadan: Heinemann Educational Books, 1998.

Pastinha, Vicente Ferreira. *Capoeira Angola*. Salvador: Escola Gráfica N.S. de Loreto, 1964.

———. *Centro Esportivo de Capoeira Angola*. Salvador, 1965.

———. *Esportivo de Capoeira Angola*. Salvador, 1963.

Patterson, Orlando. *Slavery and Social Death*. Cambridge, Mass.: Harvard University Press, 1982.

Pederneiras, Raúl. *Geringonça carioca: Verbetes para um Dicionário da Gíria*. Rio de Janeiro: Briguiet, 1922,

Peixoto, B. "Capoeira Angola: Luta de destreza." *Arquivos da Escola de Educação Física e Desportes*. Rio de Janeiro, n.d.

Pires, António Liberac. *Bimba, Pastinha e Besouro de Manganga*. Goiana: Editôra Grafset, 2002.

———. "A Capoeira no jogo das cores: Criminalidade, cultura e racismo na cidade do Rio de Janeiro, 1890–1937." M.A. thesis, Campinas, 1996.

Querino, Manuel. *Costumes africanos no Brasil*. Recife: Editôra Massangana, 1988.

———. *A Bahia de outrora*. Salvador: Progresso, 1946.

Rachum, Ilan. *Brazil*. Tel Aviv: Papirus, 1991.

———. "Futebol: The Growth of a Brazilian National Institution." *New Scholar* 7.1–2 (1979): 183–200.

Ramos, Arthur. *The Negro in Brazil*. Translated by Richard Pattee. Washington, D.C.: Associated Pub. 1951.

Ramos, D. "Community, Control and Acculturation: A Case Study of Slavery in 18th-Century Brazil." *The Americas* 42.4 (1986): 419–451.

Rego, José Carlos. *Dança do samba*. Rio de Janeiro: Aldeia, 1994.

Rego, Waldeloir. *Capoeira Angola: Ensaio sócio etnográfico*. Salvador: Itapua, 1968.

———. "Mitos e ritos africanos da Bahia." In *Iconografia dos Deuses da Bahia no candomblé da Bahia*, edited by Hector Júlio Paride Bernabó (Carybé). São Paulo: Raízes, 1980.

Reis, João José. *Liberdade por um fio: História dos quilombos no Brasil*. São Paulo: Companhia das Letras, 1996.

———. *A morte é uma festa*. São Paulo: Companhia das Letras, 1991.

———. *Slave Rebellion in Brazil*. Baltimore: Johns Hopkins University Press, 1993.

Reis, Letícia V. S. "Negros e brancos no jogo da capoeira: A reinvenção da tradição." M.A. thesis, Universidade de São Paulo, São Paulo, 1993.

Rodrigues, Nina. *Os Africanos no Brasil*. Brasília: Editôra UNB, 1988.

Romero, Silvio. *Estudos sobre a poesia popular do Brasil*. Petrópolis: Editôra Vozes, 1977.

———. "Poesia popular brasileira." *Revista Brasileira* 1 (1879): 273.

Salles, V. "Bibliografia crítica do folclore brasileiro—capoeira." *Revista Brasileira do Folklore* 8.23 (1969): 79–103.

Salvadori, Maria A. B. "Capoeiras e malandros: Pedaços de uma senora tradição popular, 1890–1950." Ph.D. dissertation, Universidade Estadual de Campinas, 1990.

Santacruz, Beatriz. "Com seus mártires e heróis: Capoeira chega a ser religião." *O Dia*, 10–11 Sept. 1978, p. 18.

Santos, Deoscóredes Maximiliano dos. *West African Sacred Art and Ritual in Brazil: A Comparative Study*. Ibadan: Institute of African Studies, University of Ibadan, 1967.

Santos, Jocelito Teles dos. "A Mixed-Race Nation: Afro-Brazilians and Cultural Policy in Bahia, 1970–1990." In *Afro-Brazilian Culture and Politics*, edited by Hendrik Kraay. New York: M. E. Sharpe, 1998.

Schwartz, Stuart B. "The Manumission of Slaves in Colonial Brazil: Bahia, 1684–1745." *Hispanic American Review* 54 (1974): 601–635.

———. *Slaves, Peasants, and Rebels*. Urbana: University of Illinois Press, 1992.

———. *Sovereignty and Society in Colonial Brazil: The High Court of Bahia and Its Judges, 1609–1751*. Berkeley: University of California Press, 1973.

———. *Sugar Plantations in the Formation of Brazilian Society Bahia, 1550–1835*. Cambridge: Cambridge University Press, 1985.

Scott, James C. *Domination and the Arts of Resistance: Hidden Transcripts*. New Haven: Yale University Press, 1990.

———. *Weapons of the Weak: Everyday Forms of Peasant Resistance*. New Haven: Yale University Press, 1985.

Shaffer, Kay. "O berimbau de barriga e seus toques." *Monografias Folclóricas*. Rio de Janeiro: Ministério da Educação e Cultura, Secretaria de Assuntos Culturais, Fundação Nacional de Arte, Instituto Nacional de Folclore, 1977.

Sleeter, Cristine E., and Peter McLaren. "Introduction: Exploring Connections to Build a Critical Multiculturalism." In *Multicultural Education, Critical Pedagogy, and the Politics of Difference*, edited by Cristine E. Sleeter and Peter McLaren. New York: State University of New York Press, 1995.

Soares, Antoni Joaquim Macedo. *Dicionário brasileiro de lingua portuguesa*. Rio de Janeiro: INL, 1954 (1st ed. 1889).

Soares, Carlos Eugênio Líbano. *A capoeira escrava e outras tradições rebeldes no Rio de Janeiro, 1808–1850*. Campinas: Editôra da Campinas, 2001.

———. *A negregada instituição: Os Capoeiras no Rio de Janeiro*. Rio de Janeiro: Prefeitura da Cidade do Rio de Janeiro, 1994.

Sobel, Mechal. *The World They Made Together*. Princeton: Princeton University Press, 1987.

Sodre, Nelson Werneck. *Panorama do Segundo Império*. São Paulo: Companhia Editôra Nacional, 1939.

Stam, Robert. "Samba, Candomblé, Quilombo: Black Performance and Brazilian Cinema." *Journal of Ethnic Studies* 13 (1985): 55–84.

Stuckey, Sterling. *Slave Culture*. New York: Oxford University Press, 1987.

Summ, Harvey. *Brazilian Mosaic: Portraits of a People and Culture*. Wilmington: Scholarly Resources Imprint, 1995.

Sweet, James. *Recreating Africa: Culture, Kinship, and Religion in the African Portuguese World, 1441–1770*. Chapel Hill: University of North Carolina Press, 2003.

"Symbol and Symbolism." In *An Encyclopedia of Religion*, edited by Vergilius Ferm. Paterson, N.J.: Littlefield Adams, 1964.

Szwed, John F., ed. *Black Americans*. Washington, D.C.: Voices of America, 1970.

Szwed, John F., and D. Roger Abrahams. *After Africa*. New Haven: Yale University Press, 1983.

———. *Discovering Afro-America*. Leiden: E. J. Brill, 1975.

Talmon-Chvaicer, Maya. "The Complexity of Capoeira: Encounter, Collision, and Fusion of Cultures. Rio de Janeiro and Bahia, Nineteenth and Twentieth Centuries." Ph.D. dissertation, University of Haifa, Haifa, 2000.

Tannenbaum, Frank. *Slave and Citizen: The Negro in the Americas*. Boston: Beacon Press, 1992.

Tavares, Júlio Cesar de Souza. "Dança de guerra." M.A. thesis, Universidade de Brasília, Brasília, 1984.

Thompson, Robert Farris. *African Art in Motion*. Berkeley: University of California Press, 1979.

———. *Capoeira*. Spoleto Festival, U.S.A., 1987.

———. "Dance and Culture." *African Forum* 2 (1966): 85–102.

———. *Face of the Gods: Art and Altars of Africa and the African Americas*. New York: Museum for African Art, 1993.

———. *Flash of the Spirit: African and Afro-American Art and Philosophy*. New York: Random House, 1983.

———. *Four Moments of the Sun: Kongo Art in Two Worlds*. Washington, D.C.: National Gallery of Art, 1981.

Thornton, John. *Africa and Africans in the Making of the Atlantic World, 1400–1800*. Cambridge: Cambridge University Press, 1998.

———. "African Dimensions of the Stono Rebellion." *American Historical Review* (1991): 1101–1113.

———. "Art of War in Angola, 1575–1680." *Comparative Studies in Society and History* 30:3 (1988): 360–378.

———. *The Kongolese Saint Anthony: Dona Beatriz Kimpa Vita and the Antonian Movement 1684–1706*. Cambridge: Cambridge University Press, 1998.

———. "On the Trail of Voodoo." *The Americas* 44 (1987–1988): 261–278.

———. *Warfare in Atlantic Africa, 1500–1800*. London: University College London Press, 1999.

Tierou, A. *Doople: The Eternal Law of African Dance*. Paris: Harwood Academic Publishers, 1992.

Tigges, Gabriela. "The History of Capoeira in Brazil." Ph.D. dissertation, Brigham Young University, 1990.

Tinhorão, José Ramos. *História social da música popular brasileira.* São Paulo: Editôra 34, 1998.

———. *Os sons dos negros no Brasil: Cantos, danças, folguedos, origem.* São Paulo: Art Editôra, 1988.

Tourinho, Irene M. F. "The Relationship between Music and Control in the Everyday Processes of the Schooling Ritual." Ph.D. dissertation, University of Wisconsin, 1992.

Turner, Victor. *The Forest of Symbols: Aspects of Ndembu Ritual.* Ithaca: Cornell University Press, 1967.

Valença, Rachel Teixeira. *Carnaval.* Rio de Janeiro: Relume Dumara, 1996.

Vansina, Jan. *The Tio Kingdom of Middle Congo, 1880–1892.* London: Oxford University Press, 1973.

Vantuono, William. *Sir Gawain and the Green Knight.* New York: Garland Publishing, 1991.

Vianna, Filho Luiz. *O negro na Bahia.* Rio de Janeiro: J. Olympio, 1946.

Vianna, Hermano. *The Mystery of Samba: Popular Music and National Identity in Brazil.* Edited and translated by John Charles Chasteen. Chapel Hill: University of North Carolina Press, 1999.

Vieira, Luíz Renato, and Mathias Röhring Assunção. *O jogo da capoeira: Cultura popular no Brasil.* Rio de Janeiro: Editôra Sprint, 1998.

———. "Mitos controvérsias e fatos: Construindo a história da capoeira." *Estudos Afro-Asiáticos* 34 (1998): 81–120.

———. Da vadiação a Capoeira Regional: Uma interpretação da modernização cultural no Brasil." MA thesis, Universidade de Brasília, 1990.

Wafer, J., and H. R. Santana. "Africa in Brazil: Culture, Politics, and Candomblé Religion." *Folclore Forum* 23 (1990): 98–114.

Walsh, Robert. *Notices of Brazil in 1828–1829.* London, 1830.

Wisser, William M. "Construction and Convention of Nineteenth-Century English-Speaking Travelers' Accounts of Brazil." Paper presented at the INCS Conference, Ohio State University, 1999.

Yvonne, Maggie. "Aqueles a quem foi negada a cor do dia: As categorias cor e raça na cultura brasileira." In *Raça, ciência e sociedade,* edited by Marcos Chor Maio and Ricardo Ventura Santos. Rio de Janeiro: Editôra Fiocruz, 1998.

Note: Italic page numbers refer to figures, maps, and tables.

LaVergne, TN USA
03 May 2010

181282LV00006B/26/P

9 780292 717244